PASSPORT
TO
PROFITS

Opportunities In
International Investing

JOHN P. DESSAUER

 Dearborn
Financial Publishing, Inc.

While a great deal of care has been taken to provide accurate and current information, the ideas, suggestions, general principles and conclusions presented in this book are subject to local, state and federal laws and regulations, court cases and any revisions of same. The reader is thus urged to consult legal counsel regarding any points of law—this publication should not be used as a substitute for competent legal advice.

Publisher: Kathleen A. Welton
Senior Project Editor: Jack L. Kiburz
Interior Design: Lucy Jenkins
Cover Design: Vito DePinto

Published by Dearborn Financial Publishing, Inc.

Printed in the United States of America

91 92 93 10 9 8 7 6 5 4 3 2 1

Library of Congress Cataloging-in-Publication Data
Dessauer, John P., 1936–
  Passport to profits : opportunities in international investing /
John P. Dessauer.
      p. cm.
  Includes index.
  ISBN 0-7931-0122-0
  1. Finance, Personal. 2. Investments, American. 3. Portfolio management.
I. Title.
HG179.D49 1990
332.6'73--dc20   90-42181
                                                                                           CIP

Contents

Preface

Despite the crash of 1987, the U.S. stock market in the 1980s turned in a respectable performance. From a low of 791.48 in 1982, the Dow Jones Industrial Average climbed to 2,810.15 in early 1990, for a gain of 255 percent. If there are gains of that magnitude available in the U.S. stock market, why bother to expand your horizons and adopt an international investment perspective?

There are several good reasons for an international perspective. The first is that the U.S. stock market's 1980s performance is misleading. All that really happened in the 1980s was that U.S. stocks made up some of the ground they lost in the 1970s. If you look at the Dow Jones Industrial Average as compared with the cost of living in the United States, the Dow should have climbed to more than 3,200 just to be even with inflation in the 1970s and 1980s. The Dow didn't make it over 3,000 in the 1980s. That means U.S. stocks didn't even keep pace with the rate of U.S. inflation in the 20 years from 1970 to 1989.

Other stock markets did much better. In terms of U.S. dollars, the Morgan Stanley Capital International Perspective world stock index climbed 467 percent in the two decades of the 1970s and 1980s. That was enough to beat U.S. inflation. In other words, holding an internationally diversified portfolio, including some U.S. stocks, was the way to keep ahead of the rising cost of living in the United States in the 1970s and 1980s.

Some foreign stock markets turned in spectacular performances in those two decades. Japanese stocks rose 3,000 percent, stocks in Hong Kong rose 1,392 percent and Swedish stocks gained 1,079 percent. Even British stocks beat the U.S. stock market with a gain of 384 percent. American investors were far better off investing in foreign markets than in their own market over that 20-year period.

Twenty years is a long time. Most investors have a shorter time horizon in deciding how to manage their money. This may come as a surprise, but if world stock markets are judged by their performance only in the 1980s, the United States still doesn't come out on top. Out of 18 major world stock markets, the United States finished in 12th place in the 1980s. There were 11 markets that were better investments for American investors than their own home market. Stock markets in England, Italy, Japan, Holland, France and Germany all were much better places for Americans to have their money in the 1980s.

In the last half of the 1980s the results were even worse for the U.S. stock market. From the end of 1984 through the end of 1989 the U.S. stock market placed 16th out of 18. Only two markets, Canada and Singapore, were worse for American investors.

The differences weren't small. The U.S. stock market gained 106 percent in the last half of the 1980s. That compares with 385 percent for French stocks, 289 percent for German stocks, 214 percent for Dutch stocks, 183 percent for British stocks and 620 percent for Japanese stocks. All of these figures are in terms of U.S. dollars. They show the real results for an American investor, including the wild fluctuations in the dollar.

Will the 1990s be different? Will the United States at last fulfill its potential and rise to the top of the performance scoreboard? It could happen. The dollar fell sharply versus the currencies of Europe toward the end of 1989. If the dollar also plunges versus the Japanese yen, American business will then gain a competitive advantage and might regain some of the markets lost both at home and abroad to foreign competition. The 1990s could be a time of greater prosperity for U.S. corporate profits and stock prices.

But the competition will be rough and tough. The Japanese led the world in capital investment in the last three years of the 1980s. Their rate of investment in new technology, new products, and more efficient factories was three times that of the United States. We fell behind and will face continued tough Japanese competition regardless of the exchange rate between the dollar and the yen.

In Eastern Europe a new army of competitors will emerge in the 1990s. Highly motivated people with lots of capital from the West will be building new factories and using the latest in computers, robots and other technologies. It won't be long before Eastern Europe develops the ability to manufacture high-quality goods for export to the United States and other world markets.

The world has changed. The United States, while still the largest of the developed economies, no longer dominates the world financial landscape. We are one of several large economic powers. To sit back myopically and think that all you need is to watch the U.S. financial markets is both foolish and wrong. The history of the 1970s and the 1980s proves that international investing can be more profitable. Common sense says that every investor needs an international perspective in the 1990s.

This book is precisely what its title says it is: a "passport," an invitation and a guide. It's not a complete study course on international investing. It is intended to open the way for you to start on a course that will allow you to develop your own practical, comfortable way of following international markets, and increase your profits in the process.

CHAPTER

1

The Truth about Investing in the 1990s

Wow! What a great few decades. Just look at all the opportunities. From 1945 to 1966 the Dow Jones Industrial Average soared 560 percent—and that doesn't include dividends. In the 20 years from 1970 to the end of 1989 the Japanese stock market did even better, rising 4,058 percent, not counting appreciation in the Japanese yen or dividends. (See Figure 1-1 for Japanese stock market monthly closings.) Over the same two decades Swedish stocks rose 955 percent; Hong Kong stocks, 1,375 percent; and stocks in Singapore, 1,146 percent.

Imagine what might have been. Suppose a lucky investor started with $1,000 in 1945, invested first in U.S. stocks and in 1970 deftly switched to Japanese stocks. By the end of 1989 the original $1,000 would have grown to $275,000. If the original investment had been $4,000 or more, there would be one more millionaire in the world today.

Forty-four years is a long time to wait to become a millionaire, especially while holding a portfolio of volatile investments such as stocks. With risky investments, most of us want to see results right away or within a year or two. The idea of setting out on a long-term investment project in stocks is, to say the least, uncommon.

We all listen to financial planners and know that a regular savings program with compounding interest can add up to a lot of money over time. But that kind of long-term program almost always has a safe interest-bearing account at the core.

Figure 1-1.   Nikkei Dow Monthly Closings, 1970–1989

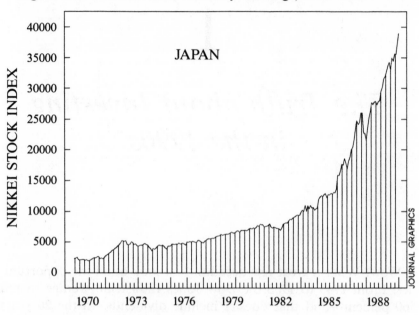

Chart prepared by Richard Andrews from data supplied by the author.

It may seem unbelievable, but the figures for the growth in the value of stocks since 1945 are, if anything, too modest. Investors who regularly added to their stock holdings or who bought more stocks when the markets plunged enjoyed gains far greater than the raw numbers for the averages. The fact is that investing in stocks, especially with an international perspective, has been the easiest route to financial security for the last four decades.

You didn't have to watch the stock market quotations every day or make many decisions along the way during those decades. What you had to do was invest in sound businesses and then have the courage to hang on for the long pull, which is usually the problem. Over the last four decades there have been a series of frightening developments, including the Cuban missile crisis, the assassination of President Kennedy, the oil crisis, several recessions, a stock market crash and more than a few best-selling books by respected experts warning of a coming economic collapse. Only the most courageous of investors could hold on in the face of so many fierce financial storms.

What is worse is that as success develops, it becomes even harder to hang on. If your portfolio is worth $1,000, it is easy. You don't have that much at risk. But when the numbers grow and the portfolio reaches $100,000, $250,000 or $1 million, even the bold rationalize that you never go wrong taking some profits. They sell, move part of the money into cash and lose out on whatever opportunity remains. Make no mistake: making a lot of money is easy only in hindsight. Some people do it, and so can you, but that doesn't mean you'll always be right. It is possible to muster the courage to hold on to a portfolio even when the market plunges and to take advantage of steep falls in stock prices (as in 1974 or 1987) to add to your holdings. You can increase your net worth without becoming a fool or a gambler.

THE FORGOTTEN TRUTH—THE WHOLE ECONOMY DEPENDS ON BUSINESS

Buying and holding a portfolio of international stocks for cash is not any riskier than holding all your money in U.S. dollars, in a bank or even in government bonds. Stocks only seem riskier because their values fluctuate and are published every day in the newspapers. If the real worth of every U.S. bank were published every day in newspapers, people wouldn't regard bank accounts as safe. In the early part of the 1980s many, if not most, U.S. savings banks were deep in the red. They were saved from disaster because they didn't have to price their mortgage portfolios at real market values. They could carry them at cost even though that was unrealistic. Government bonds aren't much better. They are denominated in U.S. dollars, and the dollar is subject to fluctuation. The appearance of the dollar in your wallet may not change from day to day, but its real value does. When stocks are compared with other investments in a realistic manner, they don't come out looking as risky as many believe.

Look at it this way. How does a government get the cash it needs to pay the interest on treasury bills and bonds? Where do banks get the cash to pay you interest on your deposit? The answer is that the money comes from individuals and business, and business is at the core of everything. Without business there would be no jobs, and people wouldn't have the cash to make their payments on loans or pay taxes to the government. No matter how you slice through a nation, you always find business at the heart of the economy. When business is good, a nation prospers; when business is not so good, the number of homeless and poor increases; and when business is bad, everyone suffers.

OUR SELF-DEFEATING ATTITUDE

We used to understand these straightforward facts of economic life. There was a time when Americans favored investing in business. Stocks used to represent a high proportion of household wealth in the United States. In the 1970s and more so in the 1980s, that fact changed. Our attitude became colored by the doomsayers' compelling warnings of coming disaster. We succumbed to fantasies and thought that by staying out of stocks we could avoid personal disaster. We spent too much time remembering the stories of those who jumped from windows in 1929, when the value of their stock portfolios plunged. We conveniently forgot that in those cases the jumpers had been borrowing to buy stocks. It wasn't the stock plunge alone that pushed so many to despair; it was the combination of margin borrowing and the stock plunge. Those who owned stocks for cash and simply held on saw some of their investments recover and a few go on to outstanding gains.

In addition to the doomsayers and memories of the crash of 1929, there has been widespread change in American attitudes about stocks, and professional investors are to blame. Money managers have become embroiled in a performance game, but they aren't entirely at fault. Their customers have hired sophisticated consultants to measure performance. Those with the best performance have succeeded the most in keeping and attracting new clients. Slowly but surely the process of measuring performance has deteriorated to a very short-term perspective. Performance quarter-by-quarter has become the most important objective, and stocks are pieces of paper to be traded for performance reasons. The basic idea that stockholders are owners of a business has vanished. The stock market has begun to behave more like a casino than a financial market. (By the end of the 1980s futures, selling short and computer program trading were the rage.) What does it matter what happens to the value of a stock in the long run if you make your fortune along the way?

Well, it matters a lot. Who cares if the professional money managers make millions? The basic idea is not to make a few rich. The idea is to build a storehouse of wealth for pension funds and mutual funds and for the millions of individuals who depend on long-term success.

After the crash of 1987 it was revealed that the General Motors pension fund had been a major seller on Black Monday. Just think about that for a moment. Here is a pension fund that is supposed to invest for the long-term financial health of workers at General Motors. After the crash, however, car sales declined, and General Motors suffered lost profits. Jobs were threatened. For a short time it was feared that the crash might tip the entire economy into a deep recession. Did it make sense for pension funds to sell and capture short-term profits if in the process they threatened the very lives they were supposed to protect? Of course not.

The computer program trading that contributed to the market's plunge in 1987 was the ultimate in shortsightedness. By the end of 1989 so many individuals had become terrified of the wild swings in stock prices caused by computer program trading that they stayed out of the stock market altogether. The brokerage firms that used computer program trading to win short-term profits suffered enormous long-run losses when individuals stayed out of the market.

Shortsightedness by professional investors came to a climax at the end of the 1980s. The transition of the U.S. stock market from a financial market to a quasi-casino had gone too far. No wonder so many individual investors lost sight of the basics. It is very difficult to think of a stock as representing part ownership in a business when the stock price swings from one extreme to the other.

However, there was a way to hang on even in the throes of the stock market crash of 1987. A stock certificate is a statement of ownership. You really do own part of a business. Suppose all the casino nonsense went to such an extreme that the stock market vanished. You would still have your certificate of ownership. You might not be able to buy or sell it easily, but you still would have an interest in a business. If you had confidence in the business, you might not mind if trading stopped. After all, many individuals buy into privately owned businesses whose stocks don't trade. In the long run you would still do well if the business did well. Gamblers can corrupt the stock market, but they can't change the basics. Business is at the heart of the stock market and the entire economy.

How did we come from such heights in the 1940s and 1950s to a nation preoccupied with gambling and doomsday fantasies? What does it all mean for the future? Will there be more opportunities to become a millionaire in stocks in the 1990s and beyond? No one knows the future. We can, however, take stock of present conditions, see how the past brought us to this point and make some judgments on what the future is likely to hold.

In the years after the end of World War II, the United States was the dominant economy in the world. Americans were full of self-confidence. Oil prices were low, and by the middle of the 1960s Americans enjoyed the highest standard of living in the history of the human race. The problem was that success had a dark side. It made Americans overconfident, self-satisfied and insular.

The ugly American was an expression used to describe the flood of tourists from the United States that visited countries around the world. We were rich and enjoyed showing off. This joke circulated in Ireland in the 1960s: An American tourist supposedly asked the price of a sweater in Dublin. The clerk gave the answer in pounds, but the American replied, "How much is that in real money?" In the 1960s most Americans thought the U.S. dollar was the only real money and the U.S. stock market was the only place to invest. Foreign markets as well as foreign currencies were regarded as risky and unnecessary. That myopic point of view cost us dearly in the 1970s and 1980s. It kept us out of the Japanese, Hong Kong and Swedish stock markets and also kept us out of many other outstanding investment opportunities outside the United States.

Clinging to a myopic, backward-looking investment perspective wasn't bad enough. After the first oil shock in the early 1970s we awakened to a changed world and concluded that it was hopeless. Pessimism became a national habit in the United States. We leapt from one doomsday fantasy to the next. By 1979 some of the best experts in the country confidently predicted that oil prices would keep rising in the 1980s, to $100 a barrel. When oil prices collapsed instead, we refused to admit error. The possibility of continued prosperity was dismissed. We quickly shifted theories, holding firmly to the conviction that an economic catastrophe was inevitable.

By late 1987 *The Depression of 1990* was a best-selling book. In October (almost on the same date as 58 years earlier) the U.S. stock market plunged. A cascade of fear swept over the nation. Doubters became convinced that the doomsayers were right and that the dis-

mal history of the late 1920s and the Great Depression were about
to be repeated.

In Orleans, Massachusetts, a day or two after the stock market
crash of 1987 an elderly gentleman was standing in line at the bank.
He withdrew $50,000 in cash, walked over to the safe deposit vault
and put the bills in his safe deposit box. He certainly was convinced
that the depression of 1990 was more than a figment of an ambi-
tious author's imagination.

In 1988, the year after the stock crash, world trade grew 8.5 percent, an astounding accomplishment. The ten-year average had
been 4.5 percent. Economists in Europe, Japan and the United
States had been convinced that the stock crash of 1987 would at
least cause a decline in the rate of world economic growth, but they
were completely wrong. The global economy rolled on as if the
stock market crash had never occurred.

The U.S. stock market was called into question as a leading indicator. How could so many supposedly well-informed investors
be so wrong? Why was there a stock market panic on the eve of a
banner year for the world's economies, including that of the United
States? In 1988 U.S. corporate profits rose by 18 percent. The logical answer is that pessimism had become so ingrained that the facts
didn't matter.

The most amazing feature of the great stock market crash of 1987
was that it did not produce a domino effect. In 1929 the crash
quickly spread to other countries, and its impact was soon felt on
all businesses. The plunge in the value of stock prices in 1929 triggered a slide into the Great Depression of the 1930s. A lot obviously
changed between 1929 and 1987, and those changes were largely
positive. By the late 1980s the world's major economies were able to
take the sudden, unexpected, severe drop in stock prices in their
stride. Little damage was done to businesses outside of the financial
industry.

THERE IS NO SUCH THING AS A SAFE INVESTMENT

Investment opportunity is only obvious after the fact. We can
look back and see what would have produced outstanding profits in
years past. The future is unknown and always full of uncertainty
and risk. There could be a serious recession or worse in our future
because there are no guarantees when it comes to markets or eco-

nomic events. On the other hand, the future might mean greater prosperity and significant new opportunities.

Investing, like life itself, demands an ability to deal with uncertainty. Imagine a person so absorbed in fear that the thought of driving to work is paralyzing. That person might even ask if there are any cement trucks on the road. Of course there almost always are, and a collision with a cement truck can be disastrous. One logical way to avoid the risks of travel is to always stay home. But is that practical? How can you enjoy life, work or play if you live in that kind of constant fear?

Most people don't stay home out of fear of cement trucks. They go out—to work, shopping, for travel and for entertainment. They know about risk and accept it. But when it comes to investing, a different attitude often emerges. Money takes on proportions greater than life itself. Out of fear of losing on a stock investment, too many keep their cash in banks or in some other "safe" investment.

The irony is that just as there are no completely safe roads, there are no completely safe investments. The gentleman who put the $50,000 in his safe deposit box in 1987 had apparently forgotten about a bank robbery in a neighboring town some months before. Helped by local police, a band of thieves had broken into a bank's safe deposit vault and had stolen the contents of hundreds of safe deposit boxes. There is no federal insurance covering items in a safe deposit box; if the cash is stolen, it is gone.

The bottom line is that no matter how you handle your money you take a risk. It is far better to stay in control of your money by taking calculated risks than to search for safety, only later to learn of significant losses. Think about all those poor people who suffered a decline in their living standards in the 1970s and 1980s as constant inflation eroded the buying power of their cash. How many millions of retired Americans decided that they couldn't afford to take chances with their money and put the cash in the bank or in treasury bills only to find that ten years later they had lost more than they could conceivably recover?

Contrast that dismal experience with someone who took chances in the stock markets of the world. Let's suppose that back in 1929 you had $3,000 to invest. At the markets' peak in 1929 you invested $1,000. As if that wasn't bad enough, assume that you invested another $1,000 when the market rallied in 1930. That made two terrible mistakes just as the worst stock market crash in history was beginning. Having lost a lot of money, assume that in 1932, when the Dow fell to 41, you decided that since you had already lost so much anyway, why not invest the last $1,000? In 1937 the U.S. stock market managed a partial recovery. At that point you would have doubled your money. The $3,000 total investment was worth $6,000 in mid-1937.

The point is that all investing and all forms of money management involve risk. Losses are common. But with a willingness to take risks, some common sense and a little discipline, you can both make mistakes and make handsome profits. If you can double your money in a circumstance as violent as the market crash of 1929 and the depression that followed, imagine what you might accomplish in good times or in times that offer opportunity as good as in the past!

OPPORTUNITY IS KNOCKING AGAIN

In the 1970s Paul Erdman made the best-seller list with his book *The Crash of 1979*. People were fascinated with the idea that the great stock market crash of 1929 might be repeated exactly 50 years later. We know that nature is cyclical. Summer returns every year, and the sun rises and sets each day. We can predict the arrival of comets. Sun spots and solar activity change in more or less a regular pattern. Wouldn't it be nice if human behavior also followed a regular, natural rhythm? If so, we could see economic changes coming in advance and enjoy huge profits.

In 1922 Nikolai Kondratieff, a brilliant Russian economist, published the results of his study of long-term economic cycles. Kondratieff observed two and a half long-term waves or cycles going back to the late 1700s. He postulated that the third wave had already peaked and would produce a panic in the late 1920s and a depression in the 1930s. He was right! The Great Depression arrived right on Kondratieff's schedule, making him a legendary forecaster. For a while his work was popular, but when the depression dragged on and World War II began, interest in economic cycles vanished. In the 1940s and 1950s the Kondratieff long-wave theory was forgotten. In the late 1970s, however, it was revived as more and more people became increasingly anxious about their financial futures. His studies were used and abused in the 1980s to support predictions of a new depression.

A philosopher once warned that those who pay no attention to the past are doomed to repeat it. He wasn't talking about economics or financial markets. He was referring to society's dismal habit of repeating past mistakes over and over again. His point was that human nature changes slowly, and then only when individuals apply extreme effort and pay close attention to the lessons of the past. His idea has often been twisted in an effort to shine up the crystal ball, predict the future and profit from studying history.

Human beings abhor chaos and struggle to find order in the world. When it comes to money, we have a passionate desire to find ways of predicting the future. We are uncomfortable with markets full of uncertainty and unknowns. We want to arrange our portfolios and other affairs in a sensible way and think that requires foresight. At times these human tendencies become perverted. They take on ugly shapes and distort our ability to see current events and trends for what they are.

In the 1980s too many Americans persisted for too long in a one-sided view of future possibilities. Pessimism dominated, optimists were often ridiculed and we behaved as if we wanted another depression. In 1982 anyone who predicted a Dow Jones Industrial Average of 2,000 was ridiculed. Just seven years later, however, the pessimists used forecasts of a Dow Jones Average at 2,000 to support their point of view. By 1989 a Dow of 2,000 was no longer the optimists' view. The Dow had risen to more than 2,700. Real events turned optimism and pessimism upside down.

Even as the Berlin Wall came tumbling down in late 1989, experts and pundits were warning that it would take a long time before business enjoyed profits from the dramatic political and economic changes in eastern Europe. Some even predicted major problems, arguing that there would be more destructive political turmoil ahead. How could so many have become so twisted that they couldn't accept the positive aspects of whole nations throwing off the yoke of dictatorship and embracing sacrifices in an effort to improve their lives? As astounding as that may seem, it was the truth. Certainly the road to peace and prosperity will not be smooth or straight. It never is, but to focus on the negatives with such fervor was overly one-sided. Too many Americans had for too long indulged in doomsday expectations. Not even the opening of the Berlin Wall shook them out of that one-sided, twisted perspective.

The opening of Eastern Europe in late 1989 was one of the most startling developments of the century. It has opened up a whole world of opportunity. The road to progress in Eastern Europe may not be an easy one, but when so many millions of people are so determined to try and improve their lives, a lot of good is sure to result.

In 1945 the United States emerged as the victor in a world war. We looked with compassion on the war-ravaged economies of Europe and Asia and did something unprecedented in history: we decided to help our former enemies rebuild their economies. The Marshall Plan was formulated, and this resulted in 20 years of unprecedented prosperity for Americans.

In 1990 the American attitude was quite different. We did look with compassion on the ravaged economies of Poland, Hungary, Czechoslovakia, East Germany and Romania, but we offered only token economic aid, arguing that our deficit-ridden nation, with its rising poverty and homelessness, couldn't afford any more. Completely forgotten were the facts that after World War II the U.S. national debt, at 125 percent of the gross national product (GNP), was twice the size of the national debt in 1989 or that after the war we faced rising unemployment and rising inflation but still went ahead with massive aid programs.

Once, not that many years ago, the United States was one of the most generous countries in the world. By 1988 the U.S. official foreign aid had fallen to 0.2 percent of GNP, one of the stingiest in the world. In fact, in 1988 only Ireland gave away to poor countries a smaller portion of its national wealth than the United States. Norway and Holland gave away, in official aid, five times the level of the United States.

Feeling poor is another aspect of the American malaise. The feeling is real, but the "facts" are not. The United States may indulge in fantasies of a coming depression, but the rest of the world is likely to ignore that dismal attitude and get on with the business of trying to improve standards of living.

After the First World War the victors, including the United States, followed historical patterns. Beggar thy neighbor, especially former enemies, was the policy. Germany, for example, was expected to pay for the damages done in the war. Keeping Germany under the heel of international debt did not work. Instead of lasting peace, the war to end all wars was followed by a depression and a new world war worse that the first. The dismal economic conditions of the Great Depression proved to be a breeding ground for fanatical political ideologies.

The Holocaust was too much for the world to bear. After World War II the victors resolved not to repeat the mistakes of the past. Instead of holding down the losers to assure that they did not have the economic strength to fight again, we provided structures and money to improve living conditions. The essence of the Marshall Plan was to provide all the help needed to lift Europe and Asia out of the war mess and back to respectable living standards. That approach worked. Not only did the people of Europe and Asia benefit, but Americans enjoyed two decades of magnificent opportunity.

The countries of the Soviet bloc were not ravaged by bombs and guns in the decades between 1945 and 1989, but they were nevertheless devastated. Central planning, the economic keystone of communism, failed to deliver on its promise of greater prosperity for the masses.

By 1988 there were 40 million personal computers in the United States and only 100,000 in the Soviet Union. The lack of this basic tool for life in the modern world is poignant evidence of how miserably communism failed. While Americans complained about Japanese competition, they were able to buy whatever they wanted, from television sets to gourmet food. In the Soviet Union and Eastern Europe the shelves were bare, and there were long lines for what few consumer goods were available.

The first immigrants to break through the wire and cement to West Germany in 1989 were astounded. They found that the tales of life in the West had not been exaggerated. To them the prosperity of West Germany was above and beyond their wildest imaginings. When the Wall came down and people flooded across the border, the earlier judgments were confirmed, and worse. Not only were conditions in the West better than imagined, conditions in the East were worse than anticipated. Politicians lived in luxury while the people fought for the basics of life.

The most telling comparison of life and death behind the Iron Curtain and in the United States came from two earthquakes. There were earthquakes of similar severity first in Armenia in the Soviet Union and later in San Francisco. In Armenia, whole towns were leveled because of poor construction, and rescue efforts were hampered by a lack of transportation and working equipment. A year later millions still lived in primitive conditions. In San Francisco, the earthquake cost lives and buildings crumbled, but the wreckage was a fraction of what Armenia suffered. In the United States communications were quickly restored, and rescue efforts were prompt and effective. Life in San Francisco was back to normal reasonably quickly. The free-market, democratic system of the United States, while far from perfect, served its citizens well. The centrally planned, Communist bureaucracy of the Soviet Union failed miserably.

OPENING THE DOOR TO OPPORTUNITY
MEANS TAKING RISKS

The final year of the 1980s was a time of exposure. The failures of one system were highlighted, while the other looked bright by comparison. The people of the Soviet Union and Eastern Europe, like those of the devastated, war-torn countries in 1945, saw clearly the task ahead. They too had to begin to rebuild. History had repeated itself, but with a new twist.

With all the attention given to Kondratieff's long-wave theories and other cycle theories it is astounding that the basic truth of what was happening in the late 1980s eluded so many. The parallels were there. In 1945 a system had been beaten with guns and bullets, and in the late 1980s a system surrendered to the success of the West. Devastated economies prepared to rebuild. The battles of 1945 to 1989 were of ideologies.

The great difference between the end of World War II and the end of the war of ideologies was that tanks, guns and bullets had played a smaller role. Free markets, entrepreneurs and capitalists led the winning side. Ideologues, bureaucrats and centrally planned economies were the legions of the losers. The differences apparently clouded the vision of many. They failed to see that a new era of prosperity might be dawning.

When the clouds of radiation settled over Hiroshima and Nagasaki, the world did not look like it held opportunity. All of Europe was in rubble, and Japan was without a political system. The parades and banners celebrated the end of barbaric dictators. The question of what to do next was hotly debated by politicians and economists. We look back now and see that the Marshall Plan produced two decades of prosperity and investment opportunity. At the time, looking forward, prosperity and opportunity were anything but obvious.

This is also true today. West Germany is moving rapidly to help East Germany recover, Western business is rushing to find opportunity in Eastern Europe and the German stock market soared in late 1989. But the future isn't certain. There is political turmoil in the Middle East, the Baltic countries have threatened to create real problems in the Soviet Union and China still clings to oppression.

There were no guarantees of prosperity in 1946, and there are none today. Investors who made their fortunes in the 1950s and 1960s took real risks. They saw the possibility of rich rewards and were willing to take a chance.

What made the decades of the 1950s and 1960s so prosperous was not just the Marshall Plan. The more important explanation was the motivation of so many people to produce prosperity in order to prevent another war. It was World War II and all its horror that gave the world the incentive needed to overcome the challenges and the blockades to prosperity, and to get on with achieving that goal.

In the 1990s there are also millions of people who have suffered a painful lesson. In America, where most are still comfortable, the motivation may not be so evident; but in East Germany, Poland, Hungary, Czechoslovakia and other devastated countries, the motivation is there. Betting on highly motivated people was the right thing to do in the 1950s. It will undoubtedly be the right thing again in the 1990s. If people really want to avoid war and depression and if they have memories so painful that they become dedicated to hard work and sacrifice, the odds are that opportunity will not be held back. The horrors of life behind the Iron Curtain are apt to provide the motivation that will produce a better world in the decade that lies ahead.

Opportunity is knocking again. It's far better to take a chance on success than to be mired in the dismal attitudes of the doomsayers.

WHY WE ARE SO STUCK ON PESSIMISM

Combining the dramatic events in Eastern Europe with mankind's basic belief in cycles makes one wonder why it hasn't become popular to embrace an optimistic attitude about the 1990s. The reason it is so difficult to recognize the past when it reappears is that history almost never repeats itself exactly. Each new cycle is accompanied by a shower of new events that are confusing and distracting.

If there had been an exact replica of the stock market crash of 1929 and the depression that followed, people today would probably be expecting a time of new prosperity. That isn't what happened. The course of the 1970s and 1980s was not an exact replica of anything. The difficulties of seeing opportunity are evident in the story of the Beijing Massacre.

The dawn of the new opportunity to rebuild Eastern Europe, the collapse of the Berlin Wall and the uprisings in Romania did not spring up out of a vacuum. They were preceded by a long chain of events, including bloodshed in Beijing.

In the 1980s China had been a leader in economic reform. The world, especially the United States, was impressed. President Nixon paved the way to what many thought would be an outstanding opportunity when he renewed diplomatic relations with China in the 1970s. For years it looked as if China was going to make the great leap into the modern world. Guangdong Province, a neighbor to Hong Kong, became a model of prosperity. Private ownership of business and property was being allowed even to the point of condominiums for sale on Chinese soil. Western business rushed to participate. Capital flowed freely into China from the West. It was widely expected that rising economic prosperity would pave the way for future political change. The theory was that once standards of living began to rise appreciably there would be no turning back.

This theory had special appeal in the United States. We felt sure that as long as a nation was mired in poverty there would be no hope for political change. We were convinced that China was traveling the right road. Our firm conviction was that if you make people richer, democracy will flower.

All along there were signs of strain. New prosperity caused new challenges. Inflation rose because demand grew faster than supplies. The road from Communist central planning to an economy ruled by free-market forces was not quick or painless. But most Western observers in the late 1980s were confident that China would manage the transition.

China's economic hopes and reputation vanished in a cloud of cordite when, in June 1989, the Peoples' Army was ordered to fire on the people. The Beijing Massacre came as a dreadful jolt. All hope that economic reform would lead the way to a more open and free China was crushed. Western plans for billions in profits from trade with China had to be scrapped.

Until the massacre, conventional Western wisdom favored the Chinese approach over Mikhail Gorbachev's *perestroika*. Western preoccupation with business and commerce produced a bias. We found it hard to believe that political reform—*perestroika*—could succeed without being accompanied by economic results. Because of our bias, we firmly believed that improving living standards had to be the first priority. We were completely wrong.

The hard-line killers in the Chinese government proved conclusively in June 1989 that political, not economic, reform is the higher priority. As long as dictators wielding military power control a country, prosperity doesn't have a chance.

The problem is that when a firm conviction is shattered, self-confidence tends to be weakened. If we can be so wrong about something as basic as how the process of economic and political reform will evolve, how can we be right about anything?

The collapse of economic progress in China produced understandable skepticism about developments in Eastern Europe. Had we been right about China and if economic reform had led to political reform, we might be more confident and not so blinded to the developing opportunity in Europe. The story of China shows how one specific development can throw up a cloud that makes it difficult to see that history really is being repeated and that new opportunity lies ahead.

THE UNNERVING TRUTH ABOUT THE FUTURE

In 1984 England negotiated a settlement of the Hong Kong issue with the Chinese government. The deal calls for British control of the crown colony to end in 1997. At the end of that year the Chinese government in Beijing is to take control of prosperous and free Hong Kong. Thus Hong Kong will be turned over to Chinese rule in 1997.

The stock market in Hong Kong was hit hard when the army opened fire in Beijing. The Hang Seng Index fell more than 35 percent in the days after the Beijing Massacre.

The reality of Hong Kong in June 1989 made a mockery of all the popular U.S. doomsday fantasies. In all the glib warnings of a coming depression, including the best-seller *The Depression of 1990*, there was a promise: if you would buy the book, subscribe to the newsletter or invest in a particular fund, you would be spared from the coming economic collapse. In fact most of the doomsayers promised more than that. They promised that if you followed their advice you would become rich while most others were swept into the pit of poverty.

What a preposterous indulgence in pure fantasy. The fact that so many otherwise intelligent people were so convinced by the crash-depression nonsense is a testimony to the gullibility of crowds, even crowds of savvy investors.

Even before the Beijing Massacre there was ample evidence in Lebanon and on the streets of American cities that the doomsayers were wrong. In the early 1970s Beirut, Lebanon, was a beautiful and incredibly prosperous city. In those days Lebanon was often called the Switzerland of the Middle East. However, there was a dark side to Lebanon's character—the drug lords. In the countryside around Beirut the climate is right for growing hashish, so while Lebanon was prosperous, the drug lords lurked in the background. Legitimate business and law and order dominated. As the economy of Lebanon came tumbling down in civil war, the balance of power shifted; the forces of chaos—the drug lords—emerged, while legitimate business was ruined. Beirut became a war zone where life itself was cheap.

Imagine what would happen if the U.S. economy followed the doomsday script and plunged into a new depression. What good would it do to have a hoard of gold coins or cash in a safe deposit box? Our jails are full now. The streets in many cities have already become battle zones. The dark side of the American character has gained in power and strength because of our hunger for drugs and our inclination to take the quick road to riches. It doesn't take much to realize that a serious fracture in the U.S. economy will lead to something much worse than the Great Depression. It will undoubtedly lead to a shift in power. Law and order could be swept away, and drugs, bloodshed and chaos could gain the upper hand.

There is a lot written about the level of debt in the United States and about the risk that entails. We sanguinely worry about how much to hold in stocks, government bonds and cash, while the real risks elude us. The economic risks are real enough. The mistake we make is believing that the past, in the form of the Great Depression of the 1930s, is the risk. The real risk is far worse. Let the United States fall into another depression, and the result will be another Dark Age, with hunger, disease and pestilence reigning the land.

In the 1930s many Americans still lived on farms or knew how to grow food, hunt and catch fish. Poverty was a problem, but most still were able to feed themselves and survive. Today too many depend on the microwave and can't make the connection between fertilizer and their last meal. Killing an animal or cleaning a fish is regarded as "gross." We are more vulnerable today than we were in the 1930s. In fact the debt level, the savings and loan crisis and the other financial challenges are the least of our worries. We are well equipped to deal with the problems of money, commerce and economics, but we aren't that well equipped to deal with a breakdown in our food distribution system or a quantum increase in lawlessness.

The doomsayers might argue that holding gold or cash is the ticket to a better land. Hong Kong shows the fallacy in that thinking. The five million citizens of Hong Kong were denied passports by the British government. London worried about a flood of immigrants that might wreck the British system. If there ever is another depression in the United States and chaos rules, how many of the 250 million Americans will be able to find a home somewhere else? A few might but certainly not all those that bought the doomsday books or followed the doomsayer's advice. If a compassionate world, with years to make preparations, cannot assure the five million citizens of Hong Kong safety, how would the world cope with a huge country like the United States in an economic mess? And if the United States plunged into a depression, it is likely that much of the rest of the world would also suffer. There simply wouldn't be the resources to provide protection, and money would be of little value to most people.

Could such an apocalypse really happen? The answer is yes. Will it happen? The answer to that depends on our attitude. If we assume that the future is dismal, that our problems are too great and that it is hopeless to try, we increase the odds of a true calamity. We do ourselves no favor by indulging in fantasies of disaster. It's better to take a lesson from the people and markets of Hong Kong.

REAL RISK PRODUCED REAL PROFITS
IN HONG KONG

After the Beijing Massacre investors in Hong Kong stocks were forced to face the ultimate financial disaster. If the hard-liners in Beijing remain powerful and treat Hong Kong in 1998 as they did the students in Beijing in 1989, stocks in Hong Kong will become almost worthless. Assets—from land to the Hong Kong dollar— will plunge in value.

In the summer of 1989 investors had no choice but to examine each Hong Kong company in light of the new political reality, and they did. The surprising result was that many stocks were found to be undervalued even if their business was significantly devalued in 1998. By year-end 1989 the Hang Seng Index had largely recovered. In 1990 the Hong Kong stock market remained relatively strong even as the political battles with Beijing wore on. Investors who added to their holdings of Hong Kong stocks after the Beijing Massacre enjoyed handsome profits.

The funny thing about fantasy is that it can blind us to reality. The investors who were swept up in popular fantasies of a coming depression looked at Hong Kong stocks in June 1989 and said "no thank you." To them, the fall in the Hong Kong stock market looked like another step along the yellow brick road to fulfillment of their disaster dreams. They held firmly and confidently onto their cash. Others more rooted in reality concluded that there was a reasonable chance for profit in Hong Kong stocks and decided to take the chance. They enjoyed the profits.

The lesson for all investors is that there really are no guarantees when it comes to the future. There is no government, no system and no formula so correct that followers can be protected from all dismal possibilities. There are only people and when people are willing to take realistic risks and make sacrifices, the odds on success improve. When it becomes too popular to avoid risk and indulge in fantasy, the odds on prosperity diminish and the chances of a slump in the quality of life increases.

A Hong Kong full of hard-working risk takers improves chances for continued freedom and prosperity. The Beijing Massacre crushed the Chinese economy and paralyzed the government. It did not eliminate the killers at the top, but it did cause fear to spread throughout the country. Bureaucrats in every province were terrified of the consequences should they make a mistake. They refused to accept responsibility for simple decisions. All issues, even the most mundane, percolated to the top. Beijing was swamped, and government processes ground down almost to a halt. After the Beijing Massacre, China headed down a road leading either to change or catastrophe. In the event that change wins the day a vibrant and prosperous Hong Kong would become a priceless jewel for China. The investors in Hong Kong reasoned that it's better to plan on that outcome than assure financial ruin by assuming the worst.

The story of the Beijing Massacre and the Hong Kong stock market in 1989 provide examples both for investors and nations. The quick recovery of the Hong Kong stock market shows that political tragedy can create opportunity. Buying after a market plunges often results in significant profits. The other and perhaps more essential lesson from Hong Kong is that investors play an important role in setting the level of national confidence. It seldom pays to be overconfident; likewise, avoiding risk and planning for the day of economic disaster does not pay.

In time Beijing may be forced to follow in the footsteps of the nations of Eastern Europe. It is doubtful that the tough, antihumanity ideology shown in June 1989 will lead to political stability and greater prosperity. It is more likely that it will lead to continued economic strife, falling standards of living and political instability. If China's people manage to change the character of their government, China will again represent significant future potential.

FOUR STEPS TO BECOMING A SAVVY INTERNATIONAL RISK TAKER

No investor can singlehandedly prevent the world from plunging into chaos or the United States from creating a new depression. If the worst happens, you'll be affected—no matter how rich you are or what investment strategy you follow. What you can do is be a savvy risk taker with a solid international perspective. Increase your wealth in the good times and minimize the impact on your personal life if the worst becomes reality.

The first step is to dismiss the fantasies of a world about to be plunged into chaos. They prevent you from taking the risks required to improve your personal fortune. Life itself is full of risks. If we live day to day in abject fear of death, illness or old age, we will not live at all. The same principle applies to investments. To live, we have to accept life's ugly side and take risks, and to prosper, we have to apply the same attitude to our financial affairs.

The second step in the dual quest for financial security and riches is to look at history and at the world around us to see how real people deal with real economic challenge. We can learn from the people of Eastern Europe and from those who have survived wars and economic deprivation.

The third step is to embrace the adventure and risks of living and investing in a world full of uncertainty.

The fourth and last step is to courageously and sensibly take the plunge into world markets in search of opportunity.

If the world is not headed for another depression in the foreseeable future, you'll enjoy a fuller and more prosperous life and in the process will make a real contribution. What better protection against the evils of economic chaos than a nation full of prosperous risk takers.

OPPORTUNITY #1: HOW TO GET A GUIDEBOOK

First of all, throw away your list of unacceptable risks. You can always make another list if you wish. Risks, most of them unacceptable, have been a part of the world since the beginning of history, and they'll be around for a long time to come.

Next, look at investing as an adventurer looks at the next journey. Take a little money out of savings and buy shares in an international mutual fund. T. Rowe Price, Templeton and Fidelity Investments are three that offer international funds. There are others, but don't fret about which one to choose. Look in one of the financial papers for an ad, call the toll-free number and get an application form. You don't have to invest a lot to start. The primary objective is to begin the adventure rather than plunge ahead, throwing caution to the wind.

After you invest, the fund's manager will start sending quarterly reports. Look at these reports as you would a guidebook for traveling to a foreign country. They are full of information prepared by professional investors. The reports will tell you about the world economic outlook and the specific countries the fund's manager thinks are attractive. Open up an atlas and find out where the various countries are located. Take an interest in one or two of the companies helped by the fund. Write to them for an annual report.

For a very small investment, an international mutual fund can give you all the information you need to begin the adventure of investing in the 1990s.

CHAPTER

2

The Next Global Investment Opportunity

The last four decades were times of wild markets but overall opportunity for investors in U.S. markets, as is shown in Table 2-1. A portfolio of $100,000 invested in the equivalent of the Standard & Poor's 500 stocks in 1950 grew to more than a million dollars by the end of the 1960s. Multiplying your money by ten in 20 years is the perfect definition of major, long-term opportunity. In an environment where a major world stock market rises that much there are thousands of individual stocks that do even better. The 1960s were the years of Xerox and IBM, where small investments became millions in a few years.

Over the last two decades the averages appear to have produced solid, if smaller, gains. The 1970s and 1980s combined produced good profits on U.S. stocks. A $100,000 portfolio invested in the Standard & Poor's 500 in 1970 grew to $177,000 by 1979 and to $890,310 by 1989. Those numbers, however, are misleading. Infla-

Table 2-1. Investment Returns on U.S. Assets

	1950s	*1960s*	*1970s*	*1980s*
Stocks (S&P 500)	+486%	+112%	+77%	+403%
Corporate bonds	11	18	83	240
U.S. government bonds	1	16	71	227
Treasury bills	20	46	84	134

Source: T. Rowe Price Associates, based on data furnished by Standard & Poor's and Ibbotson Associates.

tion was much greater in the Seventies and Eighties, as well as capital gains taxes. The real gains, after inflation and taxes, were much
less than in the great years between 1950 and 1969. The numbers for
the Seventies and Eighties look good only until you take into account the steep rise in the cost of living and the increased capital
gains tax burden. You needed good gains then just to stay even. To
put it another way, stocks would have had to rise a lot more to have
matched the real, after-tax gains of the Fifties and Sixties. The complete definition of major, long-term opportunity then is multiplying
your money by ten in 20 years and not losing most of it to either
taxes or inflation.

Twenty years of slugging it out with inflation and taxes are
enough to discourage even the most persistent optimists. We wish
that the great days of the 1950s and 1960s would return, but we're
afraid to count on it. We think it's safer to expect those dismal
trends from the recent past to continue into the future than to tantalize ourselves with dreams of real opportunity.

HOW IS MAJOR OPPORTUNITY CREATED?

When it comes to your personal portfolio, opportunity is very
specific. It means selecting stocks or bonds that rise significantly.
This very important personal perspective can be distracting. There
are always opportunities somewhere in the world. While it is important for an investor to work hard to find specific opportunity, it is
equally important to understand the background.

In 1987, after the world stock crash, the price for a share of
Hoogovens, a Dutch steel company, fell to 24 guilders. A year later
the price was 70 guilders, for a 190-percent gain in a single year.
Service Merchandise, a major U.S. retail chain, saw its stock price
fall to less than $3 after the crash and climb to $22 over the following year. The performance of these stocks shows one form of major
opportunity. After a major market setback there is almost always a
significant recovery. Market plunges create opportunity.

Outstanding companies with exciting new products are another
type of opportunity. Apple Computer, for example, dazzled the
world with its computers in the 1980s. The stock rose from $8 a
share in 1985 to $60 in 1987.

It is correct to say that in just about every year of every decade
there is one or another form of opportunity to make a huge profit

by selecting the right stock or buying stocks at the right moment. This type of opportunity will be found in the 1990s as well. The real question, however, is not whether there will be opportunity in the 1990s but rather if there will be opportunity of a major, long-term nature such as there was after World War II. The surprising answer is yes, that is a real possibility.

Theoretically, major opportunities for quantum increases in world trade and world economic growth come in two forms— development and reconstruction. Development has been illusive in the twentieth century. While there have been times when capital flowed into poor or developing countries, the development of underprivileged countries has not been a major source of growth. Nonetheless there have been exceptions. Taiwan and Korea, for example, have lifted their standards of living and become major players in world markets. Most other poor countries, however, have not been so fortunate. It would be nice if rich nations invested their capital in poor countries, took a chance on the future and tried to produce long-term growth in that way. Unfortunately that has not been the case, and development is not apt to be the source of major opportunity in the 1990s.

The great opportunity of the post–World War II period came in the form of reconstruction. We rebuilt Europe and Japan. The initial motive was to prevent another war, but the underlying condition was that reconstruction involves less risk than development. When a nation or group of nations is helped with reconstruction, the past is a guide to the future. From past experience you know that the people are capable of sustaining growth once capital is invested. In the case of developing countries, that is not so. As a practical matter, it is less risky to rebuild than to create an economy where none existed before.

This is a little like buying stocks in good companies after a market crash. You know that the chances of recovery are good because the company did well in the past. In the case of a brand-new company or product you don't know what the future will bring. We know that the nations of Eastern Europe once thrived and prospered. They are now desperate, but the people are capable and willing to make sacrifices to rebuild their lives.

Reconstruction produced opportunity in the 1950s and 1960s, and it is likely to produce similar results in the decades ahead. While there are no guarantees, the odds are that the rebuilding of

the economies of Eastern Europe will, like the reconstruction of
Europe and Japan after World War II, create major, long-term opportunities for investors.

WILL THE UNITED STATES
BE THE BIG WINNER AGAIN?

In the two decades after World War II the United States enjoyed
significant economic growth, rising corporate profits and major opportunities in its stock market (see Figure 2-1). In those days the
United States was the dominant world economy and the major provider of the long-term capital needed to rebuild Europe and Japan.

A lot changed in the last two decades, raising serious questions
about the role of the United States in the future rebuilding of the
economies of Eastern Europe. In the 1970s the Japanese profited by
selling cars, television sets and other goods to the United States.
Whole U.S. industries were wiped out by Japanese competition.
The United States suffered while the Japanese profited. In the 1980s
Japanese prosperity became enormous wealth, and they used some

Figure 2-1.   U.S. Quarterly Price Ranges, 1945–1966

Chart prepared by Richard Andrews from data supplied by the author.

of the capital to build factories in the United States, buy U.S. real estate and acquire whole U.S. businesses. By the end of the Eighties Japan had become the world's largest creditor and the United States, the world's largest debtor. We won the war but lost the markets.

There are several questions for the Nineties: Will the United States stage a comeback and emerge as a renewed, tough international competitor or languish in debt and deficit until swamped by payments to others? Will it be a full participant in the developing opportunities in Eastern Europe, or will it lose again to a new army of competitors? Will Europeans end up with standards of living much higher than those in the United States?

As the 1980s came to a close, the answer was anything but clear. By the end of 1989 the U.S. trade deficit had shrunk as a percent of gross national product. At $109 billion a year, however, the deficit was still a cloud over America's future. Allowed to go on at $100+ billion a year the deficit would eventually grow so large that the costs of servicing the debts would be a significant drain on U.S. economic resources.

The rules of international economics are harsh. Nations that allow their debts to rise too high pay a price in misery. The United States has a choice: it can voluntarily make sacrifices now to become a tougher international competitor, or it can keep pushing the issue off until the debts provide the answer. The only acceptable solution is for the United States to find a way to become a tougher international competitor. Working hard and saving more to increase exports is far better than having U.S. credit cut later and suffering a serious decline in our standards of living.

At the end of the Eighties there were unfortunately only a few signs that the United States had learned its lessons. Gnawing uncertainties remained about both the ability of U.S. business to compete in international markets and the willingness of the American people to make the sacrifices necessary to improve education and restore the national savings pool. The twin deficits—trade and federal—that hung over markets in the Eighties lingered on as the Nineties began.

In December 1989 the U.S. stock market presented a vivid picture of all these doubts and uncertainties. While many foreign stocks rose steadily, a broad range of U.S. stocks were battered down day after day. It seemed as if investors were determined to compress into a single month's trading all the popular gloomy visions of the world in the 1990s. Did the prospect of slower growth and lower interest rates in 1990 plus uncertainty about the United States later in the decade justify badly bashing so many U.S. stocks? Common sense says no. The bashing of U.S. stocks in late 1989 looked more like a comment on U.S. investor attitudes.

The excuse given for the late-1989 selling of so many U.S. stocks was that the United States was headed into a period of slower growth. That is not all bad; in fact, it is very healthy for the long term. (The worst case is to have a boom followed by a bust.) Instead, the U.S. was managing the transition from an economy that created millions of new jobs and ran into capacity utilization restraints with inflation threatening to an economy gathering its strength for a period of sustained, moderate growth in the early 1990s. You'd think that U.S. investors would slowly but surely accumulate U.S. stocks, but that isn't what happened. Institutional investors became very negative on the near-term outlook for stock prices, while individual investors preferred cash in the bank at temporarily high interest rates. The result was a disheartening sinking spell in a broad range of U.S. stocks.

The sad state of confidence in the United States had been around for a long time. On July 20, 1979, then President Jimmy Carter addressed the nation. The speech, billed as a major national address, was entitled "Energy and National Goals." The United States was faced with the consequences of soaring oil prices, a plunging dollar and double-digit inflation. Those who hoped for a rousing speech to lead the nation out of the mess were sadly disappointed.

The President told us that "the problems of our nation are much deeper—deeper than gasoline lines or energy shortages, deeper even than inflation or recession." His depressing message was that the lack of confidence "is a crisis that strikes at the very heart and soul of our national will. We can see this crisis in the growing doubt about the meaning of our own lives and in the loss of a unity of purpose for our nation." The speech has become known as "The Malaise Speech."

Political leaders sometimes lead nations to higher goals, and at other times they only put into words what is in the hearts and minds of the majority. In 1979 President Carter did the latter. He didn't create the malaise with his words; he merely spoke for the majority of Americans. That was how most felt as the 1970s came to a close.

The saddest thing is that not much changed in the 1980s. We indulged in anxiety about a crowding out of our bond markets by ever-rising government debt. Interest rates were supposed to climb above 20 percent and keep climbing, eventually crushing the life out of the economy. When that theory came up wrong, we went on to the Latin debt crisis and confidently expected most, if not all, of our money center banks to go broke. When the money center banks defied the will of so many and survived, we moved on down the list of potential catastrophic possibilities. At one time or other we worried about renewed double-digit inflation and about the opposite— a prolonged period of deflation. We agonized over the trade deficit and the loss of U.S. competitiveness. Our malaise attitudes helped produce the stock market crash of 1987, which was supposed to lead straight to a repeat of first 1929 and then the depression of the 1930s. When we survived the trials of the Eighties, we still worried about the level of U.S. total debt, a plunge in commercial real estate values and the collapse of so many savings and loans. The common thread in all our anxieties was the nagging but terrifying feeling that we are helpless, unable to cope and therefore doomed to an economic catastrophe.

The problems have been and are real. The Latin debt crisis, the trade deficit, the huge debts and the more recent collapse of so many commercial real estate deals are all real challenges. The issue is not the reality of the problems, but it is our approach to dealing with the situations that confront us.

Imagine what the world would be like today if the United States had adopted such a gloomy attitude back in the 1940s. If we had concluded that fighting the Nazis on one front and the Japanese on another was a hopeless situation, we might never have invaded Normandy or fought our way across the Pacific. If we had given up back then, the world today would be a much worse place. But we didn't give up. We fought on against tough odds and didn't know if we could win but were willing to give it our all anyway. We took a chance, we fought, many died, and we won.

In the 1980s we did reasonably well. Our economy grew, and millions of new jobs were created. We survived a huge trade deficit, periodic sinking spells in the dollar, a Latin debt crisis and other threatening challenges. The Dow Jones Industrial Average climbed 210 percent. Interest rates and inflation came down. We are now dealing with a savings and loan crisis, stubborn inflation and a slower economy, and with a bit of luck, we'll win again.

Imagine what we might do if we push the nagging anxieties out of our minds and adopt an attitude similar to what we had in the 1940s. We just might win back some lost markets, learn how to manufacture goods competitively and go on to raise our national standard of living. If we don't change our attitude, however, the 1990s look bleak, not for the world but for American standards of living. People in other parts of the world are willing to try, work hard and sacrifice in the short term for the long term. They stand a good chance of enjoying higher standards of living by the end of the 1990s. With our popular defeatist attitude, we stand a chance of falling further behind.

The United States will soon be faced with a new army of highly motivated competitors from East Germany, Hungary and Czechoslovakia. If we don't marshal our resources and fight hard, we could see our living standard slide while others enjoy greater prosperity. The key resource needed is capital. The wars in the 1990s will be fought mostly in commerce with capital and goods rather than soldiers and bullets. The greatest supplier of capital is undistributed, after-tax corporate profits.

Much is made of the U.S. savings rate. If only we could save more is the lament, but that doesn't go far enough. If Americans save more by putting money in the bank, the risk is an increased dependence on debt. After all, that is what American banks do with deposits; they lend them to others. What we need is not just savings but long-term investment that is at risk.

If after-tax corporate profits were to rise, business would have the capital to risk on new technologies, factories, ideas and jobs. With Americans buying stocks, we could continue to raise capital through the sales of new shares.

Business for its part seems to be trying. For example, late in 1989 Eastman Kodak and IBM, two U.S. giants, announced restructuring plans designed to make both companies leaner and more competitive. We need more of this, and we need to support U.S. business and show that we as individuals are willing to take risks through stock ownership. We also need to act as owners of business rather than speculators who hold stock only for this year's gains. In addition, Washington needs to change its attitudes about corporate profits and allow more realistic depreciation deductions and tax rates on business.

Will we do it? There were few signs of national change at the end of the Eighties. But we might. Americans have shown some signs of change. Look at Massachusetts, long a bastion of illusions about the wealth of its people. For ten years or more, this state indulged in the fantasy that its citizens were so rich that higher taxes could be imposed to pay for all sorts of needed but expensive programs. By the end of the Eighties Massachusetts citizens were faced with a huge state debt, the lowest bond rating in the nation and a rude awakening to the fact that there were too few wealthy residents to tax to support all the spending.

Slowly but surely Massachusetts began to awaken, learning that taking care of the elderly, the poor and the environment requires a sound economy, a growing number of wealthy people and a huge supply of corporate profits and personal income. There is a chance that this state will change for the better. Likewise, there is the chance that the nation will begin to pay more attention to the basics of modern economics.

The problem for investors is that you just don't know which way things will go in the future. We can insist on indulging in our doomsday wishes or decide to get going and fight for our future standard of living.

THE AMERICAN CHALLENGE

As we look back at the 1980s, it is relatively easy to spot the mistakes. The U.S. merchandise trade deficit, for example, did not just grow steadily. It made a quantum leap in 1984, rising from $52.4 billion in 1983 to more than $120 billion in 1985. Something obviously happened to produce such a sudden change. The answer is that the Federal Reserve went a step too far in its fight against inflation. Interest rates were raised so high that foreign capital flooded into the country driving the dollar up to impossible heights. Foreign goods became cheap and American goods too expensive. The consequence was a flood of imports and the quantum leap in the trade deficit.

As late as 1984, the U.S. Federal Reserve had not learned the importance of keeping the dollar low enough to make American goods competitive. That was a sad state of affairs. Once a large trade gap is created it is very difficult to cut it back.

Other deficits are equally difficult to correct. The federal government's budget deficit grew significantly in 1982. Tax collections plunged and expenses rose in the recession. Years later, at the end of the decade, the government was still fighting to close the gap. Why did we create the deficit in the first place? We did it to crush inflation. Why did we have to do that in such a brutal fashion? We didn't. Oil prices were about to come down anyway. If we had a little more patience and applied high interest tenderly, the huge increase in the federal deficit might have been prevented. There was no need for such a severe recession. The devastation caused to whole sections of the economy far outweighed the benefits from a temporary win against inflation.

The growth of the federal deficit and the trade deficit in the 1980s shows our ignorance about the importance of currency markets and our impatience, even brutality, with our economy. We still acted as if we could do what we wanted, as if our economy were still loaded with wealth and able to afford brutal treatment.

There is another area where our failings took an even worse toll. In 1980 undistributed U.S. corporate profits were $97.6 billion. Those are the profits left after taxes and after payment of dividends to shareholders. That is the basic raw material for any economy. Undistributed profits are those business can use to create new jobs, improve technology, build new plants and fend off foreign competition. Cash handed over to the government or to shareholders is gone from the corporate checking account. Given the bashing from the recession and from the dollar's 1984 skyrocket ride, U.S. business needed all the undistributed profits it could muster just to stay even. Sadly, that was not the case. In the closing quarters of 1989, undistributed U.S. corporate profits had fallen to an annual rate of just $29–$30 billion. That was a 69-percent plunge. The greatest scandal was that no politician, journalist, media personality and few investment advisors even noticed.

The reason the bleeding of American business went unnoticed was that business did all right before taxes and before dividend payments. Pretax corporate profits rose from $237 billion in 1980 to $274 billion at the end of the decade. The government was a winner; tax collections from business went up from $84.8 billion in 1980 to $120 billion at the end of the decade. Shareholders were winners;

dividend payments rose from $54.7 billion in 1980 to $125 billion at the end of 1989. But America's future was the loser; business was drained of desperately needed capital.

Laboring under the double burden of a rising national debt and rising debt to foreigners, the United States was not in a good position as the 1990s began. Having bled a valuable resource—business profits—the nation was faced with a daunting task.

How do you turn a nation around? How do you make teenagers stop watching television and start learning to read? How do you balance a federal budget when neither business nor the population can afford to pay? How do you become more competitive when your capital markets are in disarray and savings are too low? How do you convince Americans that they aren't rich anymore and that business profits are precious? If the United States is to prosper in the 1990s, all of these issues will have to be resolved.

The lesson from the 1980s is this: throw away the idea that all you need for prosperity in the 1990s are U.S. stocks, dollars and bonds. The future for U.S. assets is uncertain, but it is much brighter for assets in other countries.

This doesn't mean that all U.S. stocks are bad investments. The brutal environment of the United States in the 1980s made some U.S. companies become tougher. Don't be afraid to buy U.S. stocks because they can provide excellent results even if the overall economic situation doesn't improve. There will be growth in the world. Europe alone should provide a source of growth throughout the 1990s. Japan and the Pacific Rim likewise are expected to keep growing in the next few years. There will be opportunity for those American companies that are tough, international competitors. Opportunity will also exist for those with valuable assets and significant cash flows. If all else fails, they will be attractive as takeover candidates. The greatest investment error in the future is not likely to be buying selected U.S. stocks. It is more likely to be thinking that all you need are U.S. stocks.

The U.S. is still the world's second-largest stock market. This still is a land of reasonable political stability and some, albeit less, opportunity. There will be American companies that not only survive but go on to show handsome rewards for investors. Hold no illusions about the United States in the 1990s. Be realistic, and that includes a willingness to buy selected American stocks when they look too cheap.

Millions of Americans may find that life at the end of this century is not what they expected. You don't have to be one of them. You can buck the national financial trend, and in doing so, you may suffer pangs of conscience, wonder if you are less than patriotic, and wish the United States were different. You will also be making a contribution. If enough Americans awaken to the harsh realities of economics in the 1990s, there is a chance that the nation's wealth and standard of living will rise rather than fall. You can't change the nation, but you can do your part. The United States is going to need all the successful investors it can muster in the years to come.

AN OPPORTUNITY MISSED

People are equal only before God and justice. When it comes to money, there will always be great disparities. Some countries grow rich, while others languish in the muck and mire of poverty.

In a free capitalist system rich holders of capital are free to look for the best return on their money. Return is proportional to risk in a normal environment. The greater the risk taken, the greater the potential reward. Wealthy individuals never roll the dice with all their assets. What they usually do is invest some in low-return, safe assets and then take a part of their assets and go in search of a better return. Among nations, this should mean that capital flows out of the richest countries and into the poor or developing countries.

In the 1980s that normal flow of money was frustrated. Fear of a coming world economic catastrophe affected international capital flows. Money refused opportunity and preferred safety instead. Billions that might have benefited the countries of Latin America, for example, ended up in U.S. government bonds. Japanese investors were afraid of investing in businesses in Latin America, as they saw what had happened to American business and banks in that part of the world. They didn't want to lose their fortunes and fall on hard times.

It didn't matter that the Latin debt problem had a positive side. In the 1970s Americans screamed for revenge against the power of OPEC, which kept its money in American banks. What did we do? We loaned OPEC's cash to Mexico and other Latin countries. They used part of the cash to drill for oil, and that was the beginning of the end for OPEC. Looked at in this way, the U.S. lending to Latin debtors was not foolish; it was extremely clever.

The opposite of "all's well that ends well" is "a bad result sours the whole process." In the 1970s an opportunity was missed. Capital did not flow from the rich nations to those in need. Economic progress was slow and halting in Latin America and the developing world. We can wonder, but will never know, what might have been in the 1980s if the rich had invested a reasonable part of their capital in developing countries. Perhaps we would have found huge new supplies of natural resources; prevented the acceleration in the destruction of precious rain forests; saved millions from poverty; and opened up new markets for goods from Europe, Japan and the United States.

No matter. There is nothing to be gained from wishing that we could change the past. The important lesson from the opportunity lost in the 1980s is to recognize that free markets do not guarantee the fulfillment of opportunity.

The Marshall Plan worked after World War II because it was sponsored by governments and driven by an intense and compelling desire to prevent another war. Governments used their military force to assure that Japan and Germany did not rebuild their armies and launch another attack. With that commitment, business and private investors were willing to take a chance on rebuilding Europe and Japan. They had a lot to gain, as both were in ruins. The only real risk was that another war would develop before they had earned an adequate return on investment. With opportunity so obvious and governments providing the assurance of peace, capital flowed where it was needed and two decades of prosperity and profits for investors followed.

Today's world is awash with capital in need of investment. Trillions of dollars are stored away in pension funds around the world. The money has been accumulated to assure comfortable years in retirement for millions of workers. How is this money to be invested? Some of it should be in safe assets, such as government bonds; some should be invested in well-established businesses; and other money should be invested in venturesome ways to earn a higher rate of return.

The only way that all those workers can be assured of a peaceful and prosperous retirement is through the wise investment of pension funds. If the money continues to accumulate in well-developed countries such as the United States, the future will be less secure. The United States is a large country, but not large enough to provide workers to support all its own retirees in the next century plus retirees from other countries. Look at it this way. The only way that capital can be productive is if people make it so. If everyone retired and went fishing, there would be no return on anyone's capital. There has to be a large force of people young enough to keep working if older retired people are to live in prosperity. Where are enough millions of young people to be found? Japan has an aging population, and the United States is worried about how to provide social security in the next century. If enough capital flows to countries that are developing or rebuilding, the problem can be solved. Jobs and productive enterprises can be created to assure prosperity into the next century.

There is a good chance that this rosier scenario will be the one that evolves in the 1990s. Japan and the United States, among others, are well aware of the problem. They still aren't ready to take a chance on Latin America or the underdeveloped countries, but they are ready to take chances.

THE NEXT OPPORTUNITY

The collapse of the Berlin Wall and the opening of Eastern Europe is an obvious opportunity. Will capital flow into Eastern Europe or remain stuck in safe places? We already have a partial answer to that question. In the fourth quarter of 1989, record amounts of money flowed into West Germany to buy stocks and otherwise search for long-term opportunity. The German Bundesbank, afraid that the influx of workers from East Germany plus the unification of the two German currencies would produce inflation, raised interest rates significantly. Rising interest rates ordinarily push stock prices down, but that was not the case in Germany. Stocks rose sharply even though short-term interest rates rose to levels as high or higher than in the dark days of 1981. This is powerful evidence that investors around the world have confidence that the Germans will succeed in rebuilding the economy of East Germany.

There were other positive signs as well. Business invested in Hungary and Czechoslovakia to prepare for the future. The world may not have had a good experience in Latin America, but that has not deterred business and investors from trying again.

In addition to capital from outside, there will be capital in Europe that will be mobilized to help rebuild the Eastern European economies. West Germany united its strong D-mark with the weak East German mark as a part of a long-term plan to improve the economy of East Germany. This step alone opens the door to the free flow of capital from West Germany to East Germany.

There isn't any Marshall Plan for Eastern Europe. Skeptics therefore can argue that it is possible that the opportunity in Europe will be missed just as the opportunity in Latin America in the 1980s was missed. It is more likely that the inspiration from West Germany's example will be the trigger that sets loose a capital rush into Eastern Europe.

West Germany has chosen to ignore the obvious risks and plunge into a monetary union with East Germany. The profits from construction, telecommunications, consumer goods and investment are likely to be huge—so large as to whet the appetites of business leaders in Japan, Hong Kong, the United States, Canada and all other developed countries. They already have smelled the first aroma of profit.

ECONOMICS, NOT POLITICS, IS THE DRIVING FORCE

For the past 20 years the Soviet Union and its satellites have had a mutual trade pact. Called Comecon, this trade organization was a pillar of the Soviet bloc. Comecon was the vehicle used to blend politics and economics, but it failed miserably. The collapse of meaningful trade within the Soviet bloc was the catalyst that brought about the changes in 1989. Likewise, economics prevented a repeat of the past, when Soviet tanks enforced politics over the will of the people. By 1989 the Soviet economy was in shambles. Threatened by poverty within, the Soviets could not afford to use their military to "discipline" the people of Eastern Europe.

By the late 1980s, even before the dramatic changes in Eastern Europe, Comecon was disintegrating. For example, in 1989 Miraculum, a Polish-Soviet cooperative maker of cosmetics, bartered a shipment of cosmetics in exchange for a truckload of eggs. Imagine! A so-called world superpower forced to exchange eggs for cosmetics. That is how low the economy of the Soviet bloc had sunk.

Communism promised prosperity for its people. Economics was at the root of the Communist ideology. The system failed a long time ago, and military force was then used to maintain the ideologues in power as long as possible. In time, however, deteriorating economics undercut all support, forcing change. The revolution that has begun in Eastern Europe is not so much one of political change as one of economic change. The people of Eastern Europe want to improve their standards of living. They see the rejection of communism as the first step in that process.

At the end of the 1980s two things were clear. The Soviet and Comecon nations were in a desperate economic situation. Poland suffered from shortages of basic foods, Moscow's stores were short of consumer goods and virtually all Comecon countries suffered from standards of living that were unacceptable.

The first truth about the Eastern European nations is that they need economic development and reconstruction. The second is that there are no quick, handy solutions to the challenge of lifting standards of living. Switching from communism to democracy does not by itself ensure economic success.

The opportunity that has opened up in Eastern Europe is likely to follow a familiar pattern, evolving in phases. Investors will profit from understanding the process, not overanticipating the distant future.

Phase 1: From Bad to Worse

For years Hungary ran a trade surplus with the Soviet Union. By 1989 it had billions of rubles and wanted to do something with them. Its problem was that rubles can only be used to buy things from other Comecon countries and they didn't have quality goods to offer. In effect, rubles had become worthless pieces of paper.

Hungary approached Moscow with a proposition: substitute something of value for rubles, such as U.S. dollars. Moscow couldn't oblige, as the Soviets were short of hard currency. Their oil exports lagged behind expectations in 1989 because of "technical difficulties" (make that bureaucratic bungling) and strong domestic demand due to cold weather. Short of hard currency, the Russians reverted to the old ways, insisting that bureaucrats in Moscow by issuing orders could resurrect the Soviet economy and give paper rubles real value. No one, other than the bureaucrats themselves, believed that an order from Moscow would magically convert antiquated factories making useless machinery into modern plants making consumer goods.

Even in Moscow ordinary citizens had come to distrust the system. Long lines became common as people tried to buy antiques, gold coins and anything else that might hold its value better than the ruble. The ruble came under attack, and it was partially devalued for tourists in 1989. That didn't solve the problem. In the real world of real trade, Moscow's currency was worth far less than the politicians were willing to admit.

(Note: It is quite common for governments to fight hard to hold their currency at an unrealistic level. The United States, for example, held the value of the dollar too high for years. In the early 1970s, President Nixon was finally forced to cut the link between gold and the dollar. Fighting to prevent a devaluation of a currency seldom helps the underlying economy. More often it is better to accept defeat and let the value fall to a realistic level. That may hurt people financially in the short run, but at least it sets the stage for recovery.)

The Soviets and their Comecon partners will not be able to continue to support losing, state-run enterprises. The dismal combination of inflation and rising unemployment are the prices of long decades of economic failure. Inflation rises because of widespread shortages and the falling value of the ruble and other Eastern currencies. Unemployment rises because unproductive businesses, once propped up by government, finally close.

Yugoslavia devalued its currency in late 1989. The move was prompted by an annual inflation rate of 2,000 percent. In making the announcement, the government acknowledged that arresting wild inflation and establishing a foundation for future growth would mean harder times and more sacrifice in the near term. In other words, one Soviet bloc country stepped up and openly admitted that before things could get better they first must get worse.

Phase 1 in the development of Eastern Europe will mean hard times for millions of people. The future will depend on accepting the consequences of getting rid of the old ways before new ones can develop. This phase of the process began when corrupt Communist governments were thrown out in 1989.

Phase 2: Capital Inflows and a Surge in
Demand for Capital Equipment

When people are losing their jobs and things are going from bad to worse, there isn't any opportunity for outside investors. Opportunity comes when the rebuilding process really gets under way.

The reconstruction of the Soviet and East European economies requires useful currencies such as the U.S. dollar, German mark or Japanese yen. At the end of World War II the United States supplied the capital through the Marshall Plan. This time Western business will fill the role of economic angel. Even before the dust had settled on the first crumbled section of the Berlin Wall, many businesses had both seen and begun to seize opportunity.

The key to investing capital in an Eastern bloc country is finding a mechanism for repatriating profits. It does no good to make a profit if the payment is in a useless paper currency. That is why, for example, Pepsi took Russian vodka in exchange for its Soviet-made Pepsi. The problem was that the Russians and other East European countries ran out of barter opportunities. A new way of solving the worthless profits problem had to be found. Fiat and the Opel division of General Motors were among the first to find a way. They agreed to invest their own money in the Eastern bloc and to provide capital to rebuild existing auto factories and bring them up to modern, state-of-the-art standards. In return, they will enjoy the benefits of a highly motivated, low-cost labor force. Fiat and General Motors will then be allowed a percentage of the cars (25 percent is typical) for export. These cars will be sold in the West for hard currency. The hard currency realized will represent the return on capital for Fiat and General Motors.

There are likely to be literally thousands of similar deals made with the Eastern European countries. All kinds of products will be manufactured both for domestic consumption and for export.

The hallmark of phase 2 will be capital flowing into the Eastern bloc to be spent on Western technology, computers, building materials, machinery and a wide range of other capital goods. Business in the West will enjoy a significant increase in demand for capital goods. Companies in Europe, Canada, the United States and Japan will have new markets for capital equipment. Investors will have opportunity to profit in stocks in companies that supply the technology, machinery and equipment needed to rebuild the Eastern European economies.

This phase has already begun and will accelerate. It won't have to wait for the completion of phase 1. The flow of capital and the growth in demand for capital equipment will take place even as economic conditions in the Soviet bloc go from bad to worse.

Phase 3: The Emergence of a New Army of Highly Motivated Competitors

Tourists traveling in Romania, Czechoslovakia or Poland discovered a truth. There were few things to buy, but those that were available (locally made sweaters, for example) were both of good quality and very cheap. Over the next few years there will be a significant number of new factories in the East. Western business will expand to take advantage of low costs. The possibilities are almost endless. Cars, appliances, machinery, ships, television sets and even computers may one day be built in the Eastern countries for export to the West.

The West will soon be faced with a new army of competitors. The competition will be intense but not as threatening as the Japanese in the 1980s. The Eastern countries need goods for domestic consumption. Therefore, a large portion of the goods made in the new factories will be kept at home. Only a relatively small portion will be for export to provide the financiers with a profit.

Nevertheless, the United States and other manufacturing countries can expect to face stiff new competition. The idea that the development of the Eastern European nations will be a one-way street of opportunity for the West is completely wrong. The one-way aspect will be confined to the period of intense capital investment (called phase 2). The Eastern nations need Western equipment and technology. Once they have it, things will change rapidly. The United States should take notice and prepare immediately for a future of both increased opportunity and increased competition.

Fortunately, investors do not have to depend on their government. They can prepare individually for the future by establishing a practice of investing wherever a solid company that is a proven tough competitor can be found. An international investment perspective will be essential in the years to come.

Phase 4: The Development of a New Consumer Market

Assuming that the first three phases are successful, the long-term consequence will be to raise living standards in the Eastern European countries and finally enable them to become a part of the global economy, not only selling for export but having the wherewithal to buy as well.

The process of reconstructing the Eastern bloc economies is not likely to proceed smoothly, and the results are not likely to be evenly spread. Some countries (East Germany, for example) stand a better chance of succeeding than others. The Soviets appear to have the biggest problem. Surveys among Soviet citizens indicate that too many wish for the "good" old days when they didn't have to share the burden of responsibility and Moscow provided everything they needed at a fixed price. These views are unrealistic. The Soviet economy is suffering so much that these same citizens who would throw *perestroika* away will soon feel the harsh consequences of decades of ill-advised central economic planning.

Other members of the Eastern bloc are more fortunate. Their citizens not only cry out for democracy, but they appear willing to accept the burden of reconstructing their economies. The people of East Germany, Czechoslovakia, Poland, Yugoslavia, Romania and Hungary, for example, seem willing to sacrifice and to work hard for low wages as long as they have a genuine opportunity to improve the living standards of their country for themselves and their children.

From an investor's point of view, it is just as well that the entire Eastern bloc is not headed for prosperity at once. Imagine what might happen if every Soviet household suddenly had two cars. The strains on the entire global economy, not to mention the environment, would be tremendous. The possibility of a significant amount of progress in a few of the Eastern bloc nations is enough to provide encouragement. The arrival of tens of millions of new prosperous consumers later in the decade should be enough to sustain economic growth to the beginning of the next century.

TAKING ADVANTAGE OF THE OPPORTUNITY

The development of the economies of Eastern Europe is not likely to follow this script exactly, but that is not the point. The point is that there are phases or essential steps in any process of massive economic development. Once this idea is understood it becomes possible for an investor to relax. There is no need to rush into stocks at high prices. Not only will it take time for the process to unfold, but there will be unpredictable problems along the way.

Looking back to the years that followed World War II makes it appear as if that road to prosperity was smooth. It wasn't. There were major hurdles along the way, including a currency crisis in 1949 and long, hard-fought economic and political battles. In the end the prosperity developed because people were willing to work and make sacrifices. The people of Eastern Europe have the same motivation.

The way to profit from developments in Eastern Europe is to be patient and cautious. When the German stock market exploded in the fall of 1989, many people wanted to follow that crowd (see Table 2-2). All of a sudden it was popular to buy German stocks. In the rush, it was forgotten that the coming prosperity won't be limited to Germany. It will spread to other European countries and to companies in the United States and elsewhere. Paying high prices for German stocks was unnecessary. There was no need to rush into stocks in 1950, and there is no need today. If, as seems likely, we are headed into a period of major long-term opportunity, there will be plenty of chances to make a fortune in the years ahead.

The opening of the borders with Eastern Europe sparked a rush not only into German stocks but into stocks in Austria as well, as is also indicated in Table 2-2. To buy the most obvious beneficiaries of trade with the East is an understandable first reaction. In time, investors will sift through all the evidence searching for other stocks to buy. All of the stock markets in Europe are likely to benefit over

Table 2-2. Performance of Europe's Stock Markets after the Berlin Wall Came Down (Six months, 9/29/89–3/30/90)

Austria	+ 64%
Belgium	+ 1
France	+ 11
Germany	+ 39
Italy	+ 2
Netherlands	+ 8
Spain	– 19
Switzerland	– 1
United Kingdom	– 2

time not only from increased enthusiasm but from real gains in corporate profits.

By the end of 1989, wide differences in stock prices had opened up in Europe (see Table 2-3). Austrian stocks commanded 41.7 times earnings, while stocks in Holland sold at only 9.7 times earnings. These huge differences are not sustainable. The enthusiasm following the dramatic events of late 1989 produced an overreaction. Caution was thrown to the wind. These exaggerations will be corrected over time. Overvalued stocks will come down, and undervalued stocks will rise.

In early 1990 there were three sensible approaches to investing directly in Europe: (1) to wait for high-priced German or Austrian stocks to come down and then buy, (2) to buy the lower-priced stocks in countries such as the Netherlands, or (3) to combine both strategies by buying low-priced stocks immediately to be sure of participating in the long-term opportunity and then holding some cash to buy German or Austrian stocks later.

Was either of these three the right strategy? No! They all were "right," as long as you were investing for the long term. Common sense says don't invest all your money in a market after the crowd has already pushed prices up. You can invest some, but you never know. High-priced stocks sometimes stay that way because the profits develop quickly, justifying the price. Other times a market will run up and then pull back. Because you don't know how markets will behave in the short run, always use a common-sense approach. Don't try to buy at the bottom. Try instead to get an

Table 2-3.   Stock Prices at the End of 1989

Country	P/BV	P/E	Yield
Austria	2.89	41.7	1.3%
Belgium	1.84	12.7	4.1
France	2.09	12.5	2.7
Germany	2.39	17.8	2.9
Italy	1.74	14.0	2.5
Netherlands	1.45	9.7	4.3
Spain	1.31	14.0	4.0
Switzerland	1.80	16.7	2.1
United Kingdom	1.95	11.7	4.5

Source: Morgan Stanley Capital International Perspective.

average cost on your investments that makes sense in light of the long-term possibilities.

By all means, invest in Europe, but just don't get carried away by headlines or emotions.

OPPORTUNITY #2: BUY YOUR PERSONAL SLICE OF EUROPE

There are several ways of investing in Europe. You can buy individual stocks in Germany, Holland or France. There are closed-end, country funds for several European countries.

If you are just beginning your adventure in international investing, a smart way to buy a personal slice of Europe is through a normal, or open-end, mutual fund. T. Rowe Price and Fidelity Investments, to name two, have introduced mutual funds that invest exclusively in Europe. These funds offer a diversified list of European stocks and professional management. They are an excellent way of investing in Europe and of being sure that you are not left out of that emerging opportunity. Call them up. Use their toll-free numbers and ask for a prospectus and account-opening forms for a European mutual fund.

(Note: You will find a list of all U.S. mutual funds in the popular financial papers such as the *Wall Street Journal* and *Barron's*. You will also find that the fund sponsors run ads in those papers giving you their toll-free numbers. Just be sure to ask for a fund specializing in European securities.)

CHAPTER

3

International Investing Made Easy

Dessauer's Journal of Financial Markets was launched on October 20, 1980. Its purpose was to provide professional international investment information and advice for individual U.S. investors. The concept seemed sound enough at the time. In the early 1980s it was expensive, difficult or impossible for individual investors to get competent information on international investing. Offering such a service looked like a good idea, but it didn't turn out to be so easy.

For several years it was a struggle. The information was good, the record was good, but international investing was not popular in the United States. Build a better mousetrap, it is said, and the world will beat a path to your door. That works only if there is a solid demand for mousetraps. You can build the best mousetrap in history, but if there is no interest in mousetraps, there won't be anyone rushing to buy.

There are two sides to the law of supply and demand. There has to be demand or else supplying the product is not feasible. In the early 1980s individual American investors weren't hungry for international investment information, and demand was very limited.

Pension funds were active in international investing. The steep fall in the dollar in the 1970s (from 4.30 versus the Swiss franc to 1.49 by 1978) provided an incentive for U.S. pension funds to begin investing outside the United States. They reasoned correctly that investing abroad provided an advantage. When the dollar fell, the value of foreign investments rose in U.S. dollar terms. Simply holding Swiss francs produced a gain of 68 percent between 1970 and 1978. With interest or dividend payments, the profits in the 1970s for U.S. investors holding Swiss assets were even greater.

Pension funds diversified to protect their portfolios against a decline in the dollar and to try and increase their performance. The move into international investing was still timid. Only fairly large pension funds made the move and then with only 5 to 15 percent of the assets in their funds.

Sometimes individual investors follow in the footsteps of the big, professionally managed pension funds, but that was not the case when it came to international investing in the early 1980s. At least one other investment newsletter devoted to international investing gave up business by 1984.

The U.S. dollar soared in late 1984. That set back the developing U.S. interest in foreign investments. Just as a falling dollar lifts the value of foreign assets a rising dollar does the opposite. The strong dollar of 1984 scared away some of the pension funds and gave many individual investors the excuse they were looking for to stay invested at home and out of foreign markets.

When television brought pictures of crowds pushing their way into West Berlin in late 1989, interest in international investing got a boost. Americans were tantalized by the possibilities for profits in East Germany, Europe and the rest of Eastern Europe. Nonetheless, interest still remained low.

It isn't easy for Americans to deal with foreign currencies and foreign corporate names. They feel much more comfortable staying in familiar markets with companies they have come to know well.

The problem is that the world has changed. Like it or not, our daily lives are affected by developments in Europe and Japan. It's silly to think that one can prosper in the 1990s without becoming familiar with foreign markets.

Decades ago, travel was limited to the brave or the rich. The airplane changed all that, and today you can fly from the United States to any corner of the world and back for a reasonable cost. Goods are flown from one country to another quickly and easily. The world has been transformed, and only the myopic refuse to recognize that fact.

In the 1980s communications exploded. By June 1989 television was able to bring live pictures from Beijing to American viewers. Likewise, the availability of financial and investment information has changed. Today it is possible to get up-to-the-minute information on what is happening on markets in Japan, Taiwan, New Zealand, Australia and any other major world market while sitting at home with a telephone line and a computer.

A few years ago no one cared what happened to stocks in Japan. After the stock market crash of 1987, American investors were glued to their television sets to get the latest information on the Tokyo stock market. Tokyo recovered from the crash quickly and provided leadership that produced a similar recovery in the United States and the rest of the world. What happens on one market now affects the others.

International investing, like travel years ago, once was an expensive luxury for a few. Today it has become essential for the financial prosperity of every investor.

Communicating information may have become easy, but understanding that information is another matter. It is easy to turn on a computer and use a telephone line to get access to foreign financial data, but how to use that data is still difficult for many Americans. We know that international investing is here to stay, but we don't want to take the time and make the effort required to learn what we need to know to cope in a complex financial world.

WHY BE BOTHERED?

In discussing real estate, the experts often say that there are three essentials: location, location and location. International investing, however, is different. There are three reasons to suffer the work required to delve into something new, but they aren't all the same.

Reason #1: You Have No Choice

You have a choice when it comes to real estate. You can rent or own, and you can stay out of commercial real estate ventures if you wish. Similarly, with stocks and bonds you have a choice. You don't have to own any stocks or bonds at all. But in the modern world of money—whether you know it or not, whether you like it or not—you cannot hide from the challenges of international finance.

Every aspect of our lives is affected by what happens on world markets. The Japanese kept the value of their currency low for years to gain a price advantage over American competitors. They succeeded. American consumers may not have liked the idea of losing jobs to Japanese competition, but in the end they bought Japanese products anyway. In some cases they had no choice. Even products that were invented in the United States were no longer made here by the mid-1980s.

The interest rate paid on a U.S. bank account is no longer set in a vacuum. American interest rates have to take into account both the state of the economy at home and international interest rate trends. Holding dollars in a U.S. bank may not seem like international investing, but it is.

The value of the dollar in your wallet is also a function of international economic trends. As the dollar rises or falls on world currency markets, many Americans think they are not involved. What they are missing is that the dollar's value on world markets has a direct impact on the cost of imported goods, the level of prices in the United States, and the number of American jobs. A strong dollar cuts into inflation, makes foreign goods cheaper for Americans but, as in 1984, can also hurt American business and mean lost jobs. A weak dollar, on the other hand, tends to raise prices for all consumer goods in the United States. That in turn reduces the purchasing power of the dollars in every American wallet.

The bottom line is that there is no escape and no place to park money so that it won't be affected by changes in international trends. Not even gold is a completely safe haven. The value of an ounce of gold fluctuated widely in the 1980s—from a high of $850 in 1980 to a low of $300 in 1982. Even though the purchasing power of the dollar steadily declined in the 1980s, gold spent most of the decade moving between $300 and $500 an ounce.

The attitudes toward international investing are too often like those toward overpopulation, damage to the environment or the presence of nuclear arms. We wish that things were different. Sometimes we try to hide or run away by retreating to a rural area in hopes of finding a safer, easier or more peaceful life. However, there is no hiding from the environment, the strains on natural resources or the threat from irresponsible governments. These are the harsh facts of modern life on this planet. We are all better off if we face the facts and deal with them in a straightforward and informed manner.

Reason #2: The Never-Ending Adventure

The question of why be bothered wrongly implies that international investing is a chore. In fact, it is difficult only at the beginning. Once you become familiar with the basics, watching the world from a new financial perspective is as fascinating and interesting as reading the best novel. The difference is that watching the world is real and ongoing, while a novel is either fantasy or history. You can turn to the back of a novel to see how it ends. International investing is a never-ending story that keeps your attention, focuses your energy and adds a new dimension to life.

Suppose you owned Hong Kong stocks in June 1989 when the market plunged on news of the Beijing Massacre. Seeing the value of your portfolio plunge would have riveted your attention on the details of what was happening in China and Hong Kong. The casual observer watching nightly television news sees only the broad outline of what is happening. An involved investor with part of a personal portfolio at stake is both more observant and more interested. It is not fun to lose money in a stock market plunge. But markets do plunge occasionally, and no investor can expect to have perfect market timing.

Plunging markets often create enormous opportunity. An investor who owned stock in Hong Kong before the plunge in June 1989 had an advantage over a casual observer or even an international investor who didn't own Hong Kong stocks. The Hong Kong market recovered fairly quickly, so there wasn't much time to analyze investments in Hong Kong. Making a quick decision to invest required not only familiarity with Hong Kong but a knowledge of which stocks to buy. Owning Hong Kong stocks before the crash meant that it was much easier to make a quick decision and buy more after the plunge.

In any case, being involved added a new dimension to whole series of events. Even if you did not buy more but simply held on and watched the value of your stock recover, you were involved. Being involved means living life more fully. That alone was a significant, albeit qualitative, dividend from investing in Hong Kong in 1989.

Europe in the fall of 1989 was another example. An international portfolio in 1989 would have included some European stocks. When the television flashed scenes of the opening of the Berlin Wall, there wasn't much time for reflection or research. The European stock markets soared shortly after the news reports. If you were already involved and familiar with the markets and individual stocks, you could have made a quick decision.

Being an armchair observer of world events may be satisfying for some, but it is nowhere near as exciting or profitable as having some of your personal money committed to the markets of the world. If you are looking for a way of living your life more fully, international investing is the right choice.

Not only do dramatic world events produce adventure, watching the companies whose stocks you own is also exciting. You can be there as international deals are struck and can profit when management makes a right move. Investing is far more than simply throwing darts at a financial newspaper and calling a broker. Done properly, investing includes involvement and paying attention to what is happening in countries around the world and in the boardrooms of some of the world's most interesting companies.

Reason #3: To Make Money

The third reason for taking the plunge into international investing is for performance—to make money. Over the last 20 years international investing has been more rewarding than holding a portfolio made up exclusively of U.S. stocks. By the end of 1989 Japanese stocks, for example, had gained an astounding 1,555 percent since 1970. Stocks in Hong Kong had gained 1,196 percent in the same 20 years. The world stock index, a composite of 18 world stock markets, gained 365 percent in the 20 years from 1970 through 1989. The U.S. stock market rose 225 percent in the same 20-year period.

There isn't any magic in international investing. No mysterious forces make an international portfolio more rewarding. For the two decades after World War II, investors did very well holding only U.S. stocks. Today, however, many U.S. stocks are traded on foreign markets. Foreign investors hold billions of dollars worth of U.S. stocks, and they make decisions based on what they see happening on markets around the world. The U.S. stock market in the 1990s is affected by developments in other countries and on world markets. Holding a portfolio of U.S. assets, while remaining ignorant of markets in the rest of the world, can be hazardous to your financial health.

There is more to international investing than stocks. Opportunities exist for increasing the yield on cash holdings by investing in foreign currencies. There are bond markets in other countries, and sometimes they pay greater interest rates than bonds in the United States or offer better potential for capital gains.

The bottom line is that there really is a world of opportunity. You can increase the odds on making money by taking the trouble to learn about the world's major financial markets.

A USEFUL FRAME OF REFERENCE

Don't immediately dive for an international newspaper or dig into the details of even one foreign market. That can be discouraging. First choose a frame of reference.

Einstein was right. All things, including markets, are relative. In the search for opportunity and profit, you need to have a clear way of judging what makes one market attractive and another risky.

On Saturday February 10, 1990, the front page of the *New York Times* had this headline: "Soviet Consumers Face Cutbacks in Meat as Feed Grain Runs Out." One of the world's superpowers faced a shortage of meat because it couldn't pay for grain to feed the cattle. By February 1990 the Soviet Union, which at times was first in the space race and which could launch nuclear-powered submarines, ballistic missiles and supersonic aircraft, could not feed its own people. How could such a catastrophe have happened?

In the United States the popular answer was to celebrate the "death of communism." Democracy, we claimed, had won the Cold War, but that isn't exactly the right answer. Democracy itself does not ensure prosperity, nor does communism ensure poverty.

What went wrong in the Soviet Union and its East European satellites? Politics became the dominant force in the culture, and business was effectively shut out of the process. Politically appointed bureaucrats ran everything. They told everyone what to make, what to grow and how to do it.

Compare the Soviet catastrophe with the astounding prosperity and wealth of Japan or Taiwan. Japan is a democracy, with elections. The culture, however, has a strong foundation in collective well-being, the group, the emperor and the good of the nation. Those are "Communist" ideas. Japan is not a democracy exactly like the United States. However, being less than a perfect replica of the U.S. democractic model did not stop Japan from accumulating so much wealth as to become the world's largest creditor by 1990.

Taiwan became a democracy in late 1989. Until then the form of government was that of a benevolent dictatorship. Nevertheless, Taiwan has enjoyed outstanding real economic growth for decades.

Growth in Taiwan far exceeded that of the United States in the 1970s and 1980s. An honest look around the world reveals that prosperity and peace follow when business has the respect of the people and politics takes second place in determining national policy.

Letting business become too strong can also lead to wrack and ruin. A strong case can be made that the root cause of the stock market crash of 1929 and the Great Depression that followed was the dominance of business over sound government. Bankers and business leaders looked at people as economic units to exploit. *Caveat emptor* (buyer beware) was the rule. It didn't matter that big business had too much power and could extract unfair advantage over the buyer because in the 1920s, that was considered to be an essential part of life itself. The unfettered excesses of the pursuit of profits at any cost finally went too far, and the financial house of cards collapsed. The fallacies of economic thinking in the 1920s were vividly exposed in the global tragedy of the Great Depression. Government is essential to maintain order and defend a nation. Laws and taxes are needed to protect the environment and provide for the poor, elderly and disadvantaged who cannot fully provide for or protect themselves.

The Great Depression was the spawning ground for a reign of terror in Europe. It also tilted our thinking too much against business and too far in favor of politics. Business as practiced in the late 1800s and early 1900s was cruel, brutal and many times wrong. Nevertheless, business is also essential to any nation's health. The secret to peace and prosperity is to strike the right balance between the power of politics and the power of business. The lesson from the collapse of the economies of the Soviet Union and Eastern Europe is that tilting too far in favor of politics produces exactly the same poverty as tilting too far in favor of business. The lessons from prosperous countries is that business should rate the first priority, with politics taking second place.

The path of least resistance for investors is to look for those countries where the balance seems right. Buying almost any stock in Japan in 1970 produced outstanding profits over the following two decades. In the United States, where the balance was less clear and where politics at times rose to a threatening level of power, the task of finding a good investment was far more complicated. There were American companies that did just as well as the Japanese in the Seventies and Eighties, but they were few in number.

In the 1970s and 1980s the United States fell prey to a feeling of being rich enough to afford a quantum increase in the size of government. From less than 20 percent of the total economy at the end of World War II, the U.S. government became more than 35 percent of the economy at the end of the 1970s. The balance between business and politics tilted dangerously close to a critical point. The risk in a democracy is that the voters will voluntarily make the wrong choices without appreciating the consequences that follow. If voters have an antibusiness, antiprofits attitude or feel that political power can be applied to every problem, the economy will suffer. Carry these attitudes to an extreme, and even the democratic U.S.A. could find its economy crushed and poor.

The first step in international investing is to make a judgment about the world's markets based on the balance between politics and business. All you need to get the right answer is common sense. Where business prospers, the balance is favorable for investors. In countries where business struggles, the balance is unfavorable.

The final challenge for investors is to find opportunity at the right price. By 1990 the Japanese prosperity was obvious. Japanese stocks had soared to high prices, 60 times earnings in 1987. While the balance between politics and business remained favorable, the stock market fully reflected the good news. The best profits are to be found in countries where the balance has been unfavorable, driving stocks prices down, but is about to change for the better. Western Europe at the beginning of 1990 is a good example.

After World War II Western Europe faced a problem. Communism to the east threatened to spread across the borders. The appeal was powerful, as communism promised an end to poverty and guaranteed housing, health care and retirement. Even those who didn't accept communism were sufficiently tempted to promote a heavy dose of socialism. Western Europe fought to find a balance between democracy and socialism to keep communism at bay. Country after country felt compelled to err on the side of too much politics and too little business.

The fact that Soviet soldiers, missiles and tanks were at the doorstep meant that Europe was more directly threatened than the United States. Europeans were terrified of arousing the Soviet army. They were willing to do anything, including compromising their capitalistic inclinations, to maintain the peace. Until the truth about the economic devastation and poverty of Eastern Europe was exposed, many Europeans believed that communism, rather than democracy, was a better economic choice. For years they naively thought that communism delivered a stable life, free of anxiety. They knew that Communist countries had less but argued that the missing elements were unnecessary glitz and glitter. In the second half of the 1980s attitudes began to change. The dismal standards of living behind the Iron Curtain were covered up by the ruling Communist governments. Refugees from and visitors to the Soviet bloc countries nevertheless discovered the truth. Slowly at first and faster later, the facts crept into European politics. When the borders between East and West finally opened, the West was appalled at the poverty and deprivation in the East. Communism was exposed not only as an economic failure but as a fraud.

Europe after World War II suffered more than a military and political threat from communism. By the 1970s Europe felt the pressure of intense business competition from Asia, especially Japan. The balance between business and politics in Europe began to change. By 1992 a more united Europe, with fewer barriers to business, was proposed and accepted. Critics argued that the many nations of Europe would never give up their individuality and form a truly united Europe. They missed the principal point: by changing the balance between politics and business, Europe was moving in the direction of a major economic opportunity. A fully and perfectly united Europe isn't necessary for a leap in prosperity. Eliminating some of the red tape and other barriers to the free flow of capital and trade is enough to unleash the power of business to create new wealth.

The collapse of the Berlin Wall and the rejection of Communist regimes in Eastern Europe came as a bonus for Western Europe. In a rush the political climate changed. The brutality and oppression of decades of communism were broadcast for all to see. The idea that Western Europe should move closer to the Communist model died quickly. Preserving and enhancing the prosperity of Western Europe suddenly moved to the center of the political stage. Helping the devastated people behind the now-rusted and crumbled Iron Curtain became the motto. For decades to come, business rather than politics is likely to have the upper hand in Europe.

One poignant story is the environment. In 1990 U.S. environmentalists still had a distinct antibusiness attitude. Business was seen as the prime culprit in spoiling the air, water and land. (Ignored were facts, such as appeared in the *New York Times* in February 1990, indicating that the single biggest polluter in New York State was the state itself.)

When television cameras moved into East Germany, the first images were of extreme pollution. The environment had been a casualty of decades of communism and anemic economies. A woman in East Germany lamented that protecting the environment was expensive and that they weren't able to afford to keep things clean because they were too busy fighting for survival.

Protecting the environment is expensive. Unless a nation's businesses are strong and profitable and unless the people have wealth, protecting the environment is a dream. Making it a reality requires capital and wealth. Creating enough wealth to solve social ills and protect the environment in turn requires the right balance between politics and business. The harsh reality of the facts from Eastern Europe made these facts crystal clear for the people of Western Europe. Western Europe was propelled in the direction of good business and prosperity by the combination of Europe 1992 and the opening of the borders with the East. This explains the rush into German stocks that developed in late 1989 and early 1990. Investors wanted to get in as early as possible on what could become the next great stock market miracle.

Capturing profits from the shifts in the balance between business and politics means (1) using common sense to determine the balance between politics and business in the major markets of the world, (2) applying more common sense to determine how that balance is likely to change in the future and (3) applying a sense of value to see if the markets are undervalued or overvalued based on the outlook for the balance between business and politics.

START BY GETTING TO KNOW A FEW OF THE OTHER MAJOR WORLD MARKETS

The secret to any new and complex task is to break it down into manageable pieces. It isn't possible to take a giant quick leap up the international learning curve. To become an international investor, you need patience and persistence. Nevertheless, don't let that make you hesitate. We all remember our school days. Back then the words patience and persistence meant long, weary days and nights slaving over dull textbooks. Teachers used words like patience and persistence in hopes that we didn't quit before we started.

International investing isn't theoretical. No dull textbooks are required and no unpleasant homework. And best of all, there are no tests or examinations. Everyone gets an A+ no matter how far they progress up the international learning curve. There are no diplomas, just financial peace of mind and increased returns on your investments. There is one other reward: a deep sense of being unique. So few manage to get above or beyond their immediate surroundings that those with an international perspective stand out from the crowd.

There are 21 major world stock markets. They are Australia, Austria, Belgium, Canada, Denmark, Finland, France, Germany, Hong Kong, Italy, Japan, the Netherlands (Holland), New Zealand, Norway, Singapore/Malaysia, South Africa, Spain, Sweden, Switzerland, the United Kingdom (England) and the United States.

There are other exciting stock markets. Korea and Taiwan, for example, have had outstanding real economic growth and outstanding stock markets for years, but these two markets are closed to foreign investors. Buying stocks in those countries is regulated. As a practical matter, the only way for U.S. investors to participate is through the closed-end, single-country funds listed on the New York Stock Exchange. There are also the emerging stock markets of Greece, Portugal, Brazil, Mexico, Argentina, Chile, Jordan, the Philippines, Thailand and India. Ireland, Bermuda and Luxembourg also have stock markets. Before long there will probably be stock markets in Hungary, Czechoslovakia and other Eastern European countries, and even the Russians have expressed interest in a stock market.

BE PRACTICAL WHEN
PICKING MARKETS TO FOLLOW

There is a wide world of opportunity for investors. The problem is that the whole world is not available to U.S. investors.

The law of supply and demand has been at work in the United States to the disadvantage of U.S. investors. The supply of investment information and services tends to follow demand. Because so few American investors have demanded information on foreign securities, the supply of information and securities is limited.

There are few things so frustrating as spending time learning about a foreign market, having your interest piqued and then finding out that as a practical matter, you can't buy the securities you want. Investors in Switzerland, Hong Kong, Germany or England, however, have an advantage over their American counterparts. They can buy foreign securities through their neighborhood brokers easily. If an American investor calls up and asks to buy a foreign stock, the answer is likely to be "Sorry, we can't handle that purchase."

One answer is to open an account in Europe and do your international investing abroad. That is a good strategy if you are investing a reasonably large amount of money, say $500,000 or more. If your portfolio is smaller or if you don't want the bother of dealing with a foreign account, there is another way.

In the 1950s U.S. banks got together and created a system for trading foreign stocks in the United States. They issued American Depository Receipts (ADRs), which are the equivalent of the foreign shares. The original motivation was based on the fact that foreign investors frequently prefer bearer shares while Americans like registered stock certificates. We like the security of seeing our names printed right on the stock certificates. Europeans prefer to have no name on their certificates so that no government official can track the asset to them. This difference in preference made it difficult for foreign shares to be brought to the United States and traded here. The banks solved that problem because ADRs are registered.

Over the years the number of ADRs actively traded in the United States has grown significantly. There are now more than 700 ADRs, and the trading in the United States is more than $4 billion a year. ADRs make it easy for American investors to buy and sell foreign stocks. American brokers can buy or sell ADRs in the same way as any U.S. stock.

Another way American investors can get access to foreign securities is through mutual funds. There are conventional or open-end mutual funds and another breed of funds called the closed-end, single-country funds. These are exciting because they allow you to get involved in the process, but you can still have professional help.

In the 1980s closed-end country funds proliferated. They were particularly attractive for countries with closed, highly regulated or small stock markets. The Taiwan Fund and the Korea Fund are examples of this type of fund. In both of these cases the country's stock markets are closed to foreign investors. It isn't possible for an individual investor in the United States to buy stock directly in either Taiwan or Korea. However, both of these countries offer exciting opportunities, so a solution was found in the form of closed-end country funds.

A closed-end fund is an investment company. A specific number of shares in the investment company are sold to the public. After the offering, the shares begin to trade just like shares in any other company. This had appeal for the governments of Korea and Taiwan. By allowing closed-end funds, they could partially open their markets to U.S. investors while not risking a flood of new investment capital or potential wild swings in their markets if capital flowed in and out in large amounts. The amount of money to be invested was controlled and limited to the public offering of shares in the closed-end fund.

The success of the Taiwan and Korea funds encouraged other professional managers to offer closed-end funds for other countries. The next step was to offer a fund for countries with small, difficult to enter, stocks markets such as Switzerland. It isn't unusual to find Swiss stocks selling at $2,000 a share. This high price makes it impractical for individual investors to buy Swiss stocks. The Helvetia Fund, specializing in Swiss stocks, was launched to give U.S. investors an easy way of participating in the Swiss stock market.

Before long, the list of closed-end country funds trading in the United States grew quite large. Funds were offered for stocks in Australia, Austria, Brazil, Chile, Spain, the Philippines, Germany, Switzerland, India, Italy, Indonesia, Ireland, Jakarta, Japan, Korea, Taiwan, Mexico, Malaysia, Portugal, Thailand, Turkey and the United Kingdom. There are likely to be more closed-end, single-country funds offered in the future.

PRACTICAL ADVICE

Choose up to five foreign countries that seem interesting to you. In making the selection limit your list to countries where there are either ADRs in a reasonable number traded in the United States or at least one closed-end, single-country fund available in the United States. Following countries when you know there is a practical way to take advantage of opportunity when it comes along is much more satisfying than following a country only to later discover that it is expensive, awkward or impossible to invest when you are ready.

OPPORTUNITY #3: MAKING A KILLING WITH CLOSED-END COUNTRY FUNDS

Closed-end country funds open up exciting opportunities for U.S. investors. For example, after the crash of 1987 shares in the Germany Fund fell along with most other stocks. The difference was that the shares in this fund fell to a discount to net asset value. Net asset value is what the shares would be worth if the portfolio were sold and the cash distributed to shareholders. The net asset value of a closed-end fund fluctuates depending on how well the fund's professional manager does and what happens to the stocks in the portfolio. After the crash of 1987, the German stock market was depressed. The peak in Germany had come in 1986, ahead of the rest of the world.

German stocks were depressed before the crash of 1987 pushed them down even further. For months it was possible to buy shares of the Germany Fund at a 15-percent discount to net asset value. Not only were German stocks cheap, but you could buy them even cheaper through the Germany Fund. It may seem silly today, knowing what we now know about East Germany and the Berlin Wall, but in 1988 American investors were offered a bargain on German stocks.

Even without knowing what was to come, buying stock in one of the world's six largest stock markets at a discount was attractive. Nevertheless for many long months, few Americans saw it that way. The share price for the Germany Fund languished at the $6 level through all of 1988 and the opening months of 1989.

In 1989 Japanese investors decided to buy closed-end country funds in the United States. Their first target was the Spain Fund, whose share price soared. Then came the dramatic news of the collapse of the Berlin Wall and the Japanese moved into the Germany Fund. That stock also soared, reaching, at one point, more than $25 a share. Patient investors who had suffered the grueling wait through more than a year suddenly had a 317-percent profit on their investment. What's more, they could sell the Germany Fund at a substantial premium to net asset value, buy a few German stocks directly, keep their investment in Germany and pocket the difference.

The lesson from the soaring prices for selected closed-end country funds is that investors with patience who buy these funds when they sell at a discount to net asset value can enjoy outstanding profits. Not only can they profit as the underlying stock market appreciates, they might have significant additional profits if investors such as the Japanese decide to move into one of their funds.

When is a good time to buy? The best time is when there has been a world markets crash or a plunge in the particular stock market and also a plunge in the shares of the closed-end, single-country funds. That was the case with the Germany Fund in early 1988 after the crash of 1987. The problem is that world stock market crashes don't come along too often and neither do plunges in individual stock markets.

The next best time to buy is when the closed-end, single-country fund shares sell at a deep (10 percent or more) discount to net asset value. This happens more often than you might think. For example, in early 1990 shares in the ROC Taiwan Fund, traded on the New York Stock Exchange, fell to $10, when the net asset value was $14.24. Because of selling by frightened investors, the ROC Taiwan Fund shares sold at a whopping 30-percent discount to net asset value.

Finding out about closed-end country funds is easy. A list of the stock funds is published every week and carried in *Barron's,* the Monday edition of the *Wall Street Journal* and the Saturday edition of the *New York Times.* The list shows the fund, its share price, the net asset value and the discount or premium.

OPPORTUNITY #4: A BONUS FROM
CLOSED-END, SINGLE-COUNTRY FUNDS

There you are in hometown U.S.A., far from the action in London, Tokyo and Frankfurt. You dream of being well connected, having the best professional advice and making a killing in foreign stocks but may not realize that this dream can come true.

Closed-end, single-country funds are managed by experienced professionals with detailed knowledge of their particular country.

Every quarter they publish a report on the fund's assets, listing the holdings. By reading the reports and keeping track of what is being bought or sold, you can find out what the professionals in Germany, England, Italy or Spain think about the individual stocks in their country.

The managers will frequently give a specific report on one of the stocks in the portfolio. When you read a glowing report about one of the individual stocks in the closed-end country fund, call your broker or investment advisor and find out if there are ADRs available for those shares. If there are, buy some and add individual stocks to your portfolio of closed-end country funds.

What could be easier? You follow this simple three-step process. First, accumulate shares in a few closed-end, single-country funds, buying only when they sell at a deep discount (10 percent or more) to their net asset value. Most closed-end, single-country funds are traded on one of the major U.S. stock exchanges. You buy or sell them just like buying or selling stock in IBM or General Motors. Closed-end, single-country funds are generally not expensive. Except when the share prices soar (and you shouldn't buy them after they have moved up sharply anyway), these funds generally trade for $5 to $20 a share. Second, read the quarterly reports and watch for the fund manager's glowing report on an individual stock. Third, call your broker and ask if the attractive individual stock has ADRs traded in the United States. If it does, buy some.

With a little luck you can make a killing on one of your closed-end funds or on one of the individual stocks, or possibly both.

CHAPTER

4

Six Major Markets

Malcolm Forbes, the founder of *Forbes Magazine,* said, "You make more money selling the advice than following it." For the Forbes family, that turned out to be a prescription for enormous wealth.

The fallacy in his statement is that if no one wants to follow the advice, you won't be able to sell it! Malcolm knew, however, that you can always find a market for good advice. He didn't mean that the purveyors of investment advice should be rich and their clients poor. He meant that if the clients get rich, the provider of the advice might get richer. The true test of all investment theories and advice is in their practical application.

You can be an armchair tennis player, stay home rather than rough it in the wilderness or prefer the United States to strange foreign lands, but you can't be satisfied with an academic approach to investing. Sooner or later you have to take the plunge. The question is how to get started without putting your entire life savings at risk.

GO IT ALONE OR SEEK PROFESSIONAL HELP?

Not every investor finds digging into company profit and loss statements or watching market trends fun. Keeping track of financial trends can be boring and tedious. The problem is that your savings, future and financial security are at risk. Blindly trusting someone else to manage your money can be dangerous.

A large part of the total wealth in the United States is owned by women. This is because wives have outlived their husbands. One of the saddest sights is a widow suddenly faced with both grief and money management. The records are full of reports of widows who have been defrauded by people they thought they could trust. Widows, however, aren't the only ones who fall prey to the financial predators. There are plenty of men who have allowed their ignorance or greed to lure them into propositions that cost them their entire lifesavings and turned their golden years to ashes.

There are lots of things in life that are more important than money. In the modern world, however, it is all but impossible to live—never mind enjoy the finer aspects of life—without money. Money is at the root of many of our anxieties, is a cause of marital stress and can fracture relationships between parents and children. The problem isn't money itself; it is our relationship with our own finances.

Living in relative security requires a basic understanding of yourself, your tolerance for risk and of how your money should be managed. A reasonable understanding of markets and how they work is essential to a full life. Even if you decide to turn over the day-to-day management of a portfolio to a professional, you must know how to choose a money manager, mutual fund or financial vehicle.

Get involved. Apply the principles of international investing, and you won't regret the effort.

PRICE PLUS QUALITY IS THE CHALLENGE

The six major financial markets in the world are Japan, the United States, England, France, Germany and Hong Kong. Sometimes they rise and fall together, and at other times one will rise while others fall, or vice versa. As an investor, your challenge is to buy low into a market that will later rise. That sounds simple, but it isn't.

In the largest markets—Japan, the United States and England— there are almost always some investments that do well even during times when the overall market is falling. That fact of financial life can lead an uninformed investor into trouble. More often, when a market is weak, most of your investments in that market will fall. Conversely, in a rising market even the worst of investments usually manages to climb. Having a fundamental sense of value, market by market, is important.

When shopping for markets, the same principles apply as in buying a car, real estate or a major appliance. What you are looking for is the best quality at the lowest price. When it comes to markets, that means balancing risk against potential reward.

Markets that have the best long-term records tend to sell at the highest prices. Japanese stocks, for example, sold at an average of 64 times earnings in 1987. Buying Japanese stocks then was not a good idea even though the long-term outlook for Japanese business was bright. Japanese stocks fell sharply in the crash of 1987, recovered and then plunged again in early 1990. Buying high, even where the fundamentals are solid, can produce losses.

Buying low, on the other hand, leads you to markets where either the record isn't particularly good or where the outlook is dismal. This doesn't mean that the crowd is always right. Markets tend to exaggerate the feelings of investors. Those with good records and bright futures often rise too high, and those with poor records or dull futures frequently fall too low. You can buck the crowd, buy right and enjoy significant profits. To do that, you need to apply the right frame of reference.

Finding the right market at the right price begins by analyzing markets based on the balance between business and politics. What you are looking for are markets where the future is not being foreclosed by excessive politics. You don't want to buy the equivalent of Russian bonds just before the Communist takeover of a country. You are looking for bargains in a market with a better-than-even chance of future success.

Applying the business-versus-politics frame of reference is not an exact science. It requires judgment, a sense of history and practice. The principles can be applied to any market you choose. To help you develop a sense of opportunity, what follows is an analysis of the six major stock markets of the world.

THE FIRST: HONG KONG

If you never invest a penny in Hong Kong, you will profit from knowing about this British Crown Colony and its markets. Understand how to apply the basic principles of international investing to Hong Kong and other world markets will fall into place. The story of Hong Kong shows how the balance between business and politics has a direct impact on investors.

There are two parts to Hong Kong—the New Territories and the island city itself. The New Territories were leased to Great Britain for a specified time, but the island city of Hong Kong was leased in perpetuity. In 1984, when England began negotiating with the Chinese government over the future of the New Territories, the British made an awful concession. They agreed to return not only the New Territories but the city of Hong Kong itself to Beijing's control on July 1, 1997.

Hong Kong had been a bastion of free enterprise for decades. Business dominated all activity. The government's role was that of custodian to assure just enough regulation to allow business an optimum operating environment. Hong Kong enjoyed above-average economic growth throughout the 1970s and into the early 1980s.

Wide-open markets carry images of lurid, behind-the-scenes dealings, financial treachery and great risk. Over the years the Hong Kong stock market has lived up to the images, but it has also proved very profitable for long-term investors. From 1970 to the end of 1989 Hong Kong stocks gained 1,341 percent in U.S. dollars. By comparison, U.S. stocks gained 203 percent. Will 1997 mark the end of Hong Kong as a land of opportunity?

Nowhere else in the world is the balance between politics and business so clearly played out as in Hong Kong. Here is a market that both proves the value of this perspective and provides an opportunity to practice its application.

Back in 1984, long before the Beijing Massacre, Britain's agreement to turn over control of Hong Kong to Beijing in 1997 threw Hong Kong's markets into chaos. Stocks plunged, property prices plunged and the people felt betrayed. The surrender of control to Beijing was seen as the first step in changing the balance between politics and business in Hong Kong for the worse. Heavy-handed communism has never been favorable to business, and that is what Beijing practiced.

Over the next few years the Hong Kong markets recovered and returned to their old volatile but profitable selves. Hong Kong was reassured because the Chinese had set upon a course of economic reform. The right to own private property was recognized by China in the provinces neighboring Hong Kong, and Beijing seemed to be moving in the direction of business and putting politics in its place.

Then in 1989 Beijing's politicians were threatened by student protests demanding an end to corruption and more freedom. The government's answer was the Beijing Massacre. Thousands of unarmed students were brutally murdered by the Chinese army in Tiananmen Square. The Hong Kong stock market plunged again, dropping 25 percent quickly, and the balance between business and politics appeared to be tipping against business again.

By the end of 1989 the Hong Kong stock market had recovered. In early 1990 it continued to do well. On the surface this appeared to be a puzzle because Beijing had not backed down. There had been no overthrow of the Chinese government. On the contrary, the Communist leaders in Beijing had carried out reprisals against the protest leaders and had cracked down on all students. Communist ideology was once again being forced upon the people.

In the United States President Bush was severely criticized for sending high-ranking officials to visit the "murderers of Beijing." Americans despise the collective application of political principles when the consequences are murder and the denial of human rights. The United States likes to stand up for the individual rights of all human beings, and in the case of the Beijing Massacre, right and wrong, good and evil seemed clear.

What was done in Beijing in June 1989 was wrong. The United States government wanted to punish the government of China and thus imposed economic sanctions. The investment issue, however, was more complex. Americans assume that economic and diplomatic sanctions are the answer to oppression. The idea that encouraging good business might be an alternative route to the better treatment of human beings too often is brushed aside in favor of retribution and punishment. What we fail to appreciate is that our predominantly political attitude has its roots in the most brutal part of human history. Applying political power to deprive an entire people of economic opportunity has been the most popular practice throughout written history, but it has seldom accomplished its intended goal. Too often economic sanctions have produced unrest, turbulence and a fertile ground for radical political views.

We would all feel more comfortable if Beijing moved along the same path as the Soviet Union and placed an equal emphasis on democracy, human rights and economic progress. However, that was not the case in 1989 in China, and it is unlikely to be the case in the near future.

Beijing can be expected to go the other way, emphasizing economic progress while moving slowly on political reform. It is possible that over the next decade China will prove that communism can be preserved, in one form or another, and still achieve economic goals. At least investors should have an open mind when it comes to that possibility. If China manages to improve its economy and raise standards of living, the high-ranking politicians will feel less threatened and will allow more individual freedom.

This aspect of the greatest struggle in history will be played out on the stage called Hong Kong. Communism has failed because its proponents have overemphasized politics and put good business in a lowly position. If Beijing manages to do what is now regarded as impossible and allows business to fulfill its proper function, it is possible that a Communist form of government will achieve peace and prosperity.

The key for investors is to recognize that the form of government is less significant than the balance between politics and business. Don't write the Chinese off yet. They are well known for their entrepreneurial skills. If any nation on earth can find the right mix between Communist ideals and good business, it will be China.

Hong Kong is an exciting stock market for another reason. After the Beijing Massacre in June 1989, investors in Hong Kong were forced to face the ultimate investment fact—the possible liquidation of all Hong Kong companies in 1997. Analysts went to work studying cash flows, balance sheets and potential profits. They asked what people should pay for Hong Kong stocks in 1989 to realize a respectable total return if the companies were liquidated in 1997. The answers were, in some cases, shocking. The market panic that followed the June massacre drove stock prices down to a point where they were attractive even if the end came in 1997. As a result, the Hong Kong stock market began to recover. By the end of 1989 the Hang Seng Index was back to 2,836, up more than 30 percent from the postmassacre low.

The lesson from the Hong Kong stock plunge in June 1989 is that investors should always have an eye on real underlying value. Businesses generate cash and profits. Even if a business has to be liquidated under duress, there is an intrinsic value; and if the market falls to less than the intrinsic value, there is an opportunity.

Hong Kong may do more than survive to the end of June 1997. The Crown Colony may continue to be a market of opportunity for investors. At the least, investors should follow closely what happens in Hong Kong. The battle there between business and politics will provide valuable insights that can be applied in other markets as well.

More venturesome investors can buy Hong Kong stocks whenever they are battered down by changes in the political trend. No market that is so directly threatened by politics can be looked at as a safe, long-term investment. In Hong Kong, that is clear. Nevertheless, all markets are involved in the never-ending battle between business and politics. In some, such as the United States, we are lulled into complacency. We forget the basic issues and assume it "can't happen here." Hong Kong is valuable if for no other reason than it forces us to be alert to the real underlying issues that face all investors in all markets.

The threat from Communist hard-liners in Beijing doesn't automatically mean that buying Hong Kong stocks is a bad idea. It could be that Beijing will be transformed by popular demand or because of the changes in Eastern Europe. If politics is pushed into second place in China, the outlook for Hong Kong will improve.

There is another way investors might profit from owning Hong Kong stocks. The managers of the Hong Kong companies are also well aware of the risks. They don't want their jobs and business to be completely lost to hard-line politics. A few companies changed their official corporate residence from Hong Kong to Bermuda in the late 1980s. Others diversified their holdings, moving assets and manufacturing facilities to other countries. The Hong Kong companies understood the political threat back in 1984 when England gave away too much to Beijing. They began quickly, quietly and decisively to do everything they could to ensure the long-term viability of their companies.

Consider the story of the Hong Kong Shanghai Bank. This leading Hong Kong bank began diversifying in the 1970s through an initial purchase of a large stake in the U.S. Marine Midland Bank. Later the Hong Kong Shanghai Bank bought the remaining shares and became a 100-percent owner of Marine Midland. After the British giveaway in 1984, the Hong Kong Shanghai Bank moved its official corporate residence to Hamilton, Bermuda.

In late 1989, months after the Beijing Massacre, in separate transactions, three Japanese life insurance companies each bought 1 percent of the shares of Hong Kong Shanghai Bank. The Japanese bought the shares knowing full well that such large blocks of stock would be impossible to sell if there were major political problems in 1998. They bought knowing about the Beijing Massacre and about the Hong Kong brain drain as people left to take up residence in Canada, Australia and elsewhere. The Japanese had all the bad news, knew all the risks and still bought a large chunk of the bank's stock.

The purchase of Hong Kong stocks by savvy Japanese investors should make it clear that there is more to the story of Hong Kong's future than is revealed in the nightly U.S. television news. There may be significant opportunity for investors in Hong Kong stocks in the years ahead.

THE SECOND: FRANCE

Long before Hong Kong's future made headlines, on the other side of the world in France, another dramatic battle between business and politics was played out in a most surprising way. It was May 1981, and the votes had been counted in the French national elections. For investors, the worst became reality. A Socialist, François Mitterand, won the election. Stock prices plunged, and the doomsayers shouted, "We told you so." Capitalism had been defeated at the polls. It seemed that business had suffered a major loss in one of Europe's most important countries.

The Mitterand government made good on its pledge to nationalize whole industries. Banks and chemical companies, for example, were taken over by the government. Ironically, this gave the stock market a lift. The government didn't just take the shares; investors were paid fair prices. In many cases the French stock market plunge had pushed individual stocks far below the real fair value of the company. When the government nationalized those companies, stock prices recovered quickly.

This was another case when buying under adversity, after a stock market plunge, produced profits. After the Mitterand election, the future for stock prices seemed very dark. No one could have guessed that the Socialist government would become the source of investment profits. The best stock market opportunities always come cloaked in anxiety, fear and uncertainty. It is the bad news and the bleak outlook that pushes stock prices down to unduly depressed levels.

After the nationalization process, the new Socialist leader of France fooled all the experts. François Mitterand was well aware of the economic failings of socialism and communism in other countries. He was determined to prove that a Socialist could lead France to greater prosperity. When it came to financial matters, Mitterand proved to be more of a capitalist than many of his conservative political opponents. Monetary policy was kept tight to drive inflation down. Business, including the leaders of the nationalized industries, was encouraged to become more competitive. Tax incentives were enacted to encourage French citizens to make long-term investments in French stocks.

In the five years following the Mitterand victory, French stocks were among the best performers in the world. Investors who bought before the May crash suffered huge losses after the elections but saw their portfolios go on to double and triple in the subsequent years. Any investor who had the courage to buy more French stocks after the plunge saw his financial fortunes multiply.

François Mitterand proved in the early 1980s that the political badge is less important than how the balance between politics and business is struck. He was among the first world leaders from the Left to recognize that long-term political success requires sound, practical economic policies. When the history of the twentieth century is written, Mitterand is sure to have an important place as a farsighted and able politician.

By way of comparison, it should be said that the long-term success of democracy, even in the United States, also depends on sound, practical economic policies. Having a democracy is not enough. Bleeding away wealth through excessive taxation and social spending may produce short-term political results. In the long run, if carried too far, such policies will so impoverish the nation that democracy itself will be threatened.

The example of France in the 1980s demonstrates clearly that investors should keep an open mind when it comes to politics. What counts is how business and politics are blended, not the label on the political system.

Not only did French stocks do well after the Mitterand election, but France itself was transformed for the better. Good economic policies proved to be good both for business and the nation. By the end of 1989, France was well positioned to participate in the dramatic developments that were sweeping over Europe.

France is likely to remain a land of investment opportunity for a long time to come.

THE THIRD: ENGLAND

Nowhere in the world is it more difficult to determine the balance between business and politics than in England. The reason for this is that labor unions wield significant power in the United Kingdom. Their power doesn't always appear in election results. They can lose elections and still find ways of shackling business.

Britain's stock market is the third largest in the world. It is significantly more liquid than the number-four market, West Germany. For that reason, foreign investors are almost always hunting for opportunity in London. The buying and selling by foreign investors may or may not run consistent with domestic British political and economic trends. British stocks at times seem to defy economic rules and run up or down contrary to common-sense economic observation.

As with any large market, there are always some good stocks lurking somewhere in London's financial pages. The British stock market is large enough to produce some opportunity under almost any circumstances. Nevertheless, if you are investing in the British stock market rather than a special situation, it is usually a good idea to approach the market with a hefty dose of caution.

In the mid-1970s England was considered an economic basket case. Inflation was running wild, and British industry suffered from high costs and inefficiencies. Too many industries had been protected for too long. They had fallen into the inevitable state of bureaucratic decay and red ink.

England was saved by rising oil prices. Once the price for a barrel of oil rose high enough, it became economically feasible to drill offshore, in the North Sea. Huge amounts of oil were discovered, and Britain soon became an oil exporter earning billions of pounds for its government and its oil industry.

The oil revenue was more than an economic salvation; oil riches encouraged England to try harder to contain inflation and increase productivity. Success did not come easily. By the end of the 1980s, England still suffered from an inflation rate higher than most of its competitors. Nonetheless British industry made progress. British Steel, for example, had been transformed from a lethargic, bloated giant to one of the world's most efficient steel producers. The British government eliminated its deficit and ran surpluses, paying down the national debt.

In the 1990s, with oil revenues expected to peak and decline and competitive pressures increasing from Eastern Europe, it remains to be seen how the British will fare. Investors should recognize that the balance between politics and business in England was still in the dangerous range at the end of the 1980s. At the start of the 1990s, Britain, like the United States, was a place to search for unique opportunities rather than one where easy opportunities could be found.

If the balance between politics and business changes for the better in England, the investment results could be astounding. After all, in the 1980s Britain did eliminate one of the great economic scourges—a national deficit. With a modest change in political attitudes, Britain could go on to eliminate its trade deficit as well. If that happens, British standards of living will rise and investors will find profits easy to achieve.

There is another aspect of the British markets that gets little attention. The Japanese steal the limelight when it comes to any discussion of foreign investors in the United States. We moan about how dependent we are on Japanese capital. However, the official U.S. government statistics, published each month by the Federal Reserve, tell a different story.

In September 1984 the U.S. bond market was caught in one of its periodic anxiety attacks. Bond dealers and investors alike were terrified because interest rates were rising. The Fed was fighting inflation with tight money. In an environment of rising interest rates, few are willing to buy long-term, fixed-rate bonds. By September there was a virtual buyer's strike in the U.S. bond market. The strike ended when British investors stepped in and bought more than $10 billion worth of U.S. government bonds. As late as 1989, British net buying of U.S. stocks and bonds ran at twice the level of Japanese net buying.

British investors have both cash and a global view of investing. This fact of British financial life means that investors should never dismiss the British markets. British investors "saved" the U.S. bond market in 1984. They knew a bargain when they saw it. Likewise, they can be expected to recognize bargains at home. When British stocks fall to depressed levels and look like bargains compared to the other major world markets, buy. The odds are that British buying of British stocks will "save" the home stock market every time.

THE FOURTH: GERMANY

The balance between business and politics was given a favorable tilt in Germany after World War II. The victorious Allies moved to help rebuild the German economy but insisted that Germany not rebuild its military. The army is a keystone of politics, and denied a new army, Germany was forced to concentrate on business.

Behind the Iron Curtain, however, conditions were the opposite. The Soviet Union built a massive army and imposed its will on the people of Hungary, Czechoslovakia and other East European countries. The Cold War raged between the Soviet Union and the United States over the decades of the Fifties and Sixties. In Germany, however, the Cold War always seemed too close to hot war. From the lunch rooms on top of bank buildings in Dusseldorf, West Germany, you could see the trees and just make out the outline of the Russian tanks hidden by the foliage. As the postwar decades evolved, West Germany lived with the constant threat of invasion from the East. The United States tried to help by stationing troops along the borders. That, however, didn't fully calm the fears of West Germans. They worried that the presence of U.S. troops would provoke an attack. Pacifist movements sprung up, and Germans hoped that by adopting a nonviolent attitude they could keep the aggressive Russian bear behind the Iron Curtain.

By the 1970s politics had again emerged as a powerful force in West German life. Socialists, Communists, pacifists and environmental organizations gained increasing power. Business suffered, and tough Japanese competition threatened German markets. Once dominant in the camera industry, Germany, for example, lost that source of jobs and profits to the Japanese. German unemployment rose, and idle workers increased the political pressures.

Three things developed in the course of the 1970s and 1980s that saved Germany and the rest of Europe from political excesses. The first was the European Monetary System (EMS); the second was the drive to a more united Europe by 1992; and the third was the collapse of the Berlin Wall and the exposure of the truth about the poverty, corruption and deprivation in the Communist countries.

Throughout the 1970s and 1980s, in the face of the growing power of politics, Germany remained tough and disciplined in the management of its monetary policy. The Bundesbank, Germany's central bank (similar to the U.S. Federal Reserve), couldn't change the balance in favor of business but could and did do its best to prevent excessive politics from ruining the economy. The West German mark remained strong and won international respect as a safe "hard" currency. German success in checking inflation created problems for its neighbors. Unable or unwilling to be as tough on interest rates and money growth as the Germans, countries such as France and Italy suffered high inflation as their currencies remained weak compared to the German mark. In response, a system was proposed to keep the European currencies within set limits and encourage trade and investment throughout the region. Maligned at the beginning, the EMS, as it was called, accomplished its goals. Inflation came down throughout Europe and trade flourished. Through the EMS, business in Europe won an initial round over politics.

Later, the members of the EMS recognized that more was needed if Europe was to remain competitive in the 1990s. A drive to reduce the red tape and other barriers to the free flow of goods and capital within Europe was proposed. Dubbed Europe 1992, this move tipped the balance decisively in favor of business. Throughout both the development of the EMS and Europe 1992, the tough, disciplined Germans remained at the center of the efforts. By late 1989 it was becoming clear that business in Europe had been unleashed and that a long period of real economic growth was possible.

In November 1989 Germany again moved to the center of the world stage. The Berlin Wall came down, and East Germany opened its borders. West Germans moved quickly to help their neighbors, as the economy of East Germany was in shambles. People flooded into West Germany to escape dismal conditions in the East. West Germany quickly recognized that the opening of the borders, like it or not, made the two Germanys one, at least for economic purposes. Either the economy of East Germany was to be rescued or all East Germans might flee to the West. Either way, the bankrupt economy of East Germany became the burden of West Germany.

From Bonn, West Germany's capital, came a proposal for making the West German mark the currency of both Germanys. Markets in Europe convulsed. Investors worried that rescuing East Germany would be the straw that broke the discipline of the German central bank.

Forgotten in the rush was the fact that Europe is a relatively small region. In the 1980s the United States had managed to deal with the bankruptcy of its oil states and of its agricultural and mining regions without re-igniting inflation. Germany, if anything, had shown even greater discipline than the United States had. The best bet was that West Germany would manage to find a way of helping East Germany without re-igniting inflation. The reason that was a good bet was that Germany had rolled back the power of politics enough to unleash the power of its business leaders. Business, not politics, was driving Germany at the end of the 1980s.

There was nothing new or unusual about the popular skepticism and common anxiety towards uniting the currencies of East and West Germany in 1990. In 1948 U.S. General Lucius D. Clay was upset by Germany's currency reform. He questioned Ludwig Erhard, minister of finance, saying, "How can you undertake to ease our rationing system as long as we have so evident a shortage of food? My experts are predicting that your free-market economy will lead to chaos and plundering." Erhard responded, "General, I have not eased the rationing system, I have abolished it. From now on the only ration card will be the D-mark, and people will work hard to get it. Just wait."

Erhard was right. General Clay, his experts and all the skeptics were wrong. The German people worked hard and rebuilt their economy without chaos or plundering. There were no instant economic miracles, but over time West Germany emerged as a world economic power.

The uniting of the currencies of East and West Germany was greeted with the same sort of skepticism in early 1990. Experts warned that wild inflation would be the result of exchanging West German marks for East German marks. Financial markets convulsed on the news, fearing that the experts would be right. Go slower, take your time, don't rush to be so helpful to the East Germans was the advice. Had Erhard been alive, he surely would have again told the skeptics to "just wait."

Germany is likely to remain a land of investment opportunity for a long time. However, that doesn't mean that investors should buy German stocks at any price. After the collapse of the Berlin Wall, the German stock market soared. Billions flowed into Germany in search of profits. German stocks rose to prices that reflected the first year or more of expected new growth. The early profits went to those who bought German stocks in early 1989, before the good news of the collapse of the Berlin Wall made the nightly news. There were few bargains left on the German stock exchange by the last day of 1989.

Good news and excitement when business wins a major battle should push up stock prices. However, the excitement often goes too far and prices come back down later. Bad news is an investor's friend. It drives stock prices down and creates buying opportunities. Good news is a friend of investors who bought early. It isn't an enemy of those who didn't buy before the news, but it does make things more difficult. Caution, patience and insisting on paying a reasonable price for all your investments is the best rule, even when the news is so good that you are tempted to plunge at high prices.

THE FIFTH: JAPAN

Like Germany, Japan is another case where postwar regulations proved to be very favorable for the nation's long-term welfare. The Allies again wanted to rebuild the Japanese economy but not the military. This kept politics in the background while business received the resources and emphasis.

As an island nation, Japan didn't face the same immediate threats from Communist countries in its region as did Germany. Being surrounded by water helps keep enemies at bay. In addition, Japan was helped by U.S. military actions in Korea and Vietnam. When communism became violent in the 1950s, the United States launched the war in Korea. In the 1960s the United States went to war in Vietnam. These dismal wars, especially the war in Vietnam, captured the attention of every American. Missing from all the analysis, however, was the impact of the war on Japan. While Germany lived with the threat of a Communist invasion, the United States fought in Korea and Vietnam. The fighting effectively insulated Japan from anxiety about a Communist invasion of its land, as the United States sent its army, navy and air force to that part of the world. In Europe, the Germans always wondered if Americans would ever again fight for Europe's interests. That question was never answered.

When the Vietnam War ended with the effective defeat of the United States, the Communists didn't invade other regions. They were forced to turn inward because their economies had been ravaged by the fighting, and they could not afford another war. The combination of the war in Korea in the Fifties and in Vietnam in the Sixties and Seventies proved to be so expensive that another major conflict simply was not affordable.

The active fighting by the United States in first Korea and then Vietnam made a difference. Japan, unlike Germany, had solid evidence of the resolve of its military protector, the United States. As a result, the Japanese went about their business without suffering the same political anxieties as did Europe.

A lot has been written about the Japanese success. Most of it concentrates on Japanese skills and American weakness. Not enough attention is given to the impact of the two wars fought in Korea and Vietnam. When financial success is looked at from the perspective of the balance between business and politics, however, it should be clear that Japan was first forced to emphasize business and then sheltered from politics to its own reward.

Doubters should remember World War II. In the 1920s and 1930s politics dominated Japan. The result was war, not prosperity. The Japanese, just as any people, are subject to the consequences of the balance between political power and the power of business.

How will the Japanese fare in the decades to come? They became the world's largest creditor nation by the end of the 1980s. Their extraordinary wealth certainly will ensure them of a reasonable period of continued prosperity. It is possible, however, that politics will gain power in Japan to the long-term detriment of business. History indicates that this is likely in a nation that has enjoyed such significant growth for such a long time. Japan will remain a land of investment opportunity but only for investors who have the issues of business and politics clearly in mind.

THE SIXTH: THE UNITED STATES

By the end of the 1980s the United States had become a land of malaise and pessimism. The most popular indulgences were breast beating over America's failures. Rising debt, the federal deficit, Latin loans, low literacy, inadequate education, drugs, a lack of competitiveness, poor-quality products and other such obvious failures were prominent in the public mind. Americans were browbeaten by the success of the Japanese and the loss of the auto, television, and consumer electronics markets.

Forgotten in the collective weeping were some simple facts. First, the United States, perhaps more than any nation on earth, is known for its ability to make money and commercialize anything and everything. Second, this cultural ability was suppressed in the 1970s by the loss of free and easy natural resources and by an excessive reliance on political answers for the nation's problems.

In the late 1960s the United States lost its energy independence. Oil at home was depleted and had to be imported. OPEC seized the initiative, and the energy crisis began—not that the world was running out of oil. In fact, more new oil was found in each year of the energy crisis than was consumed. What happened was that the power to establish the world oil price shifted away from the United States, and Americans became furious. They wanted quick, easy solutions and applied political power in an attempt to solve the crisis.

At the same time, an unrealistic attitude swept the nation. Refusing to accept the new facts of international economics, Americans overindulged in feelings of wealth and power. We launched the Great Society and the war in Vietnam almost simultaneously, as if we still had unlimited cheap oil and unlimited wealth.

By the end of the 1970s, reality began to creep into American thinking. We recognized the mistakes and began to feel poor. Our natural instincts for making money surfaced but in a narrow application. We commercialized sports and entertainment but didn't expand that drive to include other more basic businesses. We gained international dominance in those two fields but lost in many other industries. Politics remained excessively powerful. To correct our society's ills, we passed new tax laws, imposed tough regulations on business and legislated all kinds of behavior in an effort to protect the environment. We sought to get rich as individuals through gambling on state lotteries and through lawsuits. By the last day of 1989 the United States was still stuck in its dilemma over the appeal of politics versus the need to strengthen business.

Will the United States follow the European example and place a greater emphasis on business? One thing is sure: the United States has that potential. That cultural instinct to make money remains strong. If politics can be tamed and reduced to a healthier level and business is unleashed, the United States could fulfill its potential.

Investors should look at the United States with full awareness of both the potential and the problem of excessive reliance on politics. Just as the commercial ability of the nation emerged in sports and entertainment, it can emerge in other businesses. The United States is likely to remain a land of opportunity for investors who can find the "gems" among U.S. businesses. If the balance between politics and business shifts in a more favorable way, it will become much easier to make money through investments in the United States.

SUMMARY

Hong Kong, France, England, Germany, Japan and the United States are the world's six major markets. International investing begins with a clear frame of reference and an understanding of how each of the six fit into that perspective. Once the battle between politics and business is understood for these six markets you can apply the principles in other exciting markets in search of even greater opportunity.

OPPORTUNITY #5: PROFITING FROM THE WORLD STOCK TREND

No major market can go its own independent way forever. Sooner or later they all catch up with the overall world trend. By watching the world trend and then monitoring the six major markets you can spot opportunity. When one market lags too far behind for too long, it becomes ripe for a catch-up move. Buying into a lagging market can produce solid profits.

There are several easy and practical ways to follow the world stock trend. The six major markets are covered in the popular financial press. For example, you can find them in *Barron's,* the *Wall Street Journal* and the *New York Times.* By simply reading these papers, you can become aware of the general trend of the six major markets and therefore the overall world stock trend.

For investors who wish to be more precise about trends, an easy way is to follow the Morgan Stanley Capital International Perspective World Stock Index, which is also published regularly in the popular financial papers. The problem with this index is that it is

Figure 4-1. Dessauer's International Stock Market Index

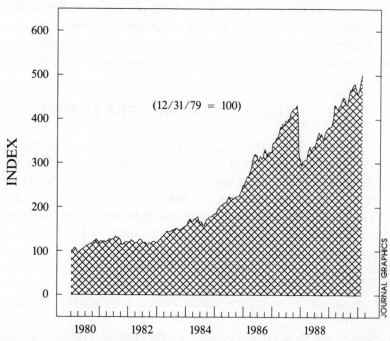

Chart prepared by Richard Andrews from data supplied by the author.

weighted in favor of the larger markets and is therefore not particularly sensitive to short or intermediate changes in direction.

Another way of watching the world trend is to construct your own index. This can be done using the six major markets. All you need do is pick a starting point and then weigh each market equally in your index. The result will be a sensitive and accurate measure of the world stock trend.

In 1980, when *Dessauer's Journal of Financial Markets* was first published, a sensitive indicator of world stock trends was needed. The approach used was to construct an index using an equal weight for each of the six major markets. Dubbed Dessauer's International Stock Market Index, the result has been a useful tool for monitoring the changes in the world stock trend. (See Figure 4-1 for an example of the index.)

Don't feel that you have to go through the mathematics of constructing an index. All you need to do is regularly watch the trends in each of the six markets. If you are proficient in mathematics or comfortable with a computer, you can use those skills to construct an index or create charts of the individual markets. While those techniques are helpful, they are not necessary for long-term investors. Believe it or not, by watching the six major markets on a weekly basis you will quickly become aware of the world stock trend.

DON'T EXPECT TO PREDICT THE FUTURE

No one likes to see the value of a portfolio decline. In October 1987, for example, the world stock trend suddenly reversed in what became known as the great stock market crash of 1987. Some were fortunate enough to be out of the markets before the crash. Most were caught and suffered temporary paper losses. After the crash it became popular to search for tools and techniques that would predict the future course for world stock markets.

Make no mistake: there are no such tools or techniques. Crystal balls that foretell the future for the markets are like Ponce de Leon's fountain of youth—a dream that is always sought after and never found. Your best guide to financial success is a well-informed, common-sense view of underlying world trends. The key is "well-informed." If you need charts, computers and indices to feel comfortable that you are well informed, then by all means construct an index and keep a detailed record of the trend. If you are confident of your knowledge by watching the weekly changes in the six major markets, you don't need the more technical, mathematically oriented techniques.

Don't make investing overly complicated. The simpler, the better. Some of the world's greatest fortunes were made by the simplest decisions—for example, to buy Japanese stocks in 1970 or to hold on to German stocks even after they plunged in 1987.

No successful investor always wins. Losses, unexpected market declines and even major setbacks like the crash of 1987 are part of the process. To be successful and to increase your personal fortune, all you need is to be right more than half the time. By following the world trend, watching a few major markets and applying the common-sense, business-versus-politics frame of reference you will increase the odds on success.

CHAPTER

5

All about Currencies

Mention any foreign currency—from the German mark to the French franc—and visions of extraordinary risks dance in the minds of most American investors. The annals of investment history are full of stories of speculators who either made or lost fortunes speculating in currencies. Even John Maynard Keynes, one of the most famous economists of our time, had to take an advance on one of his books to cover living expenses, for he had lost heavily in the currency markets.

Artists have captured the essence of speculation. One famous painting shows a man in a shoddy room lying on a bed, one arm dangling over the side, the covers in disarray, his head thrown back in agony, a bottle and a half-clad woman by his side. Its title is *Death of a Speculator.*

This particular painting doesn't mention the currency markets. The poor subject could have lost speculating in anything from tulip bulbs to commodities. Nevertheless the longest-running stories of speculation are in currencies. The reason for this is that currencies are money. Ever since the origin of nations and their specific currencies there has been speculation in currencies.

The bad image currencies have comes not from the money itself but from the techniques used by speculators. Whether you know it or not, holding dollars in treasury bills, bank deposits or cash in a safe-deposit box is a form of playing the currency markets. The U.S. dollar is only one of the world's major currencies. By holding U.S.

dollars you wittingly or unwittingly say that you prefer dollars over German marks, Japanese yen or any of the other currencies of the world. When you sell stocks, bonds or real estate and invest the cash at interest in U.S. treasury bills, you aren't being a wild speculator. That form of investment is correctly viewed as highly conservative.

The speculation emerges when high leverage is added to the investment equation. Currencies don't often fluctuate wildly in a short period of time. A 25-percent move in the value of a currency is a big event. You obviously can't make a fortune on a 25-percent move unless you start out with a fortune in the first place. However, if you borrow heavily and then have a 25-percent move on the whole investment, the gains on your equity can be enormous.

Currency speculators use high leverage: a ratio of eight to one is not uncommon. If you start out with $10,000, borrow $80,000 and then make the right move in the currency markets, a 25-percent change will produce a profit of $22,500 or 225 percent of your equity. If you roll the position over, again with an eight to one ratio, the next time you could make $73,125. Two right decisions, two 25-percent moves plus high leverage and $10,000 becomes $105,625. Of course with only one wrong move by the currency markets, your entire equity can be wiped out.

Speculators don't always go to a bank and borrow money outright. They also use the futures markets. The leverage is then built in to the contract costs and requirements. The problem with high-leveraged speculation is that you can lose more than your equity. If the markets move against you quickly, there may not be time to sell out at the zero point. If that happens, your remaining investment may not be large enough to pay off the loan or meet the margin calls on the futures contracts. More than one speculator has built a small equity into a fortune and then lost more than everything on a later trade. It is this high-leverage aspect of currency trading that produces the images of high risk and speculation.

Should you try your hand at currency speculation? The conservative answer is "no," but the temptation to try our luck can sometimes be overpowering. If you find yourself tempted by visions of the glamour of currency trading, don't be too scrupulous. Go ahead and risk what you can afford to lose but do so in options, not the futures markets.

Options are different from the futures markets in one essential respect. You can lose only what you invest and not more. Currency options are traded on the Philadelphia Exchange in the United States. You won't make as much on options when you are right, but that is a small price to pay for the assurance that you will not end up like the speculator in the painting—drunk, in debt and completely out of luck.

There are a handful of people in the world who are very good traders. Not all currency speculators end up drunk or in debt. Some make and keep fortunes. Who knows? You may be one of the few. If so, move on to the high-leveraged world of currency speculation and make your fortune. If, as is the case for most of us, you find out your trading instincts are not good enough to make a fortune, you will have learned an important lesson at a reasonable cost. It's far better to have lost a few thousand dollars on options than to be in debt and under financial pressure from excessive speculation in futures or with borrowed money in currencies.

THE RISK YOU CANNOT ESCAPE

Stop the World, I Want To Get Off was a popular Broadway play. The title is so obviously ridiculous that it set the tone for the play. We know we cannot get off the planet. A few have been in space and visited the moon, but they couldn't stay and the trips cost billions of dollars. We're stuck with this planet and all its risks. We're also stuck in a world of money and can't get out.

You may dream of a different world. A few people have even left the everyday world and headed for the wilder parts of the globe. They seek self-sufficiency and a world without money cares. Others stay but lament their plight. An artist in Rockport, Massachusetts, was engaged in conversation with an admirer of his paintings. The talk inevitably turned to price, and the artist lamented, "Isn't it a shame that each month we have to come up with a bunch of money just to live?"

Money has been dubbed "the root of all evil." Marriages are thrown into chaos more often over money than sex. The poor usually suffer their plight not for lack of trying but for lack of money. The successful and the rich often suffer severe pain born of guilt. It's not that they did anything wrong, just that they have more than others and feel the unfairness of the world's money system.

In the United States money is synonymous with the U.S. dollar. We can travel more than 3,000 miles from one coast to the other and never have to change currencies. Goods made in Tennessee can be shipped to Massachusetts, paid for in dollars and no one worries about a balance of trade. If goods are shipped that distance in Europe, the odds are that they crossed a border and moved into a country with a different currency. The two countries must have a sophisticated banking system to take care of the movements of currencies between them. Insulated from such mundane but complicated money affairs, Americans suffer a disadvantage. They see the dollar as safe and secure while other currencies are viewed as complicated and risky. Americans don't always appreciate this, but when they hold dollars, they take a currency risk.

Suppose your personal preference is for Japanese or German cars. Those cars are made in a foreign country by foreign workers paid in a different currency. The price you'll have to pay when you trade in and buy the next car will be partly determined by the changes in the value of the dollar versus the Japense yen or the German mark. To be really conservative, keep some cash in German marks or Japanese yen to reduce the cross-currency risk you have embraced by liking foreign cars. If the dollar falls in value, you will be paying more in dollars for the next car. However, if you keep cash in German marks or Japanese yen, the value of those holdings would appreciate and your next car would be more affordable.

We have grown accustomed to paying $15,000 or more for an automobile. That is a lot of cash by any measure. Nevertheless somehow we have managed to ignore the obvious currency risk inherent in any major purchase of a foreign-made product. In fact, there has been so little awareness of the currency markets in the United States that U.S. banks were not permitted to hold foreign currencies until the end of 1989. In other words, if you wanted to hold some cash in a foreign currency, you couldn't do it through a U.S. bank. You had to open an account in Canada, Europe or Asia to get access to that service. Some Americans were wise enough to go to the trouble of maintaining a bank account in Switzerland, London or another foreign country. They appreciated the value of diversifying their cash holdings. When the dollar went down, they were still able to afford a new Mercedes or Honda. When it went up, those cars became cheaper in dollar terms and the foreign bank accounts could be left alone for the next cycle. The next time you see an expensive foreign car remind yourself that the owner, knowingly or not, has plunged into the world of foreign currencies.

The point simply is that like it or not, the value of the dollars in your wallet or bank account is fluctuating in value. Just because you don't happen to visit a foreign country to see that for yourself doesn't change the facts. We can dream of a better world—one without money. We can long for a barter system or a system that uses only precious metals, but in the modern world those will remain dreams. The reality is that we live in a world of multiple currencies, and the value of all currencies fluctuates every trading day. You can't escape, so you might just as well make the best of the situation.

TWO IMPORTANT FACTS ABOUT CURRENCY MARKETS

It is natural to keep the financial score in your own domestic currency. For American investors, that's the U.S. dollar. When you add up all your assets to calculate your net worth, the final figure is in U.S. dollars. If some of your assets are foreign stocks, you have to change the currency to dollars to figure your financial condition. Because of this, it is common, but wrong, to think that foreign stocks should only be owned during times when the dollar is declining.

The first important fact about currencies is that their effect on the value of stocks and bonds is not straightforward. In fact, the best stock frequently is in a country where the currency is falling.

Throw away the idea that you should only own foreign stocks when the U.S. dollar is falling. You can also make money—sometimes lots of it—by investing in foreign stocks when the U.S. dollar is rising.

In Europe, individual investors have more choices when they visit a bank. Here in the United States banks offer only a choice of maturity and interest rate. You can choose to invest for one year, two years or longer, but the only currency choice is the U.S. dollar.

In European banks the choice is not only maturity and interest rate but currency. Investors there can choose to have their deposits in German marks, Italian lire, French francs, British pounds, Swiss francs or U.S. dollars, to name a few. The interest rates offered on the various currencies can vary quite a bit. A bank might offer 15 percent on British pounds for a one-year deposit but only 4 percent on Swiss francs. Europeans learned long ago that holding cash in several currencies reduces risk and increases yield. That is the second fact about currencies.

Used sensibly, currencies can increase your income and reduce your financial risk. That may come as a shock to those who automatically think that foreign currencies are too complicated and risky. It certainly isn't easy for any investor accustomed to only one currency to grasp.

WHAT MAKES CURRENCIES GO UP AND DOWN?

Suppose you live on a small island—one with its own currency, the island dollar. A short distance across a bay is another island where the currency is the island mark. The island dollar and the island mark start out equal, in other words, with an exchange rate of one to one. One day a freak storm sweeps through the area wiping out all the crops on your island. The storm misses the other island, and its crops are intact. As soon as the seas calm, ships sail from your island to the other taking baskets of island dollars to exchange for island marks to buy food. Within a few hours the banks are flooded with island dollars that are, for the moment, worthless. There are no crops to buy with island dollars. Your island's crops were wiped out by the storm, and there won't be anymore until new seed is planted and the sprouts have time to mature.

Savvy bankers wouldn't want their vaults empty of island marks and full of island dollars. What would they do? The answer is that they would change the exchange rate. They might say they will give only one island mark for every ten island dollars. That would save the banks and reduce the number of valuable island marks flowing out of their vaults.

The consequence of changing the exchange rate from one to one to ten to one would be a dramatic appreciation of the island mark and a devaluation of the island dollar. What caused the values of the currencies to change? One answer is the storm, but that isn't the whole answer. If the people on your island had been prepared for the storm, they wouldn't have had to rush out and buy food from the other island. Island dollars would not have flooded into the banks across the bay, and the currency exchange rate wouldn't have changed.

The immediate cause of the change in the exchange rate was the flood of island dollars. In other words, when people sell one currency and buy another, that is what changes the exchange rate. In the real world of nations and multiple currencies the situation is more complicated, but the principle remains always the same.

WHO BUYS AND SELLS CURRENCIES?

There are six broad categories of participants in the world's currency markets: tourists, central banks, investors, speculators, consumers and business. Each group commands significant power in setting exchange rates. On any given day one group may dominate the markets. Depending on the financial condition of any given country, one group may dominate the market in that currency for a long period of time.

Economists have logged hundreds of thousands of hours studying the ebbs and flows of the currency markets. Theories about how to predict the currency markets have emerged. Some have become popular, but most serve as forecasting tools only for a while. The fundamental problem is that the six categories of players have different motives and different intentions.

Speculators, for example, have simple motives. They're looking for short-term profits when currency market exchange rates fluctuate. Tourists also have simple motives: to change their money into local currency to spend while on a visit. The motives of central banks, on the other hand, are complex. They sometimes buy or sell currencies to (1) counter the impact of speculators, (2) prevent inflation, (3) establish a favorable exchange rate for business or (4) keep interest rates from rising or falling.

Investors and business likewise have various motives when they buy or sell currencies. They may be moving profits from one country to another or investing to build a factory, earn a high rate of interest or take advantage of high- or low-priced stocks.

The interaction of the buying and selling of these six categories of participants is what moves currencies up and down. Because their motives are so often in conflict, it's all but impossible to predict the day-to-day fluctuations of the currency markets.

Individual investors should understand something about the currency markets, just enough to be in awe of these global, complex and essential money machines. Once you grasp the enormity of the global currency markets, you will probably give up on the idea of finding a way of predicting their day-to-day or even month-to-month fluctuations. The best that any investor can hope to do is recognize when the currency markets have moved to an unsustainable extreme.

Purchasing power parity is a term that describes a sophisticated way of assessing the state of the currency markets. The idea is that there are certain goods, services and commodities that have an international character. There is, for example, no reason why a dinner out should cost any more or less in one major city than another. Hotel rooms, cars, television sets and basic foods are examples of goods with an international character. The world isn't perfectly efficient; therefore, there often are wide differences in the cost for even the most basic goods and services. Tourists who travel to foreign countries will find one area cheap and another frightfully expensive. One of the forces that makes things appear cheap or expensive is the currency market.

When the U.S. dollar is strong, Americans find goods and services abroad cheap. The reason is that their dollars can buy more of the foreign currency. Conversely, when the U.S. dollar is down, the cost of travel abroad rises significantly for American travelers. Purchasing power parity theories hold that money should flow into those countries where goods and services are cheap. As money flows in, it will drive the currency up and help to equalize the international cost of goods and services.

On the other side of the currency equation, the capital flowing out of an expensive country tends to drive the strong currencies down. Theoretically, money is continually flowing around the world adjusting exchange rates in a never-ending struggle to make all basic goods and services cost the same, no matter what the country or currency.

This mercantile way of looking at currency markets makes sense and has enjoyed a long history of popular appeal. When the U.S. dollar is strong, the cost of a French wine will go down for American consumers. The amount of French wine coming into the country will naturally rise and the number of dollars flowing out will also rise. Carried on long enough and for a broad array of goods or services, these sorts of price-driven capital flows certainly have an impact on the exchange rate.

Nevertheless California wine makers won't sit by and allow their businesses to be ruined by cheap imports. They will fight. It is not in the long-term best interest of American consumers to be totally dependent on foreign countries for wine, cars or other goods or services. As a result, resistance to the cheap imports builds up and can take the form of protectionist barriers to trade. Even without formal barriers, a certain amount of natural consumer resistance to foreign goods usually develops when a currency falls too far and the flood of imports becomes too large.

Resistance to the process—the free flow of capital and goods— means that the purchasing power parity theory will never be fully realized in practice. There will always be disparities in price between countries. Economists use the theory to calculate the ideal exchange rate for the major currencies knowing full well that the calculations are an ideal, not a practical reality. They use the calculations to determine which way the currency markets ought to move next. The problem is that wide disparities in price can go on for a long time, even for years. Only when currency markets take exchange rates to an unsustainable extreme do the corrections called for by purchasing power parity seem to develop. This is the clue to the practical use of the concept.

BE YOUR OWN CURRENCY EXPERT

When currency markets go to an unsustainable extreme, the disparity in prices becomes obvious to all but the most myopic. The period between late 1984 and early 1985 provides a good example of how you can call the currency markets as well as any expert. In those days foreign-made goods became ridiculously cheap in the United States. A traveler to London found that a dinner out with all the trimmings cost $40 to $50. Hotel rooms seemed inexpensive even in Paris and Tokyo.

Something was obviously out of balance. Sure enough, the U.S. dollar had soared to a level that bore no connection to the underlying economic realities. It had been driven there by wild speculation, which started when the Federal Reserve raised U.S. interest rates. That made U.S. dollars attractive, and capital flowed into the United States, moving the dollar higher on world currency markets. Once the upward trend began, speculators decided that they could make a profit by buying dollars and selling other currencies. The speculation became intense and lasted for months. In March 1985, at the end of this speculatory period, the dollar was at a peak and its overvaluation was obvious. From that peak, the dollar fell sharply.

OPPORTUNITY #6: PROFITS FROM THE "TOURIST INDICATOR"

What should an investor do when the currency markets go to such extremes? In 1984 and 1985 American investors had dollars that were grossly overvalued. (They could be used to buy a dinner in London, a German car or for investment.) When the dollar is grossly overvalued, the best strategy is to buy foreign assets such as stocks, bonds or real estate.

How do you know when the dollar is too high? Use simple common sense, called the "tourist indicator." First realize that an extreme overvaluation of the greenback won't happen very often. The tourist indicator isn't something you can use every month. (The dollar hit the ceiling only once in the 1980s.) Nevertheless, when the opportunity comes along, it can be significant. The trick is to have the tourist indicator clearly in mind. If the dollar rises too far in the future, you will know and will be ready to seize the opportunity.

This is the way the tourist indicator works. When the number of tourists visiting the United States plunges and the number of Americans traveling abroad rises dramatically, something is wrong. The dollar is too high. The indicator is called the tourist indicator to help you remember this principle. It actually covers more than tourists. If foreign goods are too cheap, imported wine or foreign luxury cars look like unbelievable bargains, and the headlines warn of a flood of foreign imports and slumping U.S. exports, you can be satisfied that the dollar is too high and is likely to come down.

Of course currency markets go both ways. The dollar can fall as well as rise. The indicator can also tell you when the dollar is too cheap. When the reverse occurs and the United States is flooded with foreign tourists, you know the dollar is cheap. What should be done during times when the dollar is grossly undervalued? If that happens, you do the opposite. You sell foreign assets at a profit and bring at least part of the funds back into the United States to buy U.S. bonds, stocks or real estate.

Most of the time, however, the currency markets are not so far out of touch with reality that there is any obvious profitable strategy. Investors usually have to content themselves with currency markets that are within bounds considered reasonable.

Be prepared for those few occasions when the currency markets offer up an obvious profit opportunity. How many American investors took advantage of the extreme overvaluation of the dollar in 1984 and 1985? Very few. Why? Because they were not prepared. They either didn't recognize the opportunity or they didn't know what to do. To be prepared, you need to have a basic understanding of currency markets and to be involved in international investing. If such opportunities come along only once every decade, they deliver profits large enough to make it worthwhile to be an international investor.

When the U.S. dollar came down from its 1985 peak, Americans with international portfolios made a killing.

CURRENCIES AND STOCK MARKETS

There is a common, but wrong, assumption that opportunity only comes when the dollar is due for a fall. Even in ordinary times, business manages to find ways of making profits by taking advantage of the currency climate.

After the French national elections in 1981, the French stock market plunged. It soon recovered, but that was not the case for the French franc. Between 1981 and 1986 France's currency entered into a long period of decline, losing 67 percent of its value versus the U.S. dollar. On the surface this would seem to have been a bad time for U.S. investors to hold French stocks. However, the contrary was the case. French stocks rose sharply in the years from the beginning of 1981 to the end of 1985—enough to more than offset the fall in the currency. U.S. investors holding French stocks saw their portfolios gain 124 percent in those years, in terms of U.S. dollars.

The reason for the excellent performance of French stocks was that the falling franc made goods manufactured in France cheaper in other countries. This gave French business a price advantage that they used to increase market share and profits. The lesson from the performance of French stocks in the early 1980s is that a low currency can be a distinct advantage for business.

HOW THE JAPANESE WON THE GAME

Japan used the currency markets to its advantage better than any other nation in this century. This is demonstrated by the story of Honda, one of the most popular Japanese cars. Until 1968 Honda made only motorcycles. The company then decided to expand into the car business in the 1960s. The first Hondas were small, not of that high a quality and cheap. Price was Honda's competitive edge. Honda made its cars in Japan, and because the Japanese yen was at a low exchange rate versus the dollar, labor costs there were lower than in the United States. Honda enjoyed huge profit margins since the cars were sold in the United States for dollars. The dollars could then be converted into Japanese yen and used to pay labor and other costs, leaving a huge profit for the company to reinvest in new technology, new factories and better cars.

We will never know what might have happened to Honda if the Japanese yen had been at a higher exchange rate versus the dollar. A change in the rate would have made a big difference in Honda's profits. Lower profits would have meant less cash available for new technology and expansion. If the yen had risen in the early 1970s, Honda might not be the profitable company it is today.

In the 1970s the dollar fell versus most of the major currencies. But, mysteriously, the Japanese yen held its own. The dollar did not fall as sharply versus the yen, and this had the effect of preserving the price advantage for Japanese companies all through the 1970s. It wasn't until 1985 that the yen finally moved sharply higher versus the dollar. Once that happened, American business began to make a comeback versus the Japanese competition.

Fifteen years of battering by the Japanese had, of course, taken its toll. Japanese companies had enjoyed huge profits and invested them well. American business had suffered anemic profit margins, lost market share and wasn't in a good position even when the yen finally rose.

The yen didn't remain undervalued by accident. It was held there deliberately by the Japanese government—not that there was a fixed exchange rate between yen and dollars. Japan had to fight hard to keep the yen from rising in the 1970s. It took tight and tough regulation of Japanese banks and bond markets to keep the yen where Japanese business wanted it to be.

The Japanese probably were surprised that the United States did not fight equally hard to push the yen up and keep the dollar down. Americans can be tough, fierce competitors. They fought hard in World War II, came back from the surprise attack on Pearl Harbor and beat the Japanese war machine. The Japanese had plenty of reason to expect the United States would be just as tough in commercial battles. We should have been even tougher because Japanese products invaded U.S. home markets, and America unfortunately proved to be an easy target. Instead of rising up and defending American business, we relished the luxury of low-cost Japanese products. We didn't mind that the yen was too low as that made it easier for American consumers to afford Japanese cars, television sets and stereos. Even after the Japanese had overtaken the United States in cars and consumer electronics, few Americans understood the significance that the currency markets played in the battle.

To be fair, the United States was riding high in the late 1960s. In 1967 a book entitled *Le Defi Americain (The American Challenge)*, by Jean-Jacques Servan-Schreiber, warned that "an invasion of Europe by American multinationals was dominating its economy and destroying its traditional industries." In those days America was a fearless economic giant. Some predicted that the United States would dominate all international commerce by the end of the 1970s and that the Japanese didn't stand a chance of competing.

In the 1960s the dollar was king. "Made in Japan" meant cheap and shoddy. Americans enjoyed significant advantages and benefits from the strong dollar. We were a rich and successful nation, and the idea that Japan, vanquished in war, could emerge as a significant competitor was not even imagined. The fact that Japan would become the world's largest creditor at the end of the 1980s didn't even seem possible in the closing days of the 1960s.

The Japanese probably never imagined their future success either. They felt the pressure of American dominance and reasoned that they needed every competitive edge they could muster, including help from an undervalued currency.

There was no excuse for the United States once the Japanese began to take significant chunks of American markets away from American business. At that point, America should have awakened and begun to fight hard, including battling to push the yen to a higher value. If we had succeeded in driving the yen up to 145 versus the dollar in 1975 instead of 1985, American industry might have fared much better. At least the Japanese would have lost their price advantage sooner.

Once you lose the game of currencies and commerce it becomes extremely difficult to come back. The yen rose in 1985 because at that time it was in Japan's favor to have a strong currency. By 1985 Japan had accumulated enormous profits that were so large that they couldn't be invested 100 percent at home. By allowing the yen to rise in 1985, Japan made foreign assets cheaper for their businesses to buy. After the upward move in the yen, it took fewer yen to buy U.S. assets. Japan effectively put the United States on sale for its prosperous businesses, and we had no choice but to cooperate. The only way that American business could begin to fight back was to change the terms of trade to our advantage. That required an upward move in the yen and a corresponding downward move in the dollar.

TINKERING WITH THE CURRENCY IS NOT ENOUGH

Driving a currency down to gain commercial advantage is a trick as old as international commerce itself. Thus it is truly shocking that the United States didn't catch on to the Japanese currency game until it was too late. There is, however, a risk associated with a low currency. The price advantage can easily be lost by too much inflation.

The secret to having an undervalued currency is that your costs are lower relative to those of your competitors. Lower costs mean that you can sell goods cheaper and still make a profit. That advantage will vanish if inflation drives costs up more than the advantage gained by the low currency.

Japan has virtually no domestic energy. It imports more than 90 percent of all its oil. When oil prices soared in the early 1970s, Japan was threatened. The Japanese could have lost their advantage easily if inflation had run up and stayed there. Costs would have soared and Japanese goods would no longer have been cheap on American markets. Japan was very sensitive to that risk and took decisive steps to adapt to higher oil prices. Inflation in Japan rose sharply for a brief time and then promptly cooled down. By the end of the 1970s Japan had a lower rate of inflation than the United States. This had the effect of amplifying their currency advantage. Just as high inflation destroys the advantage of a low currency, having both a low currency and a relatively low inflation rate amplifies the cost-price advantage.

To give the Japanese credit, not many nations have managed to accomplish both a relatively low currency and a relatively low inflation rate at the same time. A fall in the currency usually turns out to be a short-term advantage that is soon wiped out by rising costs. The French, however, did accomplish this in the mid-1980s. The French franc fell in value, but France nevertheless managed to bring its inflation rate down. It was that combination of a falling inflation rate and a fall in the currency that provided the boost to French corporate profits and stock prices.

The lesson for investors is this: The greatest stock market profits will follow from investing in a country that enjoys both a low currency and low inflation.

The problem is that this ideal situation does not come along very often. It is usually evident only from hindsight.

Looking ahead from the early 1970s, there was no guarantee that Japan would survive rising oil prices. In fact, logic indicated there was a significant risk that high oil prices would be a major problem for Japan in the 1970s. Buying Japanese stocks in the early 1970s did produce extraordinary profits. Investors who bought Japanese stocks did so with full knowledge of the risks.

In 1981 France had a relatively high inflation rate and a new Socialist president. It had suffered from relatively high inflation for years, and there were no guarantees that France would enjoy sharply lower inflation in the coming years. Investors who bought French stocks took a well-known risk in 1981.

There are never guarantees about the future. There are only risks. The more you know about risks, the easier it is to calculate when they are in your favor.

Knowing that the combination of inflation and currency are key to stock market profits provides an investment advantage.

You will ordinarily find that one or the other of these two elements is present. In the 1970s, Japan for example, had a currency advantage. Knowing that fact, it was possible to move on to a close look at how Japan dealt with rising oil prices. By the mid-1970s it was clear that Japan was doing an excellent job handling the inflation pressures from high oil prices. At that point Japanese stocks were still cheap enough. You might have missed the early gains, but you still would have enjoyed the larger share of the profits to come.

The opposite situation can also spell opportunity. A nation with low inflation often has a strong currency. Low inflation, however, can offset the disadvantages of a currency that is too high as costs in competing countries may be rising faster. In any case, countries with low inflation are always worth watching. Once in a while such countries will find a way to bring their currency down. Alert investors are ready to move in and buy stocks when a country with low inflation gains the additional advantage of a falling currency.

HOW DO YOU WATCH INFLATION RATES AND CURRENCIES?

The U.S. financial press is getting better at providing information on inflation rates and currencies in other countries. (It's getting better, but it's not good enough yet.) The best source for this information is the foreign press. Magazines such as *The Economist,* a British weekly, provide comprehensive inflation information in tables at the back of each issue. Exchange rate information is easier to find. Newsletters, such as *Dessauer's Journal,* plus the popular U.S. financial press regularly report both the current exchange rates and the long-term trend.

The fact that you have to do a little digging or subscribe to a newsletter or foreign magazine to get information indicates that the effort is worthwhile. Just as business needs a competitive edge, so do investors. The investor who watches the right trends will make the best investment decisions.

DON'T IGNORE COUNTRIES WITH HIGH INFLATION

The battle for profits is won by those who take advantage of changing trends. High inflation causes all sorts of economic problems, including high interest rates and low stock prices. Countries with high inflation must apply high interest rates not only to suppress inflation but to prop up their currencies. Inflation often pushes the currency down.

If a country with high inflation manages to bring the inflation rate down, there can be a significant and immediate improvement in corporate profits and stock prices. In the two years after the crash of 1987 French stock prices doubled. France fooled the experts and brought its inflation rate down to a level lower than that of the United States. Relatively low inflation plus a franc that suffered from memories of past mistakes gave French business an edge.

A CASE STUDY: AUSTRALIA

Could falling inflation and soaring stock prices happen again in some other country? The answer is yes, and the next time the profits may be even bigger. Australia is a possible candidate.

By 1987 inflation in Australia was up to 10 percent. The economy was overheated, consumers demanded goods, manufacturers could not keep up, prices rose and the government took action. Interest rates soared to 20 percent. The stock market languished, tending to fall more often than rise under the weight of high interest rates. Was Australia an opportunity in the making or a disaster waiting to happen?

This is a true story about a real country, but don't investigate the Australian stock market, at least not for a while. Imagine that it is January 1990. You don't know what the outcome will be. How do you go about deciding if the Australian stock market is worth the risk?

First you need more facts, one of the most important being the history of the Australian dollar. You don't want to make the right judgment on Australian stocks only to lose all the profit to a sinking Australian dollar. As you might guess, the Australian dollar had been very volatile in the late 1980s. It soared when interest rates first rose to more than 15 percent. It then sank when high, double-digit inflation persisted.

In the fall of 1989 a prestigious brokerage and merchant-banking firm released a study on the outlook for the Australian dollar, predicting that it would fall in 1990 and ultimately reach U.S. $0.60. Considering that it was U.S. $0.80 at the time, that prediction of a potential 25-percent fall in the Australian dollar was enough to frighten the most stalwart of investors.

Lesson #1: Don't be frightened by forecasts, even those made by leading experts.

In the closing months of 1989 the Australian dollar defied the dire predictions and began to climb. The reason for this was that inflation showed signs of slowing and the Australian trade deficit began to shrink. High interest rates appeared to be working. A slower economy would allow the government to lower interest rates, and that alone could be enough to push up Australian stock prices.

The reason the experts expected a steep fall in the Australian dollar was Australia's huge foreign debt. Because of its strong demand and inadequate manufacturing capacity, Australia had been sucking in imports at a record rate. Borrowing to pay for imports caused a significant increase in Australia's debt to other countries. If the import binge continued for many more years, Australia certainly would sink under the weight of too much debt, and the warnings of a plunge in the Australian dollar would come true.

The government of Australia was well aware of that risk, and in response cut spending and raised taxes to eliminate its domestic government deficit. By 1990 the Australian government was running a surplus. The Australian national debt was being reduced as the government used the surplus to buy back bonds.

You might think that running a surplus solved Australia's problems, but it wasn't so. Much of the debt owed to foreigners was due from businesses. Only a small part was a direct obligation of the Australian government. Business had purchased foreign goods and issued IOUs or promissory notes in payment. The IOUs were denominated in Japanese yen, U.S. dollars, German marks and other foreign currencies. When business sold the goods in Australia, even at a profit, they received Australian dollars from their customers. To pay the foreign firms, they had to sell the Australian dollars and buy foreign currency. That kept downward pressure on the Australian dollar.

Lesson #2: A balanced government budget is only a small part of the story of a nation's economic health.

In light of the huge foreign debt and large trade deficit, the late-1989 strength of the Australian dollar was something of a mystery to many investors. How could the Australian dollar rise when so many domestic businesses were forced to keep selling?

A rising currency means that there is more capital coming into a country than leaving it. In early 1990 the challenge was to figure out where the capital inflows were coming from. In part, they were speculative. Wealthy investors in Europe were buying Australian bonds with high interest rates in hopes of making a killing if the interest rates came down. If that were all there was to the Australian dollar's early-1990 strength, the risks would be high. Speculators can reverse directions quickly. If too many wealthy investors decided to sell their Australian bonds at the same time and take the money home, the Australian dollar would plunge. However, Australian interest rates had been high for years. Wealthy investors had been buying and selling Australian bonds for years. It was unlikely that they alone accounted for the mysterious early-1990 strength of the Australian dollar. The capital had to be coming from somewhere else.

Lesson #3: No country is an economic island.

Australia has a very prosperous neighbor—Japan. This neighbor is short of raw materials while Australia has plenty of them. By the end of the 1980s Japan was suffering a problem every nation should have—too much money. There was so much money in Japan that it was impossible to invest it all at home. Capital had to leave Japan and find opportunities in other countries. Some, for example, went to the United States to buy the Spain Fund and the Germany Fund, driving those stocks to record highs. Other capital also went to Australia to buy real estate and other assets. Capital flowing out of Japan and into Australia probably accounted for the mysterious strength in the Australian dollar in early 1990.

When making a judgment about a currency, consider a country's geographical region and use some common sense to anticipate logical capital flows. As long as Japan is flush with cash and Australia is a region rich in natural resources, it is logical to expect that capital will flow from Japan to Australia and prevent a collapse of the Australian dollar.

This story of investments and Australia shows that opportunity never comes clearly marked. Australia had serious negatives at the close of 1989 including a huge trade deficit, a huge foreign debt and high inflation. It also had a balanced budget, high interest rates, plenty of natural resources and a rich neighbor.

What would you have done in early 1990? Would you have passed Australia by or taken the risk and bought Australian stocks?

Lesson #4: Opportunity, in the form of low-priced stocks or other assets, always develops because there are real negatives. You won't get a chance to buy low as long as all the news is good. Buying low means looking at the risks, understanding them and deciding whether or not to take a chance.

CHAPTER

6

Currencies and Your Investments

It is a myth, but a popular one, that foreign stocks are riskier than American stocks because of the currency markets. The way to sort out fact and fantasy is to look at the record.

In the decade of the 1980s foreign stocks did just as well or better for American investors than U.S. stocks despite some wild fluctuations in the currency markets. Eleven out of 18 world stock markets provided better profits in U.S. dollars than the U.S. stock market. Six did worse, but there were no losers.

The performance of world currencies varied from a 37-percent decline in the Hong Kong dollar to a 67-percent gain in the Japanese yen (See Table 6-1). Sweden, where the value of the currency went down, was second only to Japan in performance for American investors. A falling currency was more than made up by outstanding gains in Swedish stocks. American investors were better off owning Swedish stocks in the 1980s than American stocks even though the Swedish currency fell sharply versus the U.S. dollar. The table shows that over a long period of time the changes in the currency markets are not all that important when it comes to profits in foreign stocks.

In March 1985 the U.S. dollar was grossly overvalued and at a peak. (An overvalued dollar provides American investors with a significant opportunity, namely, to buy foreign stocks cheap.) In the last five years of the 1980s 15 foreign markets provided significantly better gains for American investors than U.S. stocks (see Table 6-2).

Table 6-1.   Stock Markets and Currencies: A Ten-Year View
(12/31/79–12/31/89)

Country	Stock Market Performance in U.S. Dollars	Currency Change vs. U.S. Dollar
Japan	+1,007%	+66.5 %
Sweden	871.2	–33.0
Italy	517.3	–36.5
Denmark	409.1	–18.8
Netherlands	297.3	– 0.4
Austria	257.3	+ 4.4
England	265.0	–27.7
Belgium	248.6	–18.5
France	247.0	–30.5
Germany	241.6	+ 1.8
Spain	189.8	–39.6
United States	211.4	0
Singapore/Malaysia	176.7	+13.8
Switzerland	144.7	+ 3.5
Hong Kong	135.2	–37.0
Norway	135.5	–25.2
Australia	139.4	–28.8
Canada	111.6	+ 1.3

Figures in this table are based on national indices from Morgan Stanley Capital International Perspective. Dividends are not included.

The United States was in sixteenth place out of a total of 18. Only two markets did worse. Once again there were no losers. One of the reasons foreign stocks did so much better was the fall in the value of the U.S. dollar from March 1985 to December 1987. It is worthy of note, however, that Australian stocks did better for Americans than their own market even though the Australian dollar fell 4 percent.

The 1980s were a time of wild fluctuation in the currency markets. When the last day of trading was finished, the dollar had fallen sharply versus the Japanese yen but finished close to where it started the decade versus two major European currencies, the West German mark and the Swiss franc.

From these facts we can conclude that fluctuating currencies are much less of a risk when holding foreign stocks than commonly believed. The reasons for this are that currency fluctuations are only one part of the story of business profits and stock prices. Business

Table 6-2. Stock Markets and Currencies: A Five-Year View (12/31/84–12/31/89)

Country	Stock Market Performance in U.S. Dollars	Currency Change vs. U.S. Dollar
Austria	+620.8%	+85.8%
Japan	447.0	+74.6
Belgium	407.6	+78.1
France	385.5	+66.6
Spain	379.3	+58.6
Sweden	377.2	+44.8
Italy	366.1	+52.4
Germany	289.2	+86.1
Denmark	274.0	+71.1
Norway	224.3	+37.8
Netherlands	213.6	+86.2
Switzerland	209.3	+68.4
England	182.9	+39.0
Hong Kong	158.6	+ 0.2
Australia	140.1	– 4.3
United States	105.7	0
Singapore/Malaysia	99.1	+14.7
Canada	86.7	+13.9

Figures in this table are based on national indices from Morgan Stanley Capital International Perspective. Dividends are not included.

managers work hard to keep their companies competitive even when the currency goes against them. To quote a familiar adage, "When the going gets tough, the tough get going." That applies to business as well as sports or life in general. Sometimes tough times produce better business.

In 1978 Ward and Joseph Parkinson, twin brothers, decided to form their own company and make sophisticated computer memory chips. With no help from Wall Street financiers, they started in a small way, finally raised enough capital and formed Micron Technology, Inc. (traded over-the-counter; symbol: MCRN).

Micron soon faced a life-threatening challenge from the Japanese. Since memory chips are essential parts in all computers, the Japanese wanted to dominate the chip market as they didn't dominate the personal computer market. If they controlled the market for chips, they would have a competitive advantage in the entire computer field.

In the early days of Micron the Japanese yen was still undervalued. This gave Japanese makers of memory chips a price advantage, and they decided to use it. The Japanese strategy was to sell chips at or below cost and force American chip makers out of business. They nearly succeeded, as many U.S. companies gave up the chip business rather than face years of losses. Micron suffered. Its profits plunged and losses developed, but the company didn't give up even though the Japanese ended up with almost 90 percent of the market for memory chips.

Micron fought back on all fronts. They accused the Japanese of unfair trade practices and dumping chips below cost. The charge produced an agreement from the Japanese to stop the practice. (By then the Japanese practically owned the market anyway.) Shortly thereafter, prices for memory chips began to rise and Micron enjoyed a period of significant profits.

In 1985 the Japanese yen finally began to rise, and the cost-price advantage shifted away from Japan. In 1987 Micron was the low-cost producer of memory chips, and in 1988 it earned $3.38 a share, or $98 million. Those American businesses that had given up the chip business in the face of tough Japanese competition regretted their decision.

Micron used the time and profits that followed the upward move in the yen and the Japanese agreement to stop dumping to build a new factory and develop its manufacturing processes. By the end of 1989 Micron Technology (in Boise, Idaho) had become not just a survivor but a world leader in the technology for manufacturing memory chips. The story of Micron shows that tough, international competition can cause a company to become tougher and improve its long-term prospects.

OPPORTUNITY #7: THINK IN TERMS OF EXPORTS

The story of Micron Technology is the story of a U.S. company that dealt with foreign competition in its own home market. Micron survived and went on to become a tough competitor.

There are other stories and other opportunities in companies that make their products in one country and sell them in another. In these cases the currency markets often play an important and direct role. Watching currency markets and thinking in terms of exports can produce some outstanding opportunities for profits in international stock markets.

A classic example is the story of Glaxo Holdings, a British drug company whose shares are traded on the New York Stock Exchange (symbol: GLX). Glaxo makes a drug called Zantac, which is used to help people suffering from ulcers. The field of ulcer medications is highly competitive. Glaxo, however, had an advantage: the company's headquarters and a significant part of its production is located in England. In the first half of the 1980s the pound fell from 2.14 versus the dollar to a low of 1.16. That 46-percent decline had the effect of reducing Glaxo's costs compared with competitors in countries with strong currencies. Glaxo had another advantage: roughly half of the company's sales are in the United States. Those sales in dollars meant increased profits for Glaxo. Glaxo's earnings and profits rose steadily, and so did the stock. From 1980 to 1985 earnings per share rose 233 percent. The stock climbed from $1 5/8 to $11 5/8, for a gain of 615 percent. American investors sensitive to the effect of the falling pound on Glaxo's costs enjoyed significant profits.

Suppose you had your income in U.S. dollars in the early 1980s, perhaps in dividends from American companies like General Motors or Citicorp. Also assume that you were living in England, paying a monthly rent of 1,000 pounds. In 1980 your rent would have been $2,140, but in 1985 the rent of 1,000 pounds per month would have fallen to $1,160. Having your income in dollars and your housing costs in pounds meant a gain of $980 a month thanks to the currency markets. In a simple form, that is the story of Glaxo and all other companies that enjoy manufacturing in a country with a low currency and sales in a country with a stronger currency.

Novo-Nordisk, a Danish drug company whose stock is traded on the New York Stock Exchange (symbol: NVO), is an opposite story. Novo is an excellent company, and their principal drug product is insulin. The company's chief competitor is U.S.-based Eli Lilly. In the late 1980s the Danish currency was strong. The Danish krone climbed 72 percent versus the U.S. dollar between 1985 and the end of 1989. This had the effect of raising Novo's costs relative to Eli

Lilly. Since the price for insulin is set in a free market, Novo had to meet the competition even though that meant lower profits.

The impact of the currency market can be seen clearly in the profits of Eli Lilly and Novo-Nordisk. Between 1985 and 1989 Lilly's profits climbed 73 percent while Novo's advanced 35 percent. Novo's stock price climbed from $35 in 1985 to $52 in 1989, for a gain of 17 percent. Lilly's stock price rose 142 percent over the same period.

Novo-Nordisk is an excellent company. Profits and the share price could be boosted in the future if the currency markets go the other way or if Novo, under pressure to compete, finds ways of reducing costs or introducing new products. One thing is sure: investors who understand and watch the world's currency markets will have an advantage over those who myopically ignore them. If the Danish krone weakens in the 1990s, there is apt to be a significant opportunity in Novo.

The stories of Glaxo and Novo are oversimplified, but the profit potential is genuine. Think in terms of exports. In other words, look at companies and ask yourself whether they make most of their money selling things at home or through exports. If the answer is through exports, then you want to look carefully at the currency to see if there is a potential profit.

The story of Glaxo Holdings should dispel any thoughts of currency markets as one-way streets for American investors. Instead of selling stocks in a country where the currency is weak, look for companies that make goods for export to the United States or other countries with strong currencies. Making things in one country and selling them in another where the currency is stronger is an age-old formula for profit.

Having a currency advantage can be a source of enormous profit both for a company and its shareholders. The next time you read that one of the world's currencies has fallen, don't be glad you didn't invest there. Think "exports," and look for an opportunity to make a profit.

INVESTING IN FOREIGN CURRENCIES

Investing in foreign currencies means buying for cash, not borrowing. It may come as a surprise, but buying a basket of foreign currencies for cash can be one of the least risky things you can do. A second, but equally important, reason for investing in foreign currencies is to increase the income from your cash. Buying for cash does not mean taking possession of foreign bills or notes and keeping them in a safe place. That is an alternative, but it's not a sensible way to invest in foreign currencies.

Investing in foreign currencies means opening a bank account and buying a certificate of deposit, or its equivalent, denominated in one or more foreign currencies. The "magic" that reduces the risk is that certificates of deposit and other money market instruments pay interest. The riskier the currency, the higher the interest paid. For example, at the end of 1989 a bank deposit in Australia for six months paid a whopping 18 percent.

Suppose you invested U.S. $100,000 in Australia at the end of 1989. That would have purchased A$131,579. At the end of a year your account would grow to A$155,263, thanks to interest income. (Note: The currency of Australia is also called a dollar and is designated as A$.) If the exchange rate stayed the same, you would have U.S. $118,000, or 18 percent more than at the beginning of the year. If the Australian dollar, under the pressure of heavy Japanese buying, rose by 5 percent, at year-end you would have U.S. $123,900, for a profit of 23.9 percent. If things went the other way and the Australian dollar fell by 5 percent, you would end up with U.S. $112,100, or a 12 percent profit—still a respectable rate of return. The Australian dollar would have to fall from U.S. $0.76 to U.S. $0.64 before you would end up where you started, with U.S. $100,000 and no return on your money. A fall of that magnitude would be close to what the doomsayers predicted for the Australian dollar at the end of 1989.

In other words, the very high Australian interest rates protected you almost completely from the worst-case outlook for the Australian dollar. If the Australian currency did any better, you would have a profit. If it did what it started out to do in 1990—namely, gain strength—you would have a handsome return on your money.

Interest rates take into account the risk in a currency. The riskier a currency appears to be, the higher the interest rate paid. This fact of modern currency markets can be used to earn better returns on cash. What you want to do is invest in currencies that offer high interest rates—but not high nominal rates alone. The highest returns are likely to follow from taking into account both interest rates and inflation. What you want to look for are high real, or after-inflation, interest rates.

Take the Dutch guilder at the end of 1989 as an example. Holland had one of the world's lowest inflation rates, 1.5 percent, but because the guilder was tied to the German mark, interest rates in Holland were high, at 8 percent or better. An investment in guilders at the end of 1989 earned 8 percent, or 6.5 percent after inflation. That was a good bet. In the United States at that time nominal interest rates were 7³/₄ percent for six months. The United States was running an inflation rate of 4.6 percent, so real interest rates were only 3.15 percent.

WHICH CURRENCIES SHOULD YOU WATCH?

You don't have to be very exotic to enjoy above-average yields on your cash. Stick with the major currencies—the German mark, the British pound, the Swiss franc, the French franc, the Dutch guilder, the Japanese yen, the Canadian dollar and the Australian dollar.

Look to the back pages of a magazine such as *The Economist* and make a table showing nominal interest rates, inflation and real interest rates. In April 1989, when *Dessauer's Journal* first introduced a model currency portfolio, such a table looked like this:

	Short-Term Interest Rates	Inflation Rate	Real Interest Rates
Australian dollar	16.9%	7.7%	9.2%
Canadian dollar	12.1	4.3	7.8
Dutch guilder	6.6	0.8	5.8
French franc	9.0	3.3	5.7
British pound	13.0	7.5	5.5
U.S. dollar	9.0	4.7	4.3
German mark	6.6	2.6	4.0
Swiss franc	5.7	2.3	3.4
Japanese yen	4.2	1.1	3.1

The recommendation at the time was to invest one-third in Australian dollars, one-third in German marks and one-third in Canadian dollars for six months. Why invest in these three currencies? The Australian and Canadian dollars offered very high real interest rates. Having two-thirds of the portfolio in high-yielding currencies, the sensible thing was to balance the risk by selecting a "hard" currency for the remaining one-third. You could have chosen the Japanese yen or the Swiss franc, but the recommendation at the time was the German mark.

Six months later the U.S. dollar was up 5.4 percent versus the Australian dollar, down 1 percent versus the German mark and down 1.4 percent versus the Canadian dollar. Over all, the portfolio lost money based on exchange rate changes during the first six months. But because of the fact that interest was earned on the entire portfolio, the net result was a gain of 5 percent, or an annual rate of 10 percent. By investing in three foreign currencies, the portfolio did better than U.S. treasury bills, government bonds or money market accounts even though the exchange rates went the wrong way.

The advice in October was to keep the same positions and roll the deposits over for another three months. The reason for that advice was that the real interest rate table hadn't changed much in the intervening six months. By the end of 1989, after nine months holding the same three foreign currencies, the portfolio had appreciated 12.9 percent, or an annual rate of 17.25 percent.

There was nothing spectacular about the selection of Australian dollars, German marks and Canadian dollars. No advanced degrees were required to make that selection. During the nine months the results were often mixed. The Australian dollar was volatile. For a while the U.S. dollar rose versus the German mark, but at the end of the year the results were quite satisfactory.

You won't earn 17.25 percent a year every year investing in foreign currencies. Some years the results will be much lower. The purpose of looking at this portfolio is not to tantalize you with dazzling possibilities but to show that investing in foreign currencies is not difficult, is not as risky as commonly believed and can produce handsome results even when you make a few mistakes.

The simple rules for investing in foreign currencies are as follows:

1. Watch real, or after-inflation, interest rates.
2. Be sensible, not greedy. Buy one or two with the highest real interest rates and then a third with middle-of-the-road real interest rates.
3. Always invest in more than one foreign currency. Two is the minimum, three is better and four is ideal.

4.   Invest for cash. Don't speculate, borrow or buy futures.
5.   Remember that the objective is to increase the overall yield on
     your cash holdings, not to make a killing.

THERE ARE INTEREST RATES AND INTEREST RATES

In financial publications (including *Dessauer's Journal*) you will
frequently see a reference to Eurodollars, Euro-Swiss francs or
Eurocurrencies. The prefix "Euro" is used for accuracy. There are
different interest rates for different circumstances. For example,
there are interest rates on treasury bills, ordinary bank savings accounts, certificates of deposit and rates that banks charge when you
borrow money. At any given time each carries an interest rate
slightly different from the others. When interest rates are discussed,
it is important to know exactly what is involved. This is especially
true when comparing interest rates from one country to another. if
different instruments are involved, the analysis and conclusions can
be misleading or just plain wrong.

The easiest way to be sure that international interest rate compar-
isons are accurate is to always use Eurocurrencies. Interest rates on
Eurodollars can be compared with interest rates on Euro-Swiss
francs. If you venture into other instruments, such as bank accounts, you enter the confusing world of local regulation.

American banks, for example, are required to deposit a certain
percentage of their depositors' money with the Federal Reserve.
That money is not available to the bank for general lending activity.
Idling a part of the depositors' cash has the effect of increasing the
bank's cost of funds. If the bank pays you 7 percent but has to put 5
percent in reserve at the Fed, the real cost of the deposit rises to 7.4
percent. For this reason, reserve requirements have an impact on
both what banks pay on deposits and what they charge on loans.

Reserve requirements vary from country to country. Since this
part of the international playing field is not level, it can be tricky to
compare interest rates around the world. While not perfect, Eurocurrencies eliminate many of the international differences.

THE HISTORY OF THE EURODOLLAR

In 1952 the Cold War between the Soviet Union and the United
States was raging. The Soviets needed to buy grain due to one of

their chronic agricultural shortfalls. The United States had grain to sell but needed U.S. dollars in payment. The Soviets accumulated dollars through international transactions, such as sales of gold and oil. However, the Soviets didn't want to have those dollars on deposit at an American bank. They were afraid that if the Cold War took a nasty turn, the U.S. government would freeze Soviet assets.

A solution was found with the help of a cooperative French bank. The French said that they were willing to open an account for the Soviets and hold the dollars. They also said that they could not pay the full U.S. interest rate because of the difficulties involved in handling such a unique transaction. The Soviets agreed, and U.S. dollars ended up in a French bank account.

The French bank was beyond the regulatory control of the U.S. Federal Reserve. The usual reserve requirements imposed on U.S. banks didn't apply. Dollars had found their way into Europe's banking system.

The dollars held in France were the same as those held by American banks, but they were free of regulatory control. After a while, other banks caught on to this opportunity. They could accumulate dollars without having to keep part of the money idle at the Federal Reserve and could gain an advantage over their American competition. In addition, they could either pay more to attract deposits or charge less to attract borrowers. They did both.

These dollars in Europe, free of the U.S. Federal Reserve's tough requirements, were dubbed "Eurodollars." The name stuck. In the 1970s, as interest rates rose and reserve requirements became increasingly significant, the Eurodollar market grew rapidly. From a few million dollars in the 1950s, the Eurodollar market became several hundred million and then several billion dollars.

Escaping the reach of central bank reserve requirements was so attractive that innovative bankers decided to do the same with Swiss francs, German marks and other currencies. Once they were held out of the home country, they too were dubbed "Euro." A whole new market in currencies eventually developed, and that market still exists today.

The governments of the world eventually became alarmed about the huge size of the Euro markets. American banks with subsidiaries in Europe had joined the game and held significant quantities of Eurodollars by the late 1970s. The Federal Reserve then passed new regulations covering Eurodollars held by U.S. banks.

In the 1980s central banks around the world fought to gain some control over the burgeoning international currency markets. Banks, for their part, found new ways of escaping regulation. Offshore currency markets sprung up in Asia and other parts of the world.

A dollar in Asia should technically be called an "Asiadollar," rather than a Eurodollar. For a short time in the late 1970s, currencies were tagged by region. That soon became too confusing, and in the end "Eurodollar" was used to describe any dollar deposit outside of the United States. Likewise, the prefix "Euro" is added for other currencies that are held outside their home country.

At the end of 1989 the Federal Reserve changed the U.S. banking laws to allow U.S. banks to hold deposits in foreign currencies. One of the reasons was to open the way for U.S. banks to become full participants in the growing world currency markets.

By the end of the 1990s the world of bank regulation probably will catch up with the real world of international borrowing and lending. If that is the case, the word Eurodollar may disappear from common use.

HOW TO INVEST IN FOREIGN CURRENCIES

Until December 31, 1989, it was against the law for an American bank to hold deposits denominated in foreign currencies. That rule included foreign banks doing business in the United States. This made it very cumbersome for the average American to invest in anything but U.S. dollars.

The rule was imposed on the banks, and it was a shame. In the 1970s the dollar declined every year for ten consecutive years against the Swiss franc. Americans suffered from rising inflation and a loss of buying power. Worse, they were denied the opportunity of protecting themselves. If they could have gone to the local bank and bought a certificate of deposit denominated in Swiss francs, they would have protected their purchasing power. However, for all the rhetoric about freedom, the United States still denied its citizens the freedom to choose currencies.

Be suspicious when a government doesn't allow easy access to foreign currencies. Why don't they? All too often the answer is that the government is terrified about capital flight. If too many people decided to move their cash into a foreign currency, the sale of dollars and outflow of capital amounts to a run on the whole U.S. banking system.

In the second half of the 1970s, for example, U.S. interest rates were too low. The government didn't want to allow rates to rise because of another peculiar rule. For decades the federal government had imposed tough regulations on American banks, including rules on how much they could pay on deposits. The rule served its purpose in the 1950s and 1960s. The idea was to make sure the banks could lend money for home mortgages at reasonable interest rates. Since banks have to make a profit, the rule was designed to keep the interest paid on deposits low enough so that the banks would be able to make low-cost mortgage loans. In the 1970s, when U.S. oil imports soared and the nation lost its economic independence, that rule became obsolete. The government, however, was reluctant to change. Some modest changes were made, but Uncle Sam dragged his feet until it was too late.

If Americans had been allowed to move their cash easily into foreign currencies, there might have been billions of dollars making that switch in the 1970s. Deposits would have shifted into other currencies. U.S. banks would have faced a shortage of cash. Thus the government kept in place the regulations prohibiting U.S. banks from holding deposits in foreign currencies. The "trick" worked. Americans were naive about foreign currencies. They could have gotten around the rule by opening accounts abroad, but they didn't. Only a relatively few went to the trouble of opening a bank account in a foreign country and moving part of their cash into other currencies.

This story from the 1970s shows how American naiveté works to hamper the entire economic system. All governments resist facing bad economic music. In that respect there is nothing unique about the U.S. government's currency rules and regulations. In countries with citizens aware of currency markets, however, the governments are not so easily able to fool the people. They have to use more direct means, such as outright prohibition on the free flow of capital, to avoid facing bad economic music. Such controls seldom work because people are then well aware of the problem and quickly find ways around the rules and regulations.

If Americans had been aware of the international economic facts in the 1970s, the United States might have been forced to move sooner than it did to contain inflation and face the bad economic music. But that isn't the way things developed. The people allowed government to delay until inflation was out of control and the Federal Reserve was desperate. The consequence of our ignorance was the great recession of 1982. It might have been prevented—or at least reduced in impact—had the nation been more aware of currencies and the international facts of modern economic life.

Does awareness of foreign currencies help or hurt a nation? The answer is found in the interaction between a government and its people. If they work together to solve problems, the result will always be positive. If a government works against the long-term best interest of the people for political reasons, the result can be disastrous. In a democracy, however, the presumption is that government will not be able to work against the people's interests for long. Thus, in the United States it does help the country when enough people are aware of currency markets and are willing to move money in ways that protect their own personal interests.

The opposite is also true. In totalitarian systems the consequence of excessive political control is usually disastrous in the long run. In the Soviet Union, for example, it has been illegal to hold foreign currencies. This tight control of the entire economic process resulted in economic disaster and the crumbling of the entire Soviet bloc. By 1990 the people of the Soviet Union were stuck with their lifesavings in worthless rubles. They faced wild inflation and massive financial losses. If the Soviet Union had allowed the free exchange of currencies, the politicians would have been forced to face up to economic realities much sooner. The lack of a free interchange between the people and the government was one factor that helped to condemn the Soviet system to economic ruin.

Unfortunately, Americans do not seem to learn quickly. On the last day of 1989 the Federal Reserve changed the U.S. banking law to allow U.S. banks to hold foreign currency deposits. The system changed, but the people didn't. A few banks began to study the idea of offering foreign currency deposits in early 1990, but there was no rush to provide the service. Bankers worried that there would be too little demand for such deposits to cover the costs of providing the service. They probably were correct, as too few Americans understand that the U.S. dollar is just one of the major currencies in the world.

Consider this irony. In early 1990 the U.S. stock market was weak and subject to periodic sinking spells. The bankruptcy of Drexel

Burnham Lambert, a major U.S. brokerage firm and leader of the junk bond craze, was one of the reasons. Drexel's failure focused attention on the excessive level of debt in the U.S. system. Investors worried that the debt load would bring the entire economy down.

So what did U.S. investors do? They sold stocks and "invested" their cash in bank accounts and government bonds. Wall Street pundits at the time called this a "flight to quality." What utter nonsense!

What do banks do with deposits? To earn interest to pay depositors, they make loans! U.S. investors were rushing to become lenders rather than owners of business. They moaned about the high levels of U.S. debt and at the same time contributed to the problem by becoming lenders. If the only way to raise capital is by borrowing, debt levels will rise. When investors have a love affair with interest income and prefer acting as lenders to the owners of business, there is no alternative but higher and higher debt. The incredible part of this story is that supposedly savvy professional investors indulged wholeheartedly in the process. They called their move into debt as lenders a "flight to quality" while condemning the financial markets for relying too heavily on debt. If professional U.S. investors can't apply the difference between debt and investment to their own conduct, how can Americans in general be expected to understand the benefits of investing in foreign currencies?

The facts of international economic life will eventually sink into American habits. Sooner or later Americans will demand foreign currency deposits from their banks. When the demand rises, the system will move quickly. By 1990 a few American banks were offering foreign currencies to their depositors. Most, however, were too preoccupied with problem loans to consider complex new services. Until foreign currency deposits become popular in the United States, it may be easier to open an account in a foreign bank.

Contacting foreign banks is easier than you might think. A few foreign bank stocks are listed on the New York Stock Exchange. Others are traded in the U.S. over-the-counter market. Through regular stock market services found at your local library you can get the addresses for the home offices of these banks. If you write to them, they will send you information on how to go about opening an account and investing two or three foreign currencies. In some cases you will find U.S. branches of foreign banks. Several foreign banks have opened offices in the United States. If you visit one of these branches, they can give you the home office address. They may have foreign currency services available at the branch, so you will still have to do business by mail.

A WORD ABOUT U.S. TAXES

The Internal Revenue Service (IRS) does business in only one currency, U.S. dollars. Foreign banks are not obliged to provide you with 1099 forms in U.S. dollars. If you have a foreign bank account denominated in a foreign currency, it will be up to you to keep good records and convert the interest earned into U.S. dollars for tax purposes.

Don't let this record-keeping burden scare you away from foreign currencies. If you keep track of the exchange rate between dollars and the foreign currencies, you will have no problem satisfying the IRS. It is perfectly legal for Americans to hold foreign currencies. It is also legal to have a foreign bank account. If you keep good records, there will be no problem when it comes to filing and paying your federal income taxes.

By the way, this look at U.S. income tax laws sheds more light on why U.S. banks didn't rush in to offer foreign currency deposits as soon as the law changed. Banks doing business in the United States have to supply and file 1099 forms. This means that if they offer foreign currency deposits, their computers have to be able to make the conversion between foreign currencies and U.S. dollars to comply with IRS laws. Programming computers is expensive. That is another reason why bankers want to be certain that there will be enough of a demand before making the service generally available.

OPPORTUNITY #8: FOREIGN CURRENCY MUTUAL FUNDS

Fidelity Investments offers mutual funds denominated in three currencies: German marks, British pounds and Japanese yen. These funds are like money market funds only instead of investing in U.S. dollars, they invest in foreign currencies. Call Fidelity (1-800-544-8888), ask for a prospectus and begin investing your cash in more than U.S. dollars. The funds have a minimum initial investment of

$5,000, with additions of $1,000 or more. The sales charge is reasonable, ranging from 0.4 percent to 0.2 percent, depending on the amount invested.

If Fidelity is successful with these three funds, they may introduce more. Other fund sponsors may join the competition as well. American investors deserve the opportunity of investing their cash safely in a diversified list of currencies other than the U.S. dollar.

FOREIGN BONDS

Bonds are thought of as specific investments, different from cash or currencies. In a technical sense that is true, but it is wiser for investors to think of bonds as "currency in the future."

If all goes well and the borrower doesn't get into serious financial trouble, the bond you buy today will one day in the future be repaid in full, in cash. That goes for U.S. bonds and bonds in all other countries. A bond is cash to be paid in the future, and that is why it can be called "currency in the future."

Because bonds become currency in the future, they introduce the element of time into the investment question. How much will the currency be worth when the bond is repaid in the future? The answer depends on inflation, which is the great destroyer of currencies.

Bonds pay a rate of interest that is usually fixed at the time of issue. The rate usually is higher than the rate of inflation when the bond is issued, but there is no guarantee that inflation will stay down for the life of the bond. If inflation rises, interest rates rise and the value of the bond falls. This is true of both U.S. and foreign bonds.

There are two reasons for investing in bonds. One is to lock in a high rate of interest. The other is to make a profit when interest rates fall. If your primary reason for investing in bonds is to lock in a high rate of interest, foreign bonds add the element of diversification.

If you buy only U.S. bonds, you take a risk that U.S. inflation will rise and the value of the bonds will fall. The high income you locked in could turn out to be much less than you expected as inflation erodes the value of your income and principal. If you invest in bonds in several countries, you change the risk. It isn't often that inflation goes in the same direction in all countries at the same time.

One country or another usually does a better job containing its inflation rate. Germany and Japan, for example, held the line on their inflation rates in the 1970s and the 1980s. Diversifying into bonds in several countries reduces the risk from U.S. inflation.

Foreign Bonds Pay Interest in Foreign Currencies

It isn't just the principal that is paid in a foreign currency when you invest in foreign bonds. The interest that is paid along the way is also paid in that particular foreign currency. This can be one of the more attractive aspects of owning foreign bonds.

Suppose you invested in long-term, ten-year Swiss bonds in late 1984. In those days Swiss interest rates were lower than they were at the end of 1989. Because Swiss interest rates rose in the last five years of the 1980s, the principal value of your Swiss bonds declined. On the surface that looks like a bad investment, but that isn't the whole story.

Remember that you bought the bonds to lock in an income. Between 1984 and 1989 the Swiss franc rose sharply versus the U.S. dollar. The income checks you received from your Swiss bonds kept buying more and more dollars each year. The value of the bonds might have gone down on the Swiss bond market, but your personal income rose thanks to the fact that you bought Swiss bonds. An income of 1,000 Swiss francs in 1985 was the equivalent of $385.30. In 1989 an income of 1,000 Swiss francs was worth $648.90, an increase of 68 percent. That is a big difference from investing in U.S. bonds. If you buy U.S. bonds and the value falls, there is no compensating increase in your income.

Of course you might be less fortunate than buying Swiss bonds in 1984. You might buy bonds in a country where the currency falls versus the dollar. In that case your income goes down. Thus foreign bonds are not one-way tickets to prosperity. They simply introduce diversification. Because you don't know which way the dollar, U.S. interest rates or U.S. inflation will go, the safest strategy is to hedge the bet by diversifying with foreign bonds.

How To Invest in Foreign Bonds

Buying foreign bonds isn't always easy for American investors. Some are traded in the United States, and two French government bonds are even listed on the New York Stock Exchange. (They are

French Treasury Bonds or OATs. One is a 9.80-percent bond due January 30, 1996, and the other is an 8.50-percent bond due June 30, 1997.) These French bonds are exceptions. It is generally either expensive or awkward for Americans to invest in foreign bonds.

The easiest way for U.S. investors to invest in foreign bonds is through a mutual fund. Many of the U.S. mutual fund sponsors offer funds specializing in foreign bonds. Buying these shares means that the professionals managing the fund will make the selection of bonds on your behalf. It also means that you can buy or sell easily and conveniently.

The other way to invest in foreign bonds is to have a foreign bank or brokerage account and buy the bonds directly for your account. This is practical if you have a fairly large portfolio to be invested in bonds. It isn't unusual to find foreign minimum account requirements to be $100,000 or more.

Timing Your Foreign Bond Purchases

Even though you may be buying foreign bonds as a long-term investment, it is wise to make some effort at timing. At least you want to avoid buying foreign bonds at an excessively high price. The practical solution is to use your monitoring of the currency markets to determine when the U.S. dollar is strong. Buying foreign bonds after the U.S. currency has run up will reduce your purchase price on the investment.

Remember that bonds are currencies in the future. They are not investments in a business, as are stocks. If you make a bad decision and buy when the dollar is low, there will be no compensating offset from the underlying business. Watching the currency is key to making a wise decision on buying foreign bonds.

Investing in Foreign Bonds for Capital Gains

In the spring of 1989 a group of wealthy investors gathered at an expensive restaurant for lunch. The wine was excellent, and the conversation concerned how to make a profit in the markets. This savvy group was almost unanimous in their opinion that the best opportunity was in Australian bonds.

Australia had been suffering under the weight of high interest rates for a long time. Sooner or later, they reasoned, high interest rates would take effect and push down the rate of inflation. When that happened, Australian interest rates would come down and the value of Australian bonds would rise.

This glimpse into a lunch in Monte Carlo points up the way to make a profit investing in foreign bonds. A profit will only happen after interest rates have gone up so high that they are bound to come down. Bond prices rise when interest rates fall. It doesn't matter whether you are looking at bonds in the United States, Germany, England, France or Australia. The key question is this: will interest rates come down?

With foreign bonds, there is always a second question as well: what will happen to the currency when interest rates fall? If you make the right guess on interest rates and the currency falls when interest rates come down, your profit on the foreign bonds will be reduced or even eliminated.

You have to be right twice to make a killing in foreign bonds. First, you must be right about interest rates in the foreign country and second, the currency has to cooperate. Being right once is not good enough.

In the 1980s and the beginning of the 1990s currencies fell when interest rates declined. That is likely to remain the case for the foreseeable future. Currencies tend to rise when interest rates rise and fall when they come back down. The reason for this is that high interest rates attract foreign capital into short-term investments while falling interest rates do the reverse. When you buy a foreign bond in hopes of a capital gain, what you really are looking for is a bigger gain on the bonds than the loss on the currency. That is a complex challenge for even sophisticated investors.

Those wealthy investors in Monte Carlo weren't really talking about investing at all. They were talking about speculating with a small part of their holdings. They could afford the loss even if their gamble on Australian bonds didn't work out as expected.

Fortunes can be made in foreign bonds, but only those who can stand the pressure should consider buying them in hopes of a capital gain. A warning: The lure of high interest rates can be overwhelming. They often mean high risk. If you are ever tempted by high rates on foreign bonds, remember the story of the investors in Australia. If investing were as easy as buying into high interest rates wherever they can be found, the world would have many more wealthy investors.

7

Gold, Precious Metals and Mining Shares

"Gold will climb to $2,000 an ounce before the end of the decade" was a popularly acclaimed forecast in 1980. Many rushed to buy at $700 or even $800 an ounce in hopes of protecting themselves from inflation and making a profit in the process. By 1982 all such hopes had been crushed. Gold fell to less than $300 an ounce, producing losses for all but the few that bought early in the 1970s. In the 1980s gold traded between $300 and $500, never fulfilling the early expectations.

What lies ahead for gold in the 1990s? Will gold and other precious metals continue to disappoint investors, or will it at last fulfill the expectations and rise to a new record high? Is gold still attractive as financial insurance? The quick answers to these questions are (1) gold still is the best long-term financial insurance an investor can have, (2) gold is likely to trade to a higher level in the 1990s and (3) there is a chance for a new major run up to record highs in the ten years ahead.

OPEC VERSUS THE UNITED STATES, OR HOW WE MADE A MESS OF A GOOD THING

The long period of postwar prosperity came to a sudden end in the early 1970s. Oil prices rose, and the United States responded by severing the link between the dollar and gold. Financial markets became turbulent, inflation rose, interest rates rose and many blamed the termination of the gold link. They are not completely wrong, as things could have been better. We could have solved the oil problem without introducing financial market chaos and condemning the world to a severe recession. Why were we so arrogant and brutal? Ignorance is as good an answer as any.

As late as 1975 we Americans did not appreciate gold's historical character. It was not uncommon in those days to read expert U.S. opinion to the effect that gold was "just another commodity." Ignorance about gold's true character was the consequence of estrangement. If familiarity breeds contempt, a lack of familiarity breeds arrogance founded on ignorance.

In the early part of this century Americans were familiar with gold. We used to have great respect for the yellow metal. Then in the 1930s, President Roosevelt made ownership of gold illegal. That drastic step was taken in desperation. It was an effort to lift the United States out of the grip of the Great Depression. Roosevelt had to increase the U.S. money supply to stimulate the economy. However, this meant raising the official price of gold.

At the beginning of the 1930s the United States was still on an official gold standard. In the depths of the depression Americans were disillusioned and confidence was low. An official increase in the price of gold carried the risk of shattering what confidence was left. Perhaps Americans would have seen a gold price rise as a first step and expected further increases in the gold price. Under those circumstances there could have been a rush out of paper dollars and into gold. Increasing the quantity of paper money would have no impact if the new paper dollars were simply taken to the banks and exchanged for gold. The government couldn't risk such a mass move out of paper dollars and into gold.

Roosevelt understood the risks and decided to take advantage of the situation. He asked Congress for a law requiring all Americans to sell their gold to the government at the old low price. This was the first step. After the compulsory sale to Uncle Sam, the official gold price was raised to allow the printing of more paper dollars.

The Roosevelt move was at once cruel and effective. It was cruel because it took gold away from citizens at a price that was clearly too low. Americans were, in a sense, cheated by their own government. The move was effective because it closed the gold door and forced the economy to operate on paper money. Because the government's gold reserves had been increased by the forced sales, confidence in the gold backing of the new expanded paper money supply was enhanced. The economy responded, and by 1936 the United States was recovering from one of the worst economic disasters in history.

It remained illegal for Americans to own gold, other than jewelry and numismatic coins, until the 1970s. For 35 years Americans were out of the gold market. No wonder there was so much ignorance about gold in the early 1970s. During those 35 years, however, the rest of the world didn't remain ignorant about gold. In the oil-producing countries of OPEC (Oil Producing and Exporting Countries), gold was the primary form of money.

The Koran, or bible of the Islamic world, provides that no man shall live on unearned income. This was taken to mean that paying interest on bank accounts was sinful. Well into the 1970s the laws of some OPEC countries made it illegal to pay interest on bank deposits. The ideal of the Koran was that men would work hard and earn their gold. They would save regularly and be able to live in retirement on their accumulated gold hoard. Modern pressures eventually forced OPEC countries to introduce paper money. Nonetheless gold remains to this day a central part of the monetary system of the Islamic oil-producing countries.

Paper U.S. dollars are of no practical value in OPEC countries. As OPEC received more and more paper currencies, it became routine to send them back and ask for gold in exchange. Finally the United States stood its ground and refused to swap gold for paper dollars in international transactions. That was accomplished in the early 1970s by President Nixon's decree, which officially changed the rules by severing the link between the dollar and gold.

Nixon, like Roosevelt in the 1930s, had another choice. He could have increased the gold price to $100 or $150 an ounce, instead of $35. The risk was that our international trading partners either wouldn't accept a hefty increase in the gold price or would see it as a first step. In other words, in the early 1970s the United States faced the same issue it had in the 1930s, namely, confidence in the currency and the economic system.

In the 1930s President Roosevelt decided to cut the link between gold and Americans. In the 1970s President Nixon decided to cut the link between U.S. gold and foreign holders of paper dollars. Making it illegal for Americans to own gold was not excessively risky in the 1930s. In those days the nation was desperate and willing to try almost anything to effect a recovery. However, cutting the link between U.S. gold reserves and foreign holders of paper dollars carried a significant risk in the 1970s. Our trading partners were under no obligation to keep selling us oil and other necessities in exchange for paper money. The paper money was useful to them only to the extent that it could be exchanged for goods and services produced by the United States that they wanted or needed. President Nixon in effect told OPEC that when we bought oil we would pay in paper dollars and that those dollars could only be used to spend here in the United States. They could not be used to draw gold out of Fort Knox.

The OPEC countries in particular were unlikely to take kindly to such a deal. They didn't want to exchange their only valuable resource—oil—for current consumption. They wanted the option of selling oil in exchange for something of lasting value that would ensure good living for their people long after the oil was gone.

President Nixon had to find a way of satisfying our trading partners, especially the OPEC countries. His answer was to reverse the Roosevelt decision and make it legal for Americans to own gold. In addition he declared that the dollar's value in foreign currencies would no longer be set by Washington. Thus the dollar would be free to float on world markets.

The Nixon moves were clever. By making it legal for Americans to own gold again he opened the way to a global free market in gold. At the same time he opened the way for a free market in foreign currencies. The bottom line was that if OPEC didn't want paper dollars, they could sell them on the world's currency markets and turn around and buy gold. The value of the dollar and the price of gold would be determined by the marketplace. OPEC couldn't blame Washington if the price for dollars or gold wasn't to their satisfaction. This effectively ended the drain on U.S. official gold reserves and at the same time kept the oil flowing to U.S. industry and consumers.

For all his brilliance, President Nixon made one huge mistake. He underestimated the power of OPEC. After the severing of the link between dollars and gold, OPEC soon felt the weight of an unanticipated problem. When they sold dollars, the exchange rate for dollars fell. When they bought gold, the gold price increased. The free markets worked against OPEC because they were receiving so many paper dollars and wanted so much gold. The net effect was to reduce the amount of gold OPEC received in exchange for its oil.

OPEC's success in the oil business soon became their biggest problem. In the eyes of the people of the OPEC countries the U.S. dollar was transparent. What they saw was not a U.S. currency and free markets. They saw the price of a barrel of oil expressed in terms of gold. To them the dollar was an intermediate part of a process. They sold oil, received dollars, sold the dollars and bought gold. At the end of each transaction they wondered how much gold they received for each barrel of oil. That was their primary concern.

During the days when the dollar was fixed to gold at $35 an ounce and the price of oil was low, OPEC grew accustomed to receiving three to five grams of gold for every barrel of oil. As the price of gold began to rise on the free market, OPEC's gold-oil price began to decline. OPEC received less and less gold for each barrel of oil and didn't like it. Its response was to raise the dollar price of a barrel of oil, and the consequence was the first oil shock of the 1970s. The benefits of the oil price increase didn't last long. Within a year or so the price of gold began to rise again, so OPEC raised oil prices again. By the last days of the 1970s the world was caught in an oil-gold-inflation spiral.

At the time, the experts saw no end to the self-intensifying, destructive process. Oil was believed to be headed for $100 a barrel and the industrial economies for economic disaster. OPEC wasn't winning the game either.

When oil was at $25 a barrel and gold spiked to $850 an ounce, the price for one barrel of oil plunged to less than one gram of gold. The world, from any perspective, looked grim in the opening days of 1980.

Investors caught on to the OPEC-gold relationship. They became aware of OPEC's never-ending appetite for gold and bought heavily in hopes of huge profits. As the gold price rose, OPEC increased the oil price to compensate. In the end OPEC went too far. Oil became so expensive that it was profitable to drill in the sea bed and in remote regions. Huge quantities of new oil were found—more than had been believed possible. OPEC's cartel finally fell apart under the combined pressure of a high gold price and falling world oil prices.

The role of gold as world money and the OPEC connection were not well understood by Americans. They believed the forecasts of ever-higher inflation and oil at $100 a barrel. Thus they bought gold at high prices and suffered huge losses when the price later fell from $850 in early 1980 to less than $300 two years later. The OPEC-oil story ended with a steep fall in oil prices in 1986. Gold prices fell from $850 to less than $300 and never managed to climb much above $500 any time in the 1980s.

In 1980 there was no way of predicting what was to come. It wasn't possible to know how much new oil would be found, but it was possible, at that time, to understand that OPEC was losing its oil price game. Any investor with a calculator could have watched the oil price in terms of gold and seen that OPEC's real price for oil was falling. With that knowledge it was also possible to guess that OPEC would do something because OPEC's finance ministers couldn't sit idly by and keep fostering the self-destructive, oil-gold spiral. Raising the oil price wasn't working in OPEC's favor. At every upward tick in the oil price gold moved higher and the gold price for oil moved lower.

Even before vast amounts of new oil were discovered, OPEC was moving towards stabilizing the oil price. It wasn't that OPEC wanted to have mercy on the United States, but it wanted to see the gold price for oil return to the three to five gram-per-barrel level. The route to that gold price for oil was to calm down the gold market and allow gold prices, as well as oil prices, to stabilize.

In other words, you didn't have to have a crystal ball to appreciate that predictions of oil at $100 per barrel and gold at $2,000 an ounce were unrealistic in 1980. If all the new oil hadn't been found, OPEC would have forced the issue and made the United States and the rest of the oil-consuming world move back toward an official gold standard. Had OPEC held on to its power, the price for oil eventually would have been set in terms of so many grams of gold per barrel.

It's possible that the financial world of the 1980s might have been smoother, and better for all, if we hadn't found such vast amounts of new oil. OPEC and the oil-consuming countries might have agreed on a stable oil price and further agreed to guarantee that price in terms of gold. Suppose OPEC had won an agreement for three grams of gold per barrel of oil. At $15 dollars a barrel, that would have implied a gold price of $155 an ounce. In 1976 the gold price traded at less than $155. In that year it would have been possible to strike such an agreement. Even if the oil price in dollars had to be adjusted upwards from time to time, such an agreement would have produced market stability, and perhaps the United States wouldn't have found itself faced with such devastating inflation. In addition, the recession of 1982 might not have been necessary, and the 1980s might have been a decade of greater prosperity for Americans.

Of course this is all conjecture. No such agreement was reached. In the interaction of oil consumers and producers and the bitterness that ensued, and with governments at odds with each other, the free markets worked to produce a long period of wild fluctuations and instability.

The story of OPEC oil and what might have been does serve a purpose by explaining why so many people wish for a return to the gold standard. It isn't possible to turn the clocks back to an absolute gold standard for all paper currencies. However, through the story of oil and the world markets in the 1970s and 1980s, we can see that it would be better if governments found ways of settling their disputes through sensible agreements instead of opening the door to wild financial speculation.

In the final analysis that is what a modern gold standard is all about—sensible agreements between governments on the terms of trade. Gold becomes the accepted medium for such international agreements because, unlike the paper U.S. dollar, gold is still world money. It can buy goods, services, natural resources and even freedom in all corners of the globe. People will cling to gold when they view paper currencies with skepticism.

Why didn't President Nixon or those who followed him to the Oval Office strike such an agreement? The reason wasn't simply competition for wealth and prosperity; it was deep misunderstanding. OPEC didn't understand the world of modern financial markets. At the beginning of the 1970s many OPEC countries didn't even have a modern banking system. The cartel wasn't capable of considering such an agreement at the time because of a lack of experience with international markets. It had been lulled into a state of financial primitiveness during the long decades when powerful people in Texas made all the decisions on oil prices.

In the United States, panic prevented cooler heads from proposing an agreement. We looked at OPEC as a threat, an enemy to be beaten. While sophisticated in many aspects of our society, in our own way we too were inexperienced in international markets. We had for too long dominated the world economy and weren't able to accept that our fortunes had changed forever. The consequence of our mutual lack of international experience was devastating for both groups. OPEC suffered and we suffered.

The next time you hear a gold "bug" wish for a return to a gold standard, don't dismiss the idea as crazy. Recognize that wish in its broader context—that is, the quest for a world where disagreements are settled through the world currency of gold rather than in destructive battles for power fought on world markets.

GOLD'S TWO PERSONALITIES

Understanding gold's role as international money is essential. It lends perspective to world market behavior and opens the way to the use of gold in your personal portfolio.

There are two reasons for owning gold: (1) as insurance against a political or economic catastrophe and (2) to make money. Those are gold's two distinct personalities. It is both a storehouse of safe value and an asset that can be bought and sold for profit.

The last time a war was fought on American soil was in the 1860s, during the Civil War. The last time the United States felt the anguish of an economic catastrophe was in the 1930s, during the Great Depression. We have otherwise enjoyed relative peace and prosperity and have come to think of our political stability as a given, a right. The idea that our nation could be torn apart by war or political upheaval seems unrealistic. Therefore the concept of gold as insurance against that possibility has little appeal.

People in other parts of the world are not so fortunate. The Swiss watched the bloodshed of two world wars from their doorsteps. The French suffered the ravages of two wars in this century and the rest of Europe likewise has suffered war and ruin twice in this century. Japan lost World War II and suffered the destruction of two atomic bombs. China has suffered for decades under the yoke of oppression. No matter where you go—from Cambodia or Vietnam to Brazil or Poland—gold is prized. Gold buys the necessities of life, and more importantly, it can be used to buy a ticket out of a country torn by war or ravaged by oppression. During times of peace and prosperity most people accumulate some gold as insurance against another time of hardship. They don't buy gold for profit; they buy it to keep, hoping it will never be needed.

In Switzerland, accumulating gold as insurance has become so common that discussions usually center on what form of gold to buy. The Swiss take it for granted that every sensible person understands the absolute necessity of owning some gold. They argue about whether bars of gold bullion or small coins are the best insurance.

Gold is heavy and cumbersome. Owning even a few bars of gold bullion presents two challenges. The first challenge is storage, and the second is reliability. It doesn't take many bars of gold bullion to make an ordinary safe-deposit box too heavy to handle.

Reliability, however, is the bigger of the two problems. Suppose the terrible day comes when you need to use your gold. If you want to buy a ticket to another country, the provider of passage probably will want gold, not paper currency. Presenting a bar of gold bullion could be excessive. What's worse is that your provider might worry that the bar was fake or filled with lead. Gold bars have been counterfeited for centuries. Filling them with lead and covering them only with the minimum amount of gold is one common way of cheating.

The world of gold has evolved a system for authenticating gold bars. It starts with assaying. Raw gold can vary in purity. An assay provides a way of determining the purity of gold and assuring that every bullion bar is of the same value. Properly assayed bars are then marked and stored under tight security. Today gold bars can be moved from one bank vault to another without having to reassay them each time. But that practice is limited to those banks with full certification. If you buy a bar of gold, take it out of the bank, walk around the block and return, the bank will insist on a new assay. That is both expensive and time-consuming.

As a practical matter, owning a hoard of bars of gold bullion is only for the very rich. One or two bars is not enough to spread your insurance around in bank vaults in different countries—and you should never even consider taking them home or to your personal safe-deposit box for safekeeping.

What would be the advantage of owning gold bars if they were all kept in a bank vault in the United States and the United States fell into political chaos? The government might do what Roosevelt did in the 1930s and take your gold away or the bank might fall into the wrong hands. To have insurance with gold, you need many bars and they must be stored in several countries.

The practical answer for most individuals is, as the Swiss usually agree, small gold coins.

BUYING AND STORING GOLD COINS

Gold coins come in two types: numismatic and bullion. Numismatic coins are for coin collectors. Their value depends less on their gold content than on their rarity and desirability for collections. The problem with numismatic coins is that in a time of genuine crisis, there is the risk that the coins will bring only their gold value. A coin that costs thousands of dollars can end up being worth hundreds.

This is not to say you shouldn't collect gold coins. A soundly based collection of gold numismatic coins can be a storehouse of value in ordinary times. The market value of such collections increased dramatically in the 1980s and could keep on appreciating for a long time to come. The point is that collectible gold coins do not fit the purpose of financial insurance against political or economic catastrophe.

The value of collectible coins tends to follow the course of personal income. If you think about it, that makes sense. What makes a coin, with say $500 worth of gold content, worth $5,000? The answer isn't only the beauty or rarity of the coin. Those are important factors, but the overriding factor is that there is a buyer willing and able to pay $5,000—the key word being "able." There will always be individuals with the desire to own beautiful and rare coins. When a lot of those individuals have a lot of money (i.e., personal income), the value of collectible coins tends to rise. In bad times the prices tend to fall because some collectors are forced to sell and the number of collectors with cash diminishes. In hard times there can be so few collectors with excess cash that the value of numismatic coins will plunge. Under those circumstances you wouldn't want to be forced to part with your collection.

Almost all numismatic coins started out as bullion coins. They were once money used to buy and sell goods and services. Governments later stopped minting the coins, and they were no longer used as money. The old coins eventually became collectors' items or numismatic coins.

Governments are back in the business of minting gold coins. Canada, Mexico, Australia and the United States, among others, mint coins for sale to the public. While these coins are not in common use as money, their value is directly connected to the price of gold rather than to collectors' desires. A bullion coin will sell at a price equal to the value of its gold content plus a premium for the cost of minting and an additional premium based on the market. Some coins have a larger total premium over their gold content than others. The South African Krugerrand, for example, had a very low premium in the late 1980s because of world anger at South Africa for its policy of apartheid. U.S. gold coins, on the other hand, had a larger premium because Americans tended to buy their own country's coins in preference to others.

Which coins should you buy? The general answer is those with the lowest premium. In 1990 that was the South African Krugerrand. The problem with the Krugerrand, however, is that it could take on an extremely negative image as a symbol of oppression and its marketability in the United States would then vanish. You might lose your premium and find the coin valuable only for its melted gold content. Melting is expensive, and therefore it is conceivable that Krugerrands could sell in the United States at a discount to their gold value.

If the unexpected happened and the United States fell into political and economic chaos, the symbolism of the Krugerrand would be forgotten. It would be simply a gold coin. In other words Krugerrands serve their purpose as financial insurance.

A wise accumulating strategy for gold coins is to have several different bullion coins in your safe-deposit box. Be sensitive to the premiums. Don't rush and buy bullion coins that are in great demand. Concentrate on those coins that have modest premiums over their intrinsic gold content value.

You can buy coins from dealers, banks and sometimes directly from governments. If you are visiting a foreign country and want to buy coins, be sure to ask about sales or VATs (value-added taxes). Some countries are silly enough to impose these taxes on the sales of gold bullion coins. Don't pay them. Wait until you have a chance to buy the coins in a country that is not that silly.

If you have never purchased gold coins before, pick up a coin magazine and browse. You'll find yourself exposed to the worlds of both numismatic and bullion coins. Accumulating gold coins as financial insurance need not be dull or boring. The acquisition of even a few coins can be an adventure. Combining travel with the acquisition of gold coins is also exciting. You sometimes find treasures in out-of-the-way places.

Just be sure to keep your mind clear, and that isn't easy when exploring the world of gold coins. Gold's luster and attraction has seduced some of the most prestigious people in history. The yellow metal had intense religious significance in the days of the Egyptian pharaohs and is still used for religious vessels and the adornment of places of high symbolism. The magic of gold can lead you astray. It's easy to forget that what you want is financial insurance. Keep your objectives clearly in mind.

How many coins should you accumulate? This is similar to asking how much life insurance is enough. The answer in both cases is as much as you can comfortably afford.

If the day comes when you have to use gold coins for survival, you'll never have enough to ensure a comfortable standard of living. The objective in accumulating coins is not to protect your standard of living against all possibilities but rather to provide you with reasonable security and peace of mind. In truly hard times a few coins are probably enough to keep body and soul together. A hundred coins might even be enough to put you in a position to move to another country and start building your life over again. Many refugees have done just that on fewer than one hundred coins.

Buying gold coins involves the age-old process of deciding how much of today's income to put away for the unknown future and how much to spend to enjoy life now. The natural human tendency seems to be to overemphasize today and let the future take care of itself. Gold coins are a nice way to deal with this problem. The coins are beautiful and buying them tends to give you both pleasure now and protection later.

WHEN TO BUY? HOW MUCH TO PAY?

The question of price moves the issue into that middle ground between gold's two personalities. While buying gold coins for insurance doesn't mean buying to sell later at a profit, you don't want to pay too much for insurance. The challenge of buying gold coins when the market is relatively low and avoiding buying at market tops is where investment and insurance come together.

In the 1970s and 1980s the price of gold moved through a very wide range. In the mid-1970s gold traded at $100, and sometimes less. By early 1980 it sold for $850 an ounce. The gold price during this period made two round trips from $500 to $300.

One strategy is to buy coins at regular intervals. This increases the odds of getting an average cost somewhere in the middle of the price range. Having said that, there is still a problem. If you buy every month for years, you will end up with a price close to the average. If you can buy only once a year, however, the odds change. With infrequent purchases you run the risk of buying at all the wrong times.

Even dollar-averaging purchasers need a basic sense of value. You need a general idea of what an ounce of gold is really worth. Looking back, we can see that $850 an ounce was too high in 1980 and $100 an ounce was too low in the mid-1970s. The question is this: how do you take history and hindsight and turn them into a useful tool?

THE LONG-TERM, INFLATION-ADJUSTED GOLD PRICE

In the 1930s President Roosevelt raised the gold price and the economy recovered. The combination of these two events suggests that the President was correct in his decision. The gold price, money supply and U.S. economy were closely connected in the 1930s. The fact that the economy recovered from the worst of the depression after gold was raised to $35 an ounce is evidence that this was at least close to the right price at the time.

Assuming that $35 an ounce was "correct" in 1934, we can adjust the price for all the inflation and deflation since. Of course this introduces another source of possible error: government inflation figures could be inaccurate. However, there is a way of testing the results. By comparing the calculated prices with actual market activity we can find out if this method is useful for buying or selling gold. Starting at $35 an ounce in 1934 and adjusting for published U.S. consumer price inflation produces the results indicated in Table 7-1 and Figure 7-1.

The market's verdict is that these calculations have merit. They are helpful in deciding when gold is priced correctly and when it is overvalued. The market price for gold has tended to rise above the calculated value but has always fallen back. Sometimes the fall brought gold right back down to almost exactly the calculated

Figure 7-1. The Open-Market Versus Inflation Value of Gold (1971-1989) Based on Gold's 1934 Price

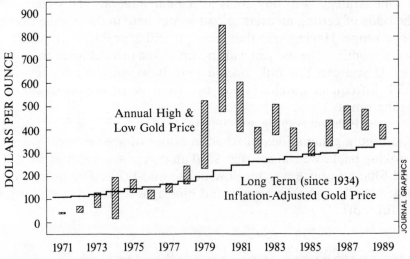

Chart prepared by Richard Andrews from data supplied by the author.

Table 7-1. Gold's Long Term, Inflation-Adjusted Intrinsic Value

Year	Inflation-Adjusted Gold Price	Market Price High	Low
1971	$109.53	$ 44	$ 37
1972	113.15	70	44
1973	120.16	127	64
1974	133.38	195	116
1975	145.52	185	129
1976	153.96	140	101
1977	163.97	168	130
1978	176.60	243	166
1979	196.55	524	232
1980	223.09	850	477
1981	246.29	604	390
1982	261.31	481	297
1983	269.67	508	375
1984	281.39	405	307
1985	291.39	340	285
1986	296.93	439	327
1987	307.62	500	399
1988	320.23	486	395
1989	334.96	418	356

value. These calculated prices for gold are obviously not far away from the market's perception of real value.

In 1981 gold sold for more than $500 an ounce. At that time, a forecast that gold was likely to fall back to $300 seemed unrealistic. Gold had come down from $850 in early 1980, and a further fall to $300 seemed impossible. But in 1982 gold did fall to less than $300. Three years later, in 1985, gold fell again to less than $300. Investors with patience had two opportunities to buy gold for protection at a reasonable price in the first half of the 1980s.

These calculations are not a trader's dream. They don't help predict the timing of moves in the gold market. All they do is help to keep gold's basic or intrinsic value in mind. The figures are useful because they will keep you from paying an inflated price for gold. When the market is far above the calculated long-term, inflation-adjusted gold price, don't buy. When it comes down to (or close to) the calculated price, that is the time to add to your collection of gold coins.

The calculated gold price is a moving target, and it has to be adjusted each year for inflation (or deflation). Here's how to adjust the price and keep your records up-to-date. Assume that inflation in 1990 was 4.4 percent and the calculated price at the end of 1989 was $334.96. The calculated price would have to be increased to take account of inflation in 1990. First take the inflation rate and divide by 100: 4.4/100 = .044. Then add 1: 1 + .044 = 1.044. Then multiply the sum by the last year's calculated price: 1.044 × $334.96 = $349.698 (rounded to $349.70). This is the "right" price after 4.4 percent inflation in 1990.

Why does gold more often than not sell at a price higher than the calculations indicate? Markets try to anticipate the future. In the case of gold that means looking ahead to future inflation rates. Since the world suffered inflation in the 1970s and 1980s, it is logical to expect that there will be more inflation in the future. For this reason, the market hasn't often come all the way down to the calculated price.

If there comes a time in the future when deflation is expected, the market price will be apt to trade consistently at a level below the calculated price.

Don't be too precise. Remember that you are accumulating gold for long-term protection—not trying to make a profit. The objective is to buy gold regularly and not pay too much. Buy whenever the market comes within 10 to 15 percent of the calculated price. Within a year or two, you will be happy that you did.

OPPORTUNITY #9: THE CANADIAN MAPLE LEAF

Canada offers a beautiful bullion gold coin called the Maple Leaf. These coins not only will provide you with long-term financial insurance, but they are also an asset you will be proud to own.

At the end of 1989 the long-term, inflation-adjusted gold price was $334.96. Assuming inflation at a 4.5 percent annual rate, the calculated intrinsic value for an ounce of gold will rise to $366 by the end of 1991.

When gold is trading at less than $370, buy a few one-ounce Canadian Maple Leafs. Keep buying as often as you can. Even if inflation stays in the single digits, these coins will have a gold value of $400 in a few years. Buying Canadian Maple Leafs when gold is below $370 will provide you with beautiful and inexpensive long-term financial insurance.

BUYING AND SELLING GOLD FOR PROFIT

Fortunes were made in gold in the 1970s. A straightforward $10,000 cash purchase of gold bullion in 1976 was worth $85,000 only four years later. Speculators and traders who used leverage (borrowed money) enjoyed even bigger profits. A few made millions in gold in the late 1970s. Gold's rise from $100 in 1976 to $850 in early 1980 was one of the most spectacular market events of the century. Cashing in on the 1980 gold rush became a worldwide rage. From London to Los Angeles people scoured their attics and safe-deposit boxes for old jewelry, coins and even tableware to sell for cash.

Silver was no slouch either. Bunker Hunt, a Texas billionaire, tried to corner the silver market. In the process he drove the price to an all-time record high of $45 an ounce (compared with less than $6 at the end of 1989). Silver dinnerware, candlesticks and tea sets suddenly became very valuable. Family treasures were sold to be melted down for their silver content.

Celebrating the new year in 1980 was a mixture of high anxiety and marvelous madness. The Soviet army invaded Afghanistan, inflation had become oppressive and President Carter's malaise speech seemed all too appropriate. This anxiety added to the lure of gold. On the second trading day of the 1980s gold closed in London at $630, a new all-time record high. Investors shouted with joy at the profits in gold and silver. Pundits confidently predicted $2,000 an ounce for gold within two years.

Then, suddenly, over the weekend of January 19 and 20, 1980, something changed. On Monday the twenty-first markets were soft. Gold and silver pulled back. On the twenty-second gold plunged, falling $145 an ounce in a single day. From $835 on Monday, gold closed at $690 on Tuesday, Investors saw portfolios of gold, silver and mining shares shrink rapidly. At first analysts tried to brush the decline aside as a normal correction following a roaring market. But as the months wore on, it became clear that the days of huge profits in gold and silver were over. By 1982 gold had fallen back to less than $300 an ounce, and analysts and investors alike were dumbfounded. Once-popular predictions of gold at $2,000 an ounce seemed ridiculous. What went wrong? How could gold fall while the world faced not only continuing inflation but a whole series of crises from the invasion of Afghanistan and Latin debts that couldn't be paid to huge U.S. government deficits?

The Swiss call gold the barometer of crisis. When the world faces turmoil, instability and financial turbulence investors are supposed to favor gold for protection. In the early 1980s there was no doubt that the world was facing turmoil, instability and financial turbulence. Fear of a total collapse of the world's financial system was common. Eminent economists published various themes with a single conclusion: the world was headed down the path of economic ruin. Under such circumstances it seemed that investors from all corners of the world had lost their minds. When they should have been accumulating gold, they didn't. Instead they sold, driving the price lower.

In 1986 oil prices collapsed, sinking to less than $10 a barrel. The rate of U.S. inflation fell to the low single digits, and deflation seemed a real possibility. Gold investors took consolation.

Inflation was one of the principal forces that drove gold to $850. Gold's fall to less than $300 in 1985 preceded the plunge in oil and the steep fall in the U.S. inflation rate. Gold's fall from the heights looked like the signal of a developing economic storm of monstrous proportions. The threat of deflation and economic collapse would make gold's value as insurance all the more significant. Analysts believed that one way or the other gold would soar again, fulfilling all the earlier expectations. Either deflation would produce the long-awaited financial chaos and drive investors into gold for safety or inflation would rise again making gold attractive as a hedge against the devaluation of paper money. Hope returned, and visions of a new opportunity flashed through the markets.

Gold, however, refused to cooperate with the optimists. It climbed only to $500 in the 1980s. Each time that level was reached, the price fell back. Hopes that either deflation or inflation would push gold to new highs were not fulfilled. The central banks of the world managed to stay on the narrow path between boom and bust. Deflation disappeared, and inflation returned but at a moderate level.

Profits in gold in the 1970s came from a buy-and-hold strategy. In the 1980s only traders who bought at the lows and sold at $500 enjoyed profits. What will the future bring? Will gold again surge as it did in the 1970s? Or will gold continue to move up and down in a narrow range indefinitely? Should you buy and hold or trade gold?

No one knew what was coming in the 1980s, and no one knows what the future holds for gold and other precious metals. One way or another there will be future opportunities to profit in gold, but to succeed as an investor in gold, you will need to understand the complex world of the gold market.

In the 1970s gold started out deeply undervalued. It had been held down by government action for decades. Once released, it was bound to rise and make up for the past. Then came the oil crises and double-digit inflation. The combination of rising gold prices plus wild inflation fears produced the spectacular rise from less than $100 at the beginning of the decade to $850 in early 1980.

Gold has been free to find its value on open markets since the early 1970s. It is no longer suppressed by governments. The spectacular combination of the 1970s is not likely to be repeated any time soon.

In the 1980s gold had to adjust to a series of circumstances. It had become overvalued by early 1980. The U.S. and world economies moved from high inflation to almost deflation and then back to moderate inflation. Gold fought to find a value that satisfied the needs of all participants.

The high price of early 1980 provided an incentive for mining companies to search for new gold and new ways of mining old mines. World production of gold grew. The supply of gold increased and had to be absorbed by the market. By the end of the Eighties the gold market had adjusted and established a range of roughly $300 to $500.

In the future gold prices are likely to respond to the old familiar factors—inflation, deflation and political turbulence.

GOLD'S OTHER PERSONALITY

Gold is more than a beautiful storehouse of value and more than insurance against economic catastrophe. Gold is also a world currency bought and sold actively on world markets. It doesn't pay dividends, but it can be bought and sold for a profit.

The world gold market is complex. Central banks buy and sell gold. Producers like South Africa and the Soviet Union regulate both production (mining) and sales. Speculators are active in the market, and investors use gold as a hedge when the U.S. dollar is weak. Commercial banks in many countries buy and sell gold. In the 1980s mining companies added a new twist to the gold market in the form of gold loans. The interaction of all the participants in the gold market make predictions and timing difficult.

The principal demand for gold comes from commercial or industrial use (a small part of the market), jewelry and investors. Jewelry demand tends to fluctuate with price. For example, when gold rose to $850, jewelry became too expensive for many buyers and demand slumped. Later in the Eighties when gold fell to $300, jewelry demand increased quickly. Investor demand for gold depends on two things: (1) investors must have the money to buy and (2) they must have a reason to hold an asset that pays no interest or dividends. Investors can raise the money to buy gold by selling other assets such as stocks or bonds. This is what happened in late 1987. World stock markets had run up to high levels by early fall. Investors, especially in the Far East, decided to take some profits on stocks and switch the cash into gold. In October the United States' stock market convulsed in fear of a possible depression. When the steep fall in U.S. stock prices spread around the world, investors rushed out of stocks and into gold, driving the price temporarily to $500 an ounce. In 1988 world stock markets recovered, fear subsided and investors switched back out of gold into stocks. The gold price fell to less than $400.

Central banks are another force in the gold market. They hold gold as a reserve to support their paper currencies. When central banks decide that gold reserves are too low, they buy more. Conversely, when gold reserves are perceived as too large, they sell.

Monitoring central bank gold trading is next to impossible. The central banks keep their gold activities secret as long as possible. Their transactions sometimes don't take place on the open market but are done in secret deals between two or more central banks. The facts about central bank gold trading usually emerge several months later.

Mining companies are somewhat easier to predict. They increase production when prices are high and slow down their gold sales during times when the market is weak. In the 1980s mining companies found a new way of dealing in gold called gold loans. They needed cash to finance expansion and didn't want to borrow through normal channels because of high interest rates. The banks found a solution. Gold from commercial banks and central banks was loaned to the mining companies. The mining firms sold the gold and raised the needed cash. In return they paid the banks low-interest rates, 2 to 3 percent in a typical deal. The mining companies expected to repay the gold out of the production of the new mines. Gold loans became so popular that total gold involved rose to more than 300 tons by 1990.

On the positive side, the borrowing and selling of gold took future production out of the market. The gold to be produced from the new mines was, to a large extent, earmarked to be returned to the banks for their reserves. This encouraged investors who saw the gold loans as assurance that gold would not suffer from excess selling in the future. A few of the gold loans went bad, and some of the new mines proved to be economically unfeasible. The mining companies were not going to produce enough gold to repay the loans. This led to a rally in gold in early 1990 based on the theory that the mining companies would be forced to buy gold on the open market to repay the loans. The rally fizzled.

The Soviet Union has at times been a major player in the world gold market. When they need cash for basic commodities, such as grain, they sell gold. At other times they withhold their production from the market to help boost the price. For the most part, the

Soviets conduct their gold trading in a sophisticated way just to make it impossible for even savvy traders to discover their true intentions.

The purpose of this look at the complexities of the world gold market is to underscore how difficult it is to analyze the basic supply and demand trends for gold. As a practical matter, it's impossible for the average investor to discover enough facts about the world current supply and demand to make a competent judgment on the likely short-term trend.

That doesn't mean that it is impossible to buy and sell gold at a profit. Profiting in gold requires patience and willingness to take advantage of opportunity when it arises. You may not be able to figure out why gold falls to an attractive price, but that isn't necessary. The objective is to buy gold when the odds are in your favor and sell after a rise that produces a reasonable profit. The long-term, inflation-adjusted gold price is the starting point for determining a safe buy point. At the end of 1989 that value was $334.96.

When gold falls to a price close to the calculated value, you can buy with confidence that at least you aren't going to suffer a huge permanent loss. What is close to the calculated value? The answer depends on your tolerance for risk. Paying 20 percent more than the calculated value worked well in the 1980s. Paying only 10 percent above the calculated value also worked. The higher the price you pay, the greater the risk that gold will fall after your purchase. The most important thing is to keep the calculated value in mind so that you don't pay $500 an ounce when the value is less than $400. That approach led to losses in the 1980s and probably will lead to losses in the future.

There is another technique that can be used to help refine the buy and sell points. Gold is traded in markets around the world. For example, it is bought and sold in London, Zurich and Hong Kong. Investors in foreign countries measure their profits and losses in their own domestic currency. Even though you may be trying for profits only in U.S. dollars, it pays to look at gold through an international perspective. One way to do that is by watching the gold price in more than U.S. dollars. Swiss francs are a good choice, although you can also choose to watch gold in German marks or Japanese yen or some other major currency. (See Figures 7-2 and 7-3.)

A chart of gold in terms of Swiss francs is valuable because the Swiss franc is the currency most watched by investors around the

Figure 7-2.   Gold in Swiss Francs, 1980–1989

Figure 7-3.   Gold in Dollars, 1980–1989

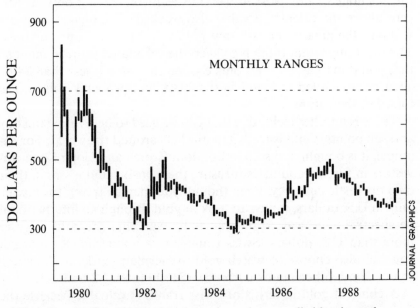

Charts prepared by Richard Andrews from data supplied by the author.

world. The chart is a proxy, allowing you to make judgments about the likely attitude of foreign investors.

In the 1980s gold in Swiss francs first fell sharply and then found a floor at 600 francs per ounce. That floor held for four years. In 1990, however, gold in Swiss francs broke down and fell significantly below 600 francs per ounce. By April it was down to 533 francs an ounce. These figures are very important.

In U.S. eyes, gold in 1990 was still well above its value in 1974. Sixteen years earlier it had reached a high of $195. At $370 in 1990, Americans still had a 90-percent profit. For investors who count their net worth in Swiss francs it was a different story. After sixteen years they had a loss on gold. Investors in other strong currencies, such as the German mark, had a similarly sad experience with gold. The chart of gold in Swiss francs should make it clear that as the 1990s began, the psychology of the gold market had been severely damaged. With 16 years of inflation, a sinking U.S. dollar and a long list of reasons why gold should be higher, the Swiss still had a loss. It should be obvious that European investors won't quickly or easily be lured back into gold. It will take a major development in the 1990s to convince European investors that there is money to be made in gold.

The chart reinforces the conclusion that in the early 1990s gold should be bought only when it trades down to or below its long-term, inflation-adjusted value.

When is a good time to sell? The answer comes from the U.S. dollar price for gold in the 1980s. Gold stopped more than once at $500 in the Eighties. For that reason alone there is likely to be heavy profit taking and some short selling whenever gold reaches $500 an ounce. A rise to that level logically represents a sensible selling point for the opening years of the 1990s. As the decade wears on, the long-term, inflation-adjusted gold price will rise, indicating that eventually the cyclical highs in gold will be above $500. By 1995, even with low inflation, gold should manage to climb to $600. By the end of the decade, a target of $750 is not out of the question.

COULD GOLD MAKE A NEW
ALL-TIME HIGH IN THE 1990s?

In the 1970s gold got a lift not only from rising inflation but also from low real interest rates. Inflation rose rapidly, and interest rates didn't keep up. Holding cash in the bank was not very attractive. Inflation eroded the value of the cash faster than the interest income refilled the account. This phenomenon created an incentive for investors to own gold, which produced real gains in the 1970s.

Interest rates stayed relatively low because the central banks found themselves in new territory. On the one hand, they didn't want to allow inflation get out of control. On the other hand, they didn't want to crush an economy already burdened with rising oil prices. Thus they opted for going slowly on raising interest rates.

Central bank policies changed dramatically in the 1980s. Oil prices came down, and the world suffered a deep recession in 1982. The booming, inflation-ridden seventies had set the stage for the bust of 1982. So many suffered that the central banks resolved to change politics in hopes of preventing a repeat. Prevention meant keeping inflation in check and that, in turn, meant keeping interest rates high enough to prevent financial excesses. In the 1980s interest rates around the world generally stayed well above the inflation rate.

High real, or after-inflation, interest rates discourage holding gold. When interest rates are well above the inflation rate, investors holding cash enjoy a real return. Why hold gold, with no interest or dividends, when cash pays so well? The case in favor of gold weakened in the 1980s. High interest rates not only kept inflation in check but also prevented gold from rising above $500 an ounce. Ten years of disappointing results for holders of gold are a powerful disincentive. Not only were investors able to enjoy real returns on cash, holding gold got them nowhere for a decade.

The harsh reality about gold is that in the 1990s it will suffer from a decade of disappointment. Of course all investors should own some gold as financial insurance, but many will refuse to follow that sensible prescription as they won't want to "park" some of their assets in an unproductive asset. It will take a considerable and powerful change in economic fundamentals to produce another spectacular run in gold in the 1990s—not that it can't happen.

There are several ways that the fundamentals could change. The continued upward climb in U.S. health costs, for example, could eventually break the U.S. economy and cause a new wild inflation. Economic progress in the Soviet Union could produce an explosion in demand for goods and services. World shortages of critical resources could develop, and inflation could break away out of control. China might find the route to prosperity. Imagine the strains on world production if every Chinese family demanded a car and a television set and had the money to pay. Some unpredictable event—from a devastating earthquake in Tokyo to a global drought—could come along and drive investors into gold. Gold could climb to new highs and could even fulfill the long-ago predictions of $2,000 an ounce; but that is in the realm of possibilities, not probabilities.

A world set on a course of peace and prosperity will be a problem for gold in the 1990s. All the dreams of rising living standards will not be fulfilled, but the effort is not likely to turn to ashes either. The odds are that significant progress towards lifting standards of living in Eastern Europe, the Soviet Union and elsewhere will be achieved in the 1990s. The world's central banks can be expected to continue to do their best to prevent the excesses that lead to higher inflation. That means relatively high interest rates.

Gold is likely to rise above $500 in the 1990s. The underlying, intrinsic value of an ounce of gold will continue to climb higher and higher even with single-digit inflation. If inflation runs at 4 percent a year for all of the 1990s, the long-term, inflation-adjusted gold price will be $495.82 at the end of 1999. There will be inflation scares along the way. Gold is likely, at times, to sell at a 25- to 50-percent premium to its underlying value. A price of $600 seems possible by the mid-1990s, and in the second half of the 1990s the price could reach $750.

Whenever gold runs, there will be forecasts of a new bull market. Don't be fooled into believing that a new long-term bull market in gold has begun when gold rises to $600 or even $750. The truth will be that continuing single-digit inflation is eroding the value of paper money, and that is simply showing up in the gold price.

For a new bull market to begin, there will have to be an outbreak of sharply higher inflation or a genuine world economic calamity. If either happens, the old forecasts from the 1980s of gold at $2,000 an ounce will come true.

PLATINUM

Platinum is another precious metal—one that can be held for long-term financial insurance or traded for a profit. Virtually all of the world's platinum comes from a very few mines in South Africa.

Supplies of platinum are limited, and demand is growing. Platinum is used in catalytic converters in automobile exhaust systems. Europe has recognized the need to cut auto emissions and protect the air. Catalytic converters will be a growing business in both Western and Eastern Europe in the 1990s.

Limited supply and growing demand might seem to be a formula for a one-way trend in platinum. How could you lose on platinum? In spite of growing demand, platinum prices were volatile in the 1980s. The reason for the volatility was that investors played a significant role in determining the price.

The story of limited supply and growing demand is well known. Investors try to take advantage of trends and in doing so move markets in anticipation of underlying fundamentals. They pushed platinum prices up in the 1980s and then pushed them back down again when it became clear that it would take a long time before industrial demand equaled or exceeded world production. Trading platinum for a profit therefore means guessing which way investors will move next. That task is never easy in any market.

There is one other uncertainty in the platinum market. At one point in the late 1980s Ford Motor Company announced that it had possibly found a new technology for catalytic converters, one that did not require platinum. If this discovery, or another, proves to be feasible, the compelling story of the growing demand for platinum will change. Investors might decide to sell large quantities of platinum, driving the price down.

The bottom line is that the platinum market has risks and uncertainties. Platinum is not an easy route to sure profits.

SILVER

The story of silver is almost the opposite of platinum. Silver is found while mining for other metals, such as copper. As a result, silver production tends to rise even during times when the price is weak.

The demand for silver is broad-based, but jewelry and investors play a significant role. The chief advantage of investing in silver over gold or platinum is that it is less expensive. Investors with less than a fortune can buy a meaningful amount of silver. Consumers can afford silver jewelry even when gold is beyond their budget. By virtue of its character as a recognized precious metal and its lower cost, silver enjoys a steady demand.

In the heady days of early 1980 silver prices followed the gold trend. The reason for this was that Bunker Hunt, a Texas billionaire, tried to corner the silver market. Once the Hunt cartel was broken, silver prices fell. From $45 an ounce, the price declined to less than $5.00 an ounce, a plunge worse than that of gold.

From time to time in the 1980s silver managed to climb, once temporarily reaching a price above $10.00 an ounce. The periodic rises in silver were a reaction to the gold market. When gold reached $500 an ounce, more investors turned to silver hoping for big percentage gains.

Investors should recognize that the silver market is normally under more downward pressure from growing supplies than gold. This means that silver should be purchased only when it is truly cheap ($5.00 an ounce or less). Buying silver when it is depressed will produce profits on the next run up in gold prices. However, like gold, silver should then be sold or else the buyer runs a risk of seeing all profits vanish.

If there is another outbreak of double-digit inflation because of burgeoning health care costs or some other economic calamity, silver will rise and the percentage gains will be greater than that of gold. Because the future is uncertain and silver is cheaper than gold, there is merit in buying silver when it is at $5.00 an ounce or less and holding it as a hedge, just in case an unexpected rise in inflation develops.

GOLD-MINING SHARES

American investors have had a long love affair with gold-mining shares. The 1930s law prohibiting Americans from owning gold did not apply to gold-mining shares, which were perfectly legal for U.S. investors.

By the end of the 1970s U.S. investors held billions of dollars worth of South African gold-mining shares. American shareholders accounted for 25 percent of the entire South African gold-mining share market at one time. It was not unusual in the Seventies to have the price for South African mining shares be determined in the United States with the market in Johannesburg following rather than leading.

Mining shares were attractive for two reasons. First, and most obvious, they were regarded as a substitute for gold. Second, mining operations were classified as "wasting assets" situations. This term describes the fact that the amount of gold in any mine is physically limited and will one day be completely gone. "Wasting" in this context does not mean careless disregard but simply "wasting away" or "diminishing." Mining companies felt a moral obligation to share profits with shareholders. Some profits were retained for development of new properties or new technologies, but for decades mining shares, especially the South African shares, paid generous dividends. When the gold price rose, the profits and dividends increased. Dividends of 20 percent and more were not unusual in the late 1970s.

In the 1980s attitudes about gold-mining shares changed significantly. So too did their characteristics as investments. It all began with the skyrocketing gold price in early 1980. That drew attention to gold, gold-mining shares and South Africa. Within a short time, anti-apartheid feelings in the United States began to affect the market for South African gold-mining shares.

The impact was not immediate and not direct. The common cry for "disinvestment" applied mostly to institutional investors and business. Gold-mining shares were the province of individual rather than institutional investors, so there was no immediate, direct attack on the mining shares. By the second half of the 1980s anti-apartheid attitudes in the United States had intensified and spilled over to other countries. At one point Congress threatened to make it illegal for Americans to own any South African assets. That law would have included gold-mining shares.

The law didn't pass, but another did. Congress changed the tax laws, taking away the foreign tax credit for taxes paid by business to South Africa. The impact was to increase the cost for Americans doing business in South Africa. Many people decided to sell out and leave South Africa. That law plus the intense feelings about South Africa and apartheid had the effect of frightening U.S. investors and depressing the price for South African mining shares.

Americans began to move their capital out of the South African shares and into gold-mining shares in Canada, Australia and the United States. The net effect was to raise the non–South African mining-share prices so high that they no longer provided generous dividends. By the last day of 1989 gold-mining shares were no longer regarded as "wasting assets" companies, no longer paid generous dividends and were bought and sold as a substitute for gold. Mining is a business, and a risky business at that. Digging deep into the earth is dangerous, and there are no guarantees as to the amount or quality of the gold that will be found. Once on the surface and ready for the market there are no price guarantees either. Investors should always remember that mining is not protected by nature, and gold-mining shares should be evaluated as the risky enterprises they are.

Mining shares are not a substitute for gold. In a political calamity mines can be closed and go out of business. Mining shares do not provide long-term financial insurance. For that you must hold gold or gold coins.

OPPORTUNITY #10: TWO GOLD-MINING SHARE STRATEGIES

Mining shares are a way of making a profit. There are two basic strategies. One is to buy shares in companies that are in the process of exploring for or developing a gold mine. If the company is successful, the share price can soar and the profits can be enormous. Speculating in gold-mining shares is exciting and with some common sense and luck, they can be very profitable. To be successful, you must either be very lucky or take the time to learn about the mining industry. Don't roll the dice on a hot tip. The best way to speculate in gold-mining shares is to have a regular program of buying shares in many different companies. Invest what you can afford to lose. If a mine doesn't prove out, you can lose 100 percent. If you buy speculative mining shares regularly and learn about the mining business, you may strike it rich!

The second strategy is to buy shares in established mining companies when they are out of favor and profit when either the group comes back into favor or when the gold price rises. There is a reasonable, but not perfect, correlation between the gold price and the prices for mining shares. They often tend to be low when the gold price is down and rise when gold recovers.

Established mining companies come in two basic types: there are those with a significant amount of debt and those with little debt.

The debt tends to accentuate the price movements of the shares in both directions. When gold prices fall, the added interest expense depresses profits and the share price. The companies with less debt do better during times when the gold price is low. When gold is rising, the opposite is the case. The leveraged companies enjoy soaring profits, and the share prices can also soar.

Pick a few gold-mining companies to watch. Make sure that one is a company with little debt (Battle Mountain Gold, New York Stock Exchange symbol: BMG, would qualify) and that another has much larger debts (Echo Bay, American Stock Exchange symbol: ECO, would fit this category). When you see that the gold price is down and the gold-mining share price has fallen out of favor, buy the conservative stock first. If you are wrong about the gold price and it falls further, you will minimize your losses this way. When your first stock is rising and gold looks ready for an upward move, buy shares in the leveraged company. When the time comes that you have handsome profits, sell the leveraged company's stock first and then sell the remaining conservative shares once you feel that the gold price is vulnerable to a sinking spell. This simple strategy will keep you from suffering huge losses and will still provide significant potential profits on gold-mining shares.

Always remember that mining is a risky business. Be cautious, and be aware that one of the risks is political. As long as the political climate in and outside of South Africa is volatile, avoid the South African shares. Investors don't need to add political uncertainty to an already risky business.

CHAPTER

8

Managing Your Personal Portfolio

Xerox is a name synonymous with copying machines and millionaires. Buying shares of Xerox in the 1960s was a strategy that led to extraordinary profits. Even investors who were late and bought in 1970 saw their investments multiply by more than 200 percent in two years. Xerox also tells the story of fortunes lost and reveals the two most common mistakes made by investors.

In 1972 one share of Xerox sold for $170, or 40 times earnings. Experts advised investors to buy growth stocks, including Xerox; and their reasoning was sound. They correctly predicted that income tax rates would rise and that the 1970s would be difficult for individual investors. They advised buying growth stocks and allowing well-managed companies to figure out how to cope with the challenges of the 1970s. In the long run the experts concluded that investors would enjoy significant profits.

The problem was that everyone was following the same advice. Xerox was driven to a price so high that it became vulnerable to a change in investor sentiment. When the stock market plunged after the first oil-price increase shock in 1973–1974, the price for a share of Xerox went into a free fall. It fell to $50, managed a partial recovery and then kept falling to a low of $27 in 1982. Following what seemed like the best advice in 1972 led to a loss of 84 percent over the next ten years.

What went wrong? Xerox didn't go out of business. In fact profits continued to grow in the 1970s. Two things changed. Xerox began to face tough Japanese competition and investors changed their opinions on the value of the stock. Instead of 40 times earnings in 1972, the market was willing to pay only seven or eight times earnings in the early 1980s.

In the early 1970s Xerox dominated the fast-growing market for copying machines. The low value of the yen and a growth market attracted Japanese competition. As more and more Japanese-made copy machines appeared in the United States, investors began to worry about the future of Xerox.

Buying Xerox in 1972 was an example of the first common mistake: assuming too much risk. Not only did investors take a risk buying a high-priced stock, but they also took the risk of an undervalued Japanese yen and the threat of Japanese competition. Of course at that time very few investors were sensitive to the exchange rate between dollars and yen. That is the saddest of all the mistakes an investor can make: assuming a risk you don't even know exists. Today every investor is sensitive to Japanese competitors. We have come full circle. In 1972 it was believed that Xerox could cope with any competitor. By 1989, as exemplified by the case of Micron Technology, the opposite was the assumption; it was impossible for Micron to survive in the face of stiff Japanese competition. Today it is hard to remember that in 1972 investors were unaware of one of the major risks they took in buying Xerox.

The first lesson from the Xerox story is that even back in 1972 it was essential to have an international perspective, and that's still the case today. Now, however, an international perspective is more likely to turn up opportunities that others are missing than raise the flag over a hidden risk.

This look back at Xerox is more than proof of the necessity of having an international perspective. It is a case study in personal portfolio management. After ten years of holding a sinking stock, even the most patient investor would be discouraged. When Xerox fell again in 1982, buying more probably was the last thing to contemplate, but it would have salvaged the entire investment. A purchase of 100 shares of Xerox in 1972 cost $17,000. In 1982 $17,000 bought 560 shares. In 1987 Xerox rose to $80. At that point the entire investment of $34,000 was worth $52,800. The case of Xerox is an extreme example, but it's intended to show that even with stocks that go down and stay down there can be opportunities to profit in the process.

The example of Xerox is one of patience tried to the limit, and it highlights the second most common mistake: refusing to take risk at the appropriate time. When the market price of a stock goes down, we not only become discouraged but we also assume there must be a major, fundamental problem at the company. When a stock falls from $170 to $27 over ten years, both of those attitudes are reinforced. Buying more Xerox in 1982 required the patience of a saint and the courage of a gladiator.

It's easy to say that the two mistakes most frequently made by investors are (1) taking too much risk and (2) refusing to take risk. Once you know that these are the primary challenges, the solution seems simple: resolve to be a well-informed risk taker. In practice, however, avoiding these mistakes in the pursuit of profits is anything but easy.

The Xerox story shows how at times when risk is the greatest we can be fooled into thinking we aren't taking a great gamble. In the early 1970s, the prestigious Ford Foundation published articles on the merits of buying and holding growth stocks such as Xerox. They were fooled and didn't fully appreciate the risks. When Xerox was a real buy in 1982, the experts advised staying away from the stock because of its poor performance record and all the then-obvious risks from Japanese competition.

Even the most experienced and skilled professionals have trouble knowing when to take a risk and when to avoid it. Striking the right balance between risk and opportunity and making money consistently isn't easy. The principal challenge is not the markets; they always provide hefty doses of risk and opportunity. The problem is our own personal feelings. We tend to swing from fear to greed and back again to fear. When we're afraid of the markets, we look for safe investments, forgetting that in this world there are no truly safe investments but only illusions of safety. After the sources of anxiety dissipate, we feel confident again and then try to make up for lost time with overly aggressive or poorly timed investments.

So common is this pendulum pattern of human behavior that it appears regularly in whole markets. In 1982, when the great rising stock market of the 1980s began, most individual investors were left out. They were still worrying about the next depression or looking back at the deep recession of 1982. It took a long time for them to build up enough confidence to venture into the stock markets. When they finally returned and bought stocks, they helped push the market up to 20 times earnings. That was August 1987: a market peak that was followed by a terrifying crash. In October fear and anxiety returned with a vengeance; the stock market crashed; and individuals sold stocks and ran back into bank accounts, cash and money market funds.

Following the crowd into stocks at high prices and selling after a crash isn't the way to make money. Mistakes and losses are a part of the investment process. They cannot be completely avoided, but you can avoid the classic mistakes, especially the ones that produce consistent losses rather than consistent profits.

WORRIED MONEY NEVER WINS

Increasing your personal wealth starts with this motto: "Worried money never wins." Anxiety is the principal enemy of profits. No matter how good the investment, if it causes you to lose sleep, worry and become anxious, the odds are that you are going to make bad decisions that will cost you money. Having said that, another issue immediately surfaces. When a stock plunges, anxiety usually isn't far behind. What may have been a comfortable investment at the beginning can become the source of anxiety later.

How can you follow the motto and avoid worrisome investments when the markets are so volatile and unpredictable? The story of Service Merchandise provides some insights. Service Merchandise's stock fell from $17 in 1983 to $10 in 1984. For a year or so, it traded in a range of $7$1/2$ to $10. Then in 1987, while the U.S. stock market was rising, Service's stock price fell to $3$1/2$. It rebounded in August only to fall to $2$1/4$ after the crash in October. Buying a stock at $17 and seeing the price, four years later, at $2$1/4$ (for an 87 percent loss) is enough to make the most hardened professional upset and anxious. Patience is hard to muster when a stock falls year after year for a long time.

Not all stocks recover. Some go down and stay down. That, however, was not the case with Service Merchandise. From $2$1/4$ in 1987, the stock rose to $22 two years later. A purchase of $10,000 of Service stock at $17, a second purchase of $10,000 at $10 and a third purchase of $10,000 at $2$1/4$ produced an investment worth $132,000 in 1989, for a gain of 340 percent in seven years. In 1989 Service paid a special onetime dividend of $10 per share. If you simply held on and didn't sell at $22, you received a check for $60,000, or twice your total investment, when that dividend was paid.

All the anxiety and worry when Service traded at $2¼ in 1987 was for nothing. The stock's fall set up the conditions for an outstanding profit. If Service had not plunged but had simply gone from $17 to $10 and then to $22, the profits would have been much smaller. The plunge in 1987 was both a source of great anxiety and the prelude to enormous profit.

The motto "worried money never wins" has to be understood in the context of stocks such as Service Merchandise. Being comfortable with your investments doesn't mean selling when a stock plunges and causes anxiety. It doesn't mean staying out of risky investments. Following the motto means preventing volatile personal emotions from dictating investment decisions. The weapons against anxiety are hard work, knowledge and a disciplined approach to investing.

Suppose when Service Merchandise fell to $2¼ in the fall of 1987 you knew the company was having the best quarter in years. If you knew that Service was about to report a substantial profit in early 1988, you might not have worried about the stock. With that information, perhaps you would have had the confidence to buy more and enjoy the huge profits that followed.

Service Merchandise did report earnings of $1.15 a share for the fourth quarter of 1987. The stock at its low sold at less than three times fourth-quarter earnings. Of course the U.S. insider-trading rules would have prevented you from finding out the exact earnings in advance. However, a call to the company in late 1987 would have revealed that Service was having a "good quarter" and that the company was not in financial trouble and certainly not going bankrupt. Surprising as it may seem, few investors—professional or individual—bothered to call Service and ask for whatever information could be made public.

In the case of Service Merchandise, the answer to anxiety was a call to the company. Knowing about the company's past record of excellence also helped. Service has a long record of excellence in retailing. The company even made a profit during the deep recession of 1982. The problems that produced losses and set up the steep fall in 1987 were connected with acquisitions that went sour. But long before the 1987 crash, management had set out on a course to correct those mistakes. If you were knowledgeable about Service Merchandise and called them in 1987, you avoided anxiety and enjoyed a huge profit. The stock's plunge had pushed shares of Service into the category of worried money. Investigation would have eliminated that worry.

Investing successfully is the result of having well-informed and well-placed confidence, not in the markets, but in the underlying businesses whose stocks you own.

THE IMPORTANCE OF HAVING A DISCIPLINE

Dealing with the combination of wild stock prices and volatile human emotions is a challenge that can be met by developing a specific investment discipline, sometimes referred to as a "philosophy." An investment discipline is more than a set of rules; it is a way of approaching the task of developing a personal portfolio and producing consistent profits.

There are several proven ways of making money through investing. Some advocate trend following; others suggest trading. There are growth-oriented disciplines and value-oriented methods. Don't fret about choosing the best discipline. The most important thing is to have a well-defined discipline and stick to it even when it isn't producing profits.

The mistake often made even by professional investors is abandoning a long-standing discipline when it isn't working and switching to another method in hopes of better performance. Value investing, for example, was out of favor for years in the 1980s. Those who bought low-priced stocks watched their portfolios languish while so many others enjoyed significant gains.

Professional investors are at a disadvantage. Their clients expect performance, and many won't wait four or five years until their portfolios show results. Clients often switch advisors after a year or two in search of better results. Professional advisors know this and become discouraged when their particular discipline isn't working and they're losing clients. Individual investors, however, don't have to worry about losing clients. They have the luxury of adopting a discipline and sticking with it as long as it takes. Nonetheless, many individual investors make an even bigger mistake than switching disciplines: they never adopt a specific discipline in the first place. They are traders one day, long-term investors the next and out of the markets altogether the third day.

The way to maximize your time, energy and effort in any endeavor is to find out what you do well and then do it over and over again. That way you become an expert in your chosen field. This applies to carpenters, bricklayers, physicians, advertising executives, writers, lawyers and particularly investors.

Discipline in investing doesn't mean specialization. You don't have to concentrate on one industry or one country. Discipline means knowing your limits and being acutely aware of what you cannot do. Turning away from what looks like an obvious opportunity is what successful investors do best. It isn't humanly possible to follow every good investment idea. You must be selective. The financial press produces more potentially profitable investment ideas in every daily issue than any single investor can follow in a year. Having a discipline means creating your own ideas, or at least having a way of screening the ideas from others down to a list that suits your personal circumstances.

There are tens of thousands of possible investments in the active markets of the world. On any given day a certain number of stocks are rising in value. Some may be skyrocketing. Look at any financial paper for the list of biggest gainers. They are always there.

In the fourth quarter of 1987, the time of the last great world stock crash, there were some stocks that did very well. For example, Tokyo Rope Manufacturing rose 58.3 percent; Martell, 37 percent; and Britoil, 29.3 percent in the final quarter of 1987. These lists of top-performing stocks are tantalizing. They are also distracting. It's natural to wish that somehow we could manage to hold at least a few of the top-performing stocks every quarter. It is that quest for a list of winners that leads investors down the wrong road. There isn't any method that will screen out all the losers and produce only winners. Losses, sometimes large ones, are a part of the investment process.

The objective of a discipline is to screen the list of possible winners down to a manageable number and then to have a way of dealing with problems when things go wrong. A sound investment discipline involves the following elements:

1. A method for limiting the number of selections
2. A way of converting the selections into a portfolio
3. Rules for when and at what price to buy
4. Rules for selling

AN INTERNATIONAL DISCIPLINE
YOU CAN FOLLOW

The more stocks you own, the greater the odds that your portfolio will do no more than match the market. Very few investors have ever managed to produce above-average gains with a large portfolio. However, Peter Lynch, the legendary manager of the Fidelity Magellan Fund, is the exception to this rule. With more than $12 billion and hundreds of stocks in the fund, Peter Lynch beat the U.S. market. He rose to fame and fortune precisely because he accomplished what few had ever achieved. If it were easy to beat the market with a long list of holdings, Mr. Lynch never would have received the attention he did. Even then he turned in his quotron in early 1989 because he wanted to spend more time with his family. Following so many companies had become a burden he no longer chose to carry.

For the most part, Peter Lynch concentrated on U.S. stocks. When you turn to international markets, the range of opportunities increases. In all likelihood, not even Peter Lynch could have developed a large portfolio that beat all the markets all the time.

Performance aside, the objective in developing a personal discipline is to reduce the task of managing money to a size that will be comfortable for years. You and your money are partners for life. The last thing you need is to create a monstrous job that will be tedious, burdensome or cause you to burn out from excess effort. Limit the number of companies you follow, and also limit the number of issues in your portfolio. A small portfolio (anything up to $50,000) needs no more than four to ten holdings. Larger portfolios (from $100,000 to millions) need only 14 to 20 holdings.

The first step in developing your discipline is to look at the size of your current portfolio and choose the maximum number of stocks you will hold when fully invested. Take that number and multiply it by three, but in all cases stop counting at 40. This number becomes the target for your personal "universe," or companies that you will get to know well.

CHOOSING THE COMPANIES TO FOLLOW

You don't have to fill up your universe all at once. In fact, it's better to let it develop over time. Get to know companies one at a time.

The place to start is with a foreign company, although it is easier for Americans to get information about companies in the United States. It's important to prove to yourself that you can pick a foreign stock and track both the company's progress and the stock's activity.

Don't make things too difficult. Pick one of the companies listed on a major U.S. exchange. Here are a few suggestions: Novo-Nordisk, a Danish drug company; Philips N.V., a Dutch electronics company; British Petroleum, a world-class oil company based in England; or Glaxo Holdings, a British drug company. All are listed on the New York Stock Exchange, and their reports can be found in the normal U.S. services such as Value Line and Standard & Poor's.

As you develop your universe, choose companies that are different from the standpoint of country, industry, size and balance sheet configuration. Also follow small companies, growth companies, highly leveraged companies and highly conservative companies.

HOW DO YOU FIND FOREIGN COMPANIES?

Living in the United States makes it seem difficult to find foreign companies that might make good investments. Americans are familiar with U.S. companies, see their products advertised on television and also see the factories when traveling. Finding out about companies in faraway places seems problematic. But it is just as easy to find foreign-made products in our communities as it is to find American-made goods. Look at car dealers or goods in a department store and you will find plenty of foreign-made products for sale. Likewise, take a look at the labels on the shelves in your local drug store and you will find that a large number are made by foreign companies.

In the 1970s and 1980s many U.S. businesses were purchased by foreign companies. More than a few familiar American brands are now owned by foreign firms. The reason we think it's hard to find and follow foreign companies is that we don't ordinarily pay close attention to the labels on the items we purchase or remember that the company in the next town was bought by a foreign firm. The more observant of the world around us we become, the more we recognize that the United States is host to hundreds of foreign companies, their subsidiaries and their products.

In 1988, for example, Akzo N.V., a Dutch chemical and pharmaceutical company, bought salt operations from Diamond Crystal.

How many Americans pick up the familiar Diamond Crystal salt box at the grocery store and never realize that a Dutch company is involved? The lighting division of Philips, N.V., another Dutch company, sponsored the Olympic games on U.S. television. Their commercial theme, "we light the Olympics," was seen in millions of American homes. But how many recognized that a foreign company was involved? People suffering from ulcers know that the least-expensive medicine is Zantac, but do they also know that the drug is manufactured by a British company, Glaxo Holdings?

Finding foreign companies is just as easy as finding U.S. investment opportunities. The same powers of observation and investigation that produce profitable U.S. stocks can uncover profitable foreign stocks.

CREATING A PORTFOLIO

There should always be a difference between the companies you follow and the companies you actually own in your portfolio. Don't rush out and buy every interesting stock you find. Follow a company and its stock's action on the market for a period of time before considering a purchase.

There are very few times when there is a reason to rush in and buy. One such time was after the crash of 1987. For a relatively short period there was extraordinary opportunity, but you had to move quickly because the markets recovered quickly. Those broad, market-generated opportunities don't happen very often. In normal times individual stocks rise and fall independently.

Don't be like the child in a candy shop who rushes to grab what he or she can out of fear that there won't be another chance. Investors with an international perspective enjoy a never-ending world of opportunity. If you miss the chance to buy one stock, there will be another chance in another stock. Take your time and stick to a disciplined approach to investing.

Balancing risks is the key to successful portfolio management. Similar to diversification, balance is a practical way of controlling risk while preserving opportunity. The following are seven types of risk that should be balanced:

1. debt
2. geography
3. company size

4. liquidity of shares
5. industry
6. earnings
7. value

Suppose you decide to buy stock in a well-known international company that has a lot of debt. The next stock should be in a company that has little or no debt. Debt or leverage can be a major plus when business goes well. Debt enhances profits in the good times and can push the stock price up in a dramatic way. When either the business or the economy turn the wrong way, however, debt punishes earnings and the stock price can tumble. The idea behind balancing a portfolio is to answer this question: what if I am wrong about this particular stock? Buying shares in a second company that has little or no debt balances the risk assumed with the highly leveraged company.

Geographic risk also requires balancing. You don't want to have all your stocks in one country because that could lead to economic or political setbacks.

Company size is important because buying stock in a fast-growing but small company carries the risk of illiquidity. There may be too few shares for the stock to trade actively. In a tough situation it could be hard to sell shares in a small company without suffering an unnecessary loss. Balance that risk by holding a very liquid stock in a large company.

Liquidity refers to how easily shares can be bought or sold. Some stocks trade only a few shares a day. Others, particularly those of large companies, trade hundreds of thousands of shares a day. Pay attention to the number of shares traded. Small companies with few shares can be outstanding investments. Therefore don't be afraid to buy stock in a small company. Just be sure to balance that risk by also owning shares in a larger company that trade easily.

Just as you don't want all your companies bunched together in a single location, you also don't want all your holdings to be in a single industry. If you own shares in a forest products company, you might want to balance that by acquiring stock in a high technology firm. Cutting trees and making computers are about as different as industries can get.

Value and earnings are both categories not ordinarily associated with risk. In these categories risk more concerns timing than anything else. Timing is important, as you don't want to wait years for profits on your entire portfolio. Markets are fickle. Sometimes investors favor stocks in companies with lots of assets; at other times, they want only companies with growing earnings. Predicting which type of company the markets will favor next is difficult to impossible. The only answer is to balance the risk of holding an out-of-favor stock by including both types in your portfolio.

HOW BUYING OPPORTUNITIES ARE CREATED

"Buy low" means buying an individual stock after the price has fallen significantly. Stocks fall for a good reason. The most common explanation for a stock falling to a bargain-basement price is that earnings have vanished and the company is suffering losses. Buying stocks that are down for this particular reason can produce extraordinary profits when the business recovers. You never know when the stock will rise, so you can't sit by and wait for business to improve. The stock may move up in anticipation of better earnings. The way to be sure of buying low is to buy while the news is bleak. If you buy a stock under these circumstances, you have taken the risk that either earnings will never recover or that it will take a long time for recovery to come along.

This risk can be balanced by buying stock in a company with good current earnings and prospects for future growth. The problem is that you may not find such a company at the right price. Patience is the only answer. If you buy one or two stocks at bargain prices and then wait for one of them to begin reporting good earnings, you will have balance in the portfolio even if there wasn't a good balance initially. Buying one or two down and out-of-favor stocks is a risk that can be balanced by holding on to cash until at least one of your initial investments recovers.

You can make a much longer list of risks that should be recognized and balanced. The list of seven risks outlined earlier is not complete, nor is it a formula for portfolio construction. Portfolios should evolve from study, research and intuition rather than be constructed based on a preconceived formula. The art of balancing risk begins with identifying risk.

The process probably will go like this: One of the companies you have studied looks very attractive. The stock comes down and you think you know why, so you become enthusiastic and buy some shares. After making the initial investment, there is a news release from the company that highlights a risk you didn't see in the initial study. The stock falls in price. Now that you own the stock, it suddenly looks less attractive and you become discouraged. This is the point where risk analysis really begins. Your early enthusiasm is necessary to provide the spark that leads to the purchase of shares. The awakening later to additional risk develops your understanding of the company and its stock. Now all the pieces are in place. You know the risks and the potential rewards and can finally make a truly well-informed decision. At this point you are likely to be right when you choose to sell, hold or buy more.

Investment books always advise investigating before investing. That seems like good advice, but it doesn't explain how to cope with the normal human reactions in the process of investigating and buying stock. The advice is actually misleading. It implies that by investigating you can find the exact right time and price to buy a stock. Such a wish is understandable but unrealistic. Nevertheless, it's a good idea to investigate before investing, but don't think that investigation will insure your portfolio from losses.

Investing means taking risks, and risks aren't always fully appreciated in advance. They tend to emerge as you proceed with the process of constructing a portfolio. As you learn more about the risks in a particular stock, you can take steps to balance those risks by buying shares in other companies with different risks. In the end, your portfolio will always include a reasonable amount of risk. If the major risks are balanced, you won't be overly exposed to adverse market conditions or unpleasant surprises from individual companies.

MANAGING A PORTFOLIO

After the crash of 1987 many investors decided they were better off in bonds or cash and out of the stock market. They missed a major opportunity: stocks that go down increase the chances for above-average profits.

Suppose you bought $5,000 worth of two stocks, each selling at $10 a share. Your initial portfolio would look like this:

500 shares of X	$5,000
500 shares of Y	$5,000
Total	$10,000

After six months, the price for X falls to $5 and the price for Y rises to $20.00. The portfolio now looks like this:

500 shares of X	$2,500
500 shares of Y	$10,000
Total	$12,500

The natural inclination at this point is to be pleased with a 25-percent gain on the portfolio in six months and to wish that there were more funds available to buy more of the stock that went down. But ordinary investors often find that their cash is low just when a stock is really cheap. The answer is to adjust the portfolio so that the two stocks are again equally weighted.

1,250 shares of X	$6,250
312.5 shares of Y	$6,250
Total	$12,500

In the next six months the price of Y doubles and the price of X falls by 50 percent. They are both back to $10 a share. If you had done nothing after six months, your portfolio would be back to $10,000 and you would have a loss of $2,500, or 20 percent in the second six months.

(Notice how the percentages work. Up 25 percent in the first six months and down 20 percent in the second means that you are even, not ahead by 5 percent. Percentages can be misleading if you fail to pay close attention. When you read about the performance of investment advisors or mutual funds, be sure to figure out in dollars if you would be ahead or behind with the advertised performance.)

In this example the investor acted wisely. The portfolio was adjusted so that the holdings were again equally weighted in terms of dollars. At the end of the year the adjusted portfolio looked like this:

1,250 shares of X	
(back to $10)	$12,500
312.5 shares of Y	
(also back to $10)	$ 3,125
Total	$15,625

The adjusted portfolio showed a profit of 56.254 percent in a year. The unadjusted portfolio showed no gain at all. The same two stocks, with different managers, showed distinctly different results.

The foregoing example shows that you don't need a never-ending supply of cash to keep buying stocks. You simply need to be willing to sell some of the winner's shares and invest the money in the loser. That strategy worked even after the crash of 1987. There were many stocks that didn't plunge in the crash. Utility stocks, for example, held their ground. Telecommunications stocks also performed well after the crash. By selling those stocks that held up and using the money to buy more shares of the stocks that plunged, a portfolio not only recovered quickly but went on to show a good profit.

Balancing a portfolio is the secret to making this strategy work. A well-balanced portfolio will have conservative and aggressive stocks. When markets crash, the aggressive stocks may fall sharply but at last some of the conservative holdings will hold their value. After a dramatic event such as the crash of 1987, the best approach is to "unbalance" the portfolio by temporarily concentrating the money in stocks that fell.

A STOCK MARKET CRASH CAN BE
YOUR BEST FRIEND

In June 1989 the Hong Kong stock market crashed (see Figure 8-1). Stocks such as Cheung Kong, a property development company, fell from U.S.$1.45 to U.S.$0.90. Other world markets were unaffected. Hong Kong crashed because of the Beijing Massacre and fear of what might happen when China takes over the rule of Hong Kong in 1997. That didn't bother markets in Taiwan, Japan, Australia, New Zealand, Europe or North America. The Hong Kong crash was an opportunity to switch some cash out of other markets and into Hong Kong. Over the six months from June to December 1989, the Hong Kong market recovered (also shown in Figure 8-1). By April 1990 Cheung Kong was back at $1.45, for a 61-percent gain from the postcrash low.

Having an international perspective opens up the opportunities that develop when one market, for its own unique reasons, decides to fall sharply. Moving money around to take advantage of market crashes when they come along enhances the overall portfolio results. When a stock falls precipitously or a whole market crashes,

Figure 8-1. 1989 Hang Seng Stock Index

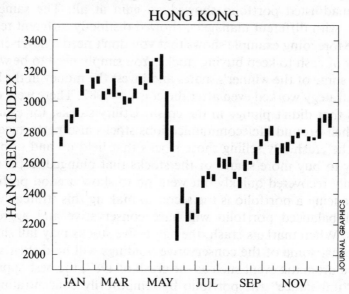

Chart prepared by Richard Andrews from data supplied by the author.

it's natural to feel anxiety and hesitation. Buying into a declining market takes depth of understanding and courage. The usual problem faced by investors during times of market anxiety is that all the news is bad and it is very difficult to believe there is opportunity in the making. The root of these feelings, however, lies not in awareness of the risks but in the false illusion that there are safe havens for investment.

In the first four months of 1990 the Japanese stock market plunged, falling more than 30 percent in terms of U.S. dollars by the middle of April. On April 4, 1990, in the late afternoon, the U.S. stock market plunged 20 points on the Dow Jones Industrial Average. U.S. government bonds soared at the same time. Analysts described the event as a "flight to safety." How silly!

In April the headlines in Massachusetts reported that the state deficit was $800 million and rising. The bond rating for Massachusetts municipal bonds was already the lowest in the nation and might be downgraded to less than investment grade. Holding bonds from one of the oldest states in the Union was certainly not "safe" in 1990.

Imagine what would happen if the fantasies of doom that prevailed on the afternoon of April 4, 1990, came true. The rate of U.S. unemployment would soar from the 5.3-percent rate at the time to something at least as bad as in the recession of 1982 (9.5 percent). The U.S. federal deficit would grow and probably at least double. The rates of U.S. savings would plunge, and the United States wouldn't have the cash at home to finance the deficit. The U.S. government would become totally dependent on the whims of foreign investors to finance the growth in the deficit. Those investors would demand higher interest rates to compensate for the risk, and the value of U.S. government bonds would plunge as interest rates rose. U.S. government bonds were no safer than common stocks on April 4, 1990.

There is an important fact about government bonds that can be seen from this example. When you cut through to the core of what gives government bonds value, you find that it is the underlying economy, or good business. The safest government bonds are in those countries with sound economies and profitable businesses. These countries provide jobs and the tax base needed to produce the income to pay the interest and principal on government bonds. Countries with poor economies or anemic businesses, on the other hand, are a poor place to look for sound government bonds. If the U.S. economy were ever battered by the winds of depression, U.S. government bonds wouldn't provide protection for investors. The idea that these bonds were somehow safer than stocks on April 4, 1990, was no more than one of the periodic fantasies that become popular and dominate the markets. Savvy investors know better than to fall prey to such illusions. The best strategy on April 4, 1990, was to do the opposite of the crowd: to stay rooted in reality and not get caught up in the fantasy and buy or hold on to common stocks.

When the Hong Kong stock market crashed in 1990, there were no illusions, just the reality of an oppressive political regime in China run amuck. It's one thing to run against a crowd-induced fantasy and another to buy in the face of harsh reality. No investor in his or her right mind should have considered investing in 100 percent of a portfolio in Hong Kong after the crash. But because business is just as important for the longevity of an oppressive political regime as for an open democratic one, there was the chance that the Hong Kong stock market might recover. Moving part of a portfolio into Hong Kong stocks was a strategy that indicated an awareness of the real risks and a willingness to take the chance that the market would recover.

The Hong Kong stock crash in June 1990 is a perfect case study for investors because it brings to light the essential elements of portfolio management. Most investors fool themselves into believing they are taking only "calculated risks." What they really mean by that expression is that they personally aren't taking any risk at all. They somehow have the ability to cut through the fog of the future and to know what will happen. Those investors sometimes get lucky and enjoy profits. More often, however, they suffer extreme anxiety when the markets sooner or later go against them and they feel the shock of what real risks are all about.

The investor who avoids this pitfall and steps into the world of real risk also needs luck. But an investor who bought into a real risk and lost is further ahead in the long run than an investor who lives in the world of financial illusions. Taking real risks and losing is sobering. Once done, it tends to cut through all the false notions and reduce the world of investing to what it is: taking real risks and hoping for the best.

Constructing a list of companies to follow, getting to know them, balancing your portfolio and adjusting for extraordinary opportunities is a discipline. While practicing the discipline won't guarantee you wealth, it will keep you from losing everything and becoming overly discouraged. It will also load the odds in favor of your portfolio making above-average profits over the long run.

WHAT ABOUT BONDS IN A PORTFOLIO?

The word *bond* is usually used generically as if all bonds were alike, but that's not the case. There are U.S. government bonds, bonds issued by agencies of the government, debentures, mortgage-backed bonds, corporate bonds, bonds issued by foreign governments and municipal bonds, to name a few. Each type of bond has its own characteristics, risks and merits.

A buyer of bonds has to look at the details of a specific bond to see what collateral, if any, there is behind the bond, what call protection there might be and if there is a sinking fund provision. Call protection refers to a guarantee that a bond paying a high rate of interest won't be called (paid off) when interest rates fall. Buying a bond that pays 14 percent won't be satisfying if, when interest rates are down to 8 percent, you are paid in full and have to reinvest at a much lower rate of interest. Sinking fund provisions are just the opposite. Sometimes the legal details require that the borrower regularly buy back a certain number of the outstanding bonds. A lottery usually determines which bonds are paid off.

When you move offshore and begin to look at foreign bonds, the level of complexity rises. Currency considerations come into play, as well as the particular features of the foreign market and legal system of a given country.

There are two principal reasons to buy bonds. One is to increase income, and the other is to make a profit if the value of the bond increases. Using bonds to make a profit means predicting the direction of long-term interest rates. That is a task that has forever eluded the best economists and market analysts. If you make a mistake in buying a bond and the price falls, there is no way of recovering until interest rates reverse course and go back down. Interest rates can remain high for years. When that happens, you have locked in a loss with no way out.

For example, in 1977 long-term interest rates on Moody's Aaa U.S. corporate bonds were 8 percent. In 1981 rates rose to 14 percent, and the price of Aaa bonds plunged. Between 1977 and 1981, $100,000 in long-term bonds lost 43 percent of the principal value. After holding the bonds ten years, they were still not back to even in 1987, when long-term interest rates were 9.1 percent. At that rate, the bonds bought in 1977 for $100 sold for $88, a loss of 12 percent.

The 1970s and 1980s made it very clear that bonds can and do produce significant losses for those investors unlucky enough to buy them just before a major rise in interest rates. This applies to U.S. government bonds as well as to all other long-term bonds.

In addition to the unpredictable interest rate risk, there is the risk that a borrower will get into financial trouble. A bond is a loan. There is a borrower and a lender. The investor who buys the bond is the lender. The company or government issuing the bond is the borrower.

There are people who won't loan money under any circumstances—not to a friend, a relative or a stranger—but they will hold a portfolio full of bonds. If you point out the inconsistency, they usually reply that bonds are "different." They think that because there is a market for the bonds but not for loans to relatives, it is therefore safe to buy bonds. That is another common financial illusion. Bonds are not "safe." Their value depends on interest rates, the ever-changing ability of the borrower to pay interest and principal, and the markets' view of the future for interest rates and the borrower's finances.

Perhaps the worst aspect of a bond is that the income never changes. Once issued, the bond will pay the specified amount of interest and no more for the life of the bond. The 8-percent bonds issued in 1977 paid the same $8.00 a year per $100 face value all through the 1980s. When interest rates soared to 14 percent in 1981, those old 1977 bonds paid the same $8.00 per $100. If an investor bought $100,000 worth of 8-percent bonds in 1977, the annual income was $8,000. It stayed at $8,000 in the 1980s even though the cost of living soared. Nonetheless many investors persist in the view that bonds are safer than common stocks.

One category of stocks that is periodically regarded as highly risky by investors is bank stocks. They didn't do that well even in the roaring bull market of the 1980s. Analysts worried first about Latin loans, then about the U.S. savings and loan crisis and later about the commercial real estate crunch of 1989 and 1990. Suppose that in 1977 instead of a government bond an investor bought shares in Citicorp, one of America's leading banks. Citicorp then paid a dividend of $0.53 per share. In 1987 the dividend was increased to $1.32. Investors who held shares of Citicorp saw their income rise by 149 percent. In a time of rising living costs that can mean the difference between survival and despair. Which do you think was safer: a government bond, the income from which declined in real terms, or stock in Citicorp that increased the dividend by 149 percent?

There was a time to buy bonds. That was in 1981, when interest rates were up to 14 percent and bond prices were depressed. Between 1981 and 1987, as interest rates came down, the value of bonds rose. A bond purchased for $50 in 1981 rose to $77 in 1987, for a capital gain of 54 percent plus the 14 percent per year in interest. Those were the good times for bonds. That experience in the 1980s (when interest rates came down) colored the judgment of investors. They saw bonds as a way of enjoying income plus capital gains.

Between 1981 and 1987 the price for a share of Citicorp rose from $10⅞ to $34, for a gain of 212 percent. Even in the good times for bonds, Citicorp shares did better. After the crash of 1987, Citicorp shares fell temporarily to $16. Even at that, they were still 47 percent higher than in 1981.

The point of this comparison is not to prove conclusively that stocks are always better than bonds. The purpose is to show that many popular conceptions about bonds aren't correct. Bonds, like stocks, are complicated and risky. If interest rates ever soar to double-digit rates again, that will be the time to look at bonds for capital gains. Otherwise, you should look to stocks for increases in income and capital gains.

The attraction of bonds is that at any given time they offer a yield higher than the rate from common stocks. At the end of 1989, for example, the average U.S. stock provided a yield of 3.6 percent, while long-term U.S. government bonds paid 8.5 percent. On $100,000, that is a difference in income of $4,900 a year. For investors who have limited capital and need maximum income, it's very tempting to buy bonds rather than stocks. The risk they take is that a few years later their cost of living will have increased but their income will be the same. It takes more capital to generate the same current income from stocks, but over the long run, rising dividends on stocks are far superior to the fixed income from bonds.

Investors in need of income shouldn't have a portfolio of 100-percent long-term bonds. They should instead keep part of their portfolios in cash, short-term bonds and high-yielding stocks and the rest in stocks that seem likely to provide dividend increases in the years ahead.

Above all, don't fall into the popular trap where the risks in common stocks are obvious but bonds seem safe. There are risks in common stocks, but there also are risks in bonds. Whenever you are tempted to buy bonds, remember these true stories:

1. Retired investors bought "safe" bonds in Washington Public Power Service in the 1980s. They paid high yields and were issued by a government-sponsored agency that was to use the money to build nuclear power plants. The project failed. Hundreds of individuals who couldn't afford to lose lost their income and principal. They found out the hard way that bonds are risky.

2. Retired investors moved to the country on what looked like an adequate fixed income from a portfolio of "safe" U.S. gov-

ernment bonds. Ten years later their general cost of living was
up 50 percent, but their income was the same. They couldn't
make financial ends meet. When one of their bonds came
due, interest rates were down. They got their principal back
but had to invest it at a lower interest rate. Their income went
down while their cost of living went up. Financially strapped,
their "golden years" were anything but golden.

These stories are only examples, but they are based on stories of real
financial misery caused by the misconception that bonds are safe.

WHAT ABOUT FOREIGN BONDS IN A PORTFOLIO?

Foreign bonds in a portfolio introduce a currency risk. Currencies don't always go in one direction. If you buy a bond in a foreign
country and that currency plunges, you will lose twice. First, the
value of the bond will fall as foreign interest rates rise; and second,
you will lose in terms of dollars when the foreign currency falls.

Suppose you invest $100,000 in bonds in a country where the ex-
change rate is two to one with the U.S. dollar and interest rates are 8
percent. That country later runs into economic problems, and the
value of the currency falls to three to one versus the U.S. dollar and
interest rates rise from 8 percent to 12 percent. The value of the
bond would fall by 33 percent in foreign currency terms. Your holdings in dollars would fall further because the foreign currency
plunged. The original $100,000 would then be worth only $44,444.

In U.S. bonds, you run the risk of rising interest rates. In foreign
bonds, you run the double risk of rising interest rates and a falling
currency. It is often popular in the United States to disparage the
country and the currency. It can be popular to worry about a dollar
decline. That in turn can lead to the false notion that a fall in the
dollar means a fall versus all other currencies in the world. There
are lots of currencies in the world—from Panama's balboa to Switzerland's franc. The value of each is determined by local economic
conditions, supply and demand factors and the speculators on
world currency markets. It isn't all that unusual to have the dollar
falling against some currencies while rising in value against others.

The first step in evaluating foreign bonds is to realize that all currencies are not alike. Before venturing into a foreign bond, take a
close look at local economic conditions and make a judgment on

the likely future value for that particular currency. Forming an intelligent opinion on the currency markets is one of the most difficult tasks in the investment world.

There is one way in which foreign bonds increase the range of opportunity. In the early 1980s U.S. interest rates soared and the value of U.S. bonds plunged. Investors who bought depressed U.S. bonds in 1981 enjoyed high income and capital gains when interest rates later fell. The problem with this strategy is that double-digit interest rates on U.S. bonds don't come along very often. There was only one such opportunity in the United States in the 1980s. But if you watch several countries, one of them might get into economic trouble and be forced to raise interest rates to double-digit levels. By watching bonds in several countries, at least you increase the possibility that a bond-buying opportunity will come along.

If you decide to hold foreign bonds in your portfolio, apply the risk-balancing principle. Balance the risk of a currency decline by also owning stocks in that country in companies that are heavy in exports. If the currency falls, the profits of such companies will rise, and that in turn is likely to mean rising dividends and a higher stock price to offset the currency loss on the bonds. The risk that interest rates might rise can be offset by holding cash in a money market fund.

Above all, don't be lured into the false assumption that foreign bonds are somehow less risky than U.S. bonds or other forms of investment. They are risky. They have their merits, but the risks should be appreciated and balanced in a portfolio.

THE FINAL PRODUCT: YOUR PORTFOLIO

After constructing a universe of companies to follow and considering mutual funds and foreign bonds, the final step is to build a portfolio of your own.

Before you buy a single stock, bond or fund, think about what the final product will look like. How many issues should you have in the portfolio? The question of how much diversification is enough probably will never be answered. Formal studies on performance produce conflicting results. Some say the more issues, the better. Others say that too many issues dilute performance. Common sense and your personal circumstances will resolve the issue.

Suppose you have 100 different issues in a portfolio. If one suffers a setback and falls by 50 percent, that means only a one-half of

1 percent decline in your total portfolio. That's the benefit of having a lot of issues. When one goes wrong, you don't lose too much. The other side of a large number of issues is that when you get it right, the benefit is small. A stock that doubles produces only a 1-percent overall gain.

It's important to know in advance how many issues you want in your portfolio before you buy the first stock. The reason for this is that you may be either too timid or too bold taking the first step unless you know exactly where you are headed. A good number is between 14 and 20. If you decide on 20, an even distribution would call for 5 percent of the portfolio in each issue. In a $100,000 portfolio, that means $5,000 in each selection. If you find a stock you like selling at $10 but are not sure of yourself, it can be tempting to buy 100 shares, or $1,000 worth. That is a common mistake.

It is far better to adopt a rule that says you will have no more than 20 holdings and further, that the minimum purchase will be 5 percent and the maximum 10 percent. This 14 to 20 positions with a minimum of 5 percent and a maximum of 10 percent works well in practice. It gives you flexibility to add to stocks that decline in value, to sell those that rise and to alter the weighting in favor of those companies where you have above-average confidence in the outlook.

This method of portfolio management works even for large multi-million-dollar portfolios. It runs into its limits, however, with small portfolios of less than $25,000, where a 5-percent position is only $1,250. Limiting yourself to 5 percent means buying less than 100 shares of many stocks. Less than 100 shares is called an odd lot, and the commissions are higher. Generally speaking, buy and sell in round lots of 100 shares or multiples of 100.

If your portfolio is less than $25,000, here are few suggestions.

1. Include mutual funds or closed-end country funds. One holding of a fund will give you a participation in all the issues held by the fund. You can accomplish a lot with a little when you buy funds.
2. Look for a few exciting stocks that sell for less than $10 a share. This will give you round lots and capital gain potential.
3. Don't be afraid to buy a round lot in an expensive stock even if it means having more than 10 percent of the portfolio in a single issue.

4. Reduce the number of issues to a minimum of four and maximum of ten. That will give some diversification while still building a sensible portfolio.
5. Be especially sensitive to the risk-balancing part of portfolio management. When you have only four issues, be sure that they are in four different parts of the world, that they represent four different industries and that they are investments with four distinct and different characteristics. For example, you might buy shares in a closed-end fund in Europe, a stock in Australia, a stock in the United States and a stock in Japan. In selecting the stocks, look for one large company with little debt, one large company with considerable debt and one small company with a solid balance sheet.

With these few rules and an international portfolio, you can enjoy the benefits of international diversification with a small portfolio.

Don't hesitate. Dig in and start developing your universe of companies. Begin your own personal, never-ending, exciting adventure into the real world of risks and rewards!

OPPORTUNITY #11: BUYING A LOW-PRICED STOCK

Look at the financial pages of a national or international newspaper. What you are looking for is an industry group or whole market that is down, out of favor and near all-time lows. In 1990, bank stocks and the New Zealand stock market fit that description.

The next step is to look for the best company in that industry or the best company in the country. J.P. Morgan and Citicorp, for example, are the best banks in the United States. Fletcher Challenge, a forest products and agricultural company, is the best company in New Zealand. Invest 5 percent of your portfolio in such a depressed stock. Then be patient. In time, all stocks have their day in the sun. When the recovery develops, you will enjoy profits and see that buying low is a practical way of managing your portfolio.

CHAPTER

9

The United States in the 1990s

A lot happened in the 1970s and 1980s. The United States lost its energy independence, and Americans didn't adjust easily to that loss. We hated OPEC, protested high oil prices and demanded revenge. We also accelerated our involvement in the war in Vietnam and at the same time launched a drive to eliminate poverty at home. We Americans acted as if we not only had the oil, but were rich enough to afford both the war and the antipoverty program.

In the 1980s U.S. after-tax corporate profits were anemic. Business didn't have the capital to invest in new factories and technologies. Whole markets were lost to foreign competition. Our government couldn't make ends meet, and the national debt soared. Business and consumers, who were faced with inadequate savings, borrowed heavily. Indebted Latin countries couldn't make their payments, and the U.S. banking system suffered. A speculative real estate binge, which produced huge losses for U.S. savings and loans, created the second banking crisis in a single decade. In the second half of the 1980s, the federal government—faced with continuing deficits, unable to raise taxes and desperate—pushed spending obligations back to the individual states. Although once running surpluses, an increasing number of states reported deficits by the last day of 1989.

The sad story of the U.S. economy can be seen in the facts of life on Cape Cod, in Massachusetts. In 1990 the cost of a family Blue Cross and Blue Shield contract for health insurance rose 41 percent to $7,600 a year. In 1989 the cost of electric utility bills rose 25 to 40 percent. Real estate taxes rose 25 percent, and Massachusetts increased income taxes by 15 percent. Making ends meet had become more than a challenge; it had become an exercise in frustration. The cost of living on Cape Cod was rising so fast that no individual could hope to keep up, and Cape Cod was not an exception. The same story was repeated in communities across the nation. Something had obviously gone very wrong for the U.S. economy.

A nation in need of more savings and investment was faced with out-of-control costs for essentials such as medical care, utilities, insurance and basic social services. For the nation as a whole, the problem was symbolized in health-care spending, which had grown to 12 percent of GNP (gross national product, or the entire economy), a level so high as to be threatening.

In 1989 everyone knew what the problems were—excessive health-care costs, too little capital investment, too much private debt and persistent government deficits—but no one had a solution. How can you raise taxes if people can't afford to pay? How can you cut spending while so many are in such desperate need?

In the 1970s the nation's problems seemed to come from outside (e.g., oil shortages and foreign competition). That changed in the 1980s. The new and more difficult problems were purely domestic.

The severity of the problems doesn't mean they cannot be solved. Other countries have faced similar or worse problems and have found the answers. In principle the solutions are easy. We Americans have to accept the fact that we are deeply in debt and no longer rich. Then we can get on with the business of making enough money to pay our bills. If we placed less emphasis on politics and more on business, the nation's wealth would eventually increase enough to solve our problems. But that is easier said than done.

The drug problem alone shows just how difficult it will be for the United States to do the right things. Drugs have sapped our energy, increased crime, destroyed lives and battered schools. As if that were not enough, we are also faced with the AIDS epidemic and an aging population in need of care. The challenge is enormous, but we will try. Mistakes will be made, and we will be forced by events to accept the fact that we aren't as rich as we'd like to be. Deficits and debts won't diminish quickly, but we are not alone in this world nor without resources. Our nation of 250 million, with its long history of political stability, will continue to attract foreign capital. That will help to finance the debts and deficits and give us time to work out the solutions to the more fundamental problems.

The greatest challenge for most of us in the 1990s will be to make enough money to maintain our standards of living. The costs of health care, insurance and taxes will continue to rise faster than most household incomes. Those who aren't able to keep ahead of rising costs will be forced to cut back on their standards of living. Vacation money will go for taxes or insurance. There will be fewer luxury cars, expensive television sets and stereo systems. More and more of the average income will be devoted to necessities.

The trends of the 1980s unfortunately point in the direction of lower standards of living for the average American, at least until the nation's businesses have been restored to a more competitive position and there are enough profits to pay our debts and deficits. Only then can real wages rise enough to restore purchasing power and living standards.

In the 1970s President Carter followed a course of redistribution of income and wealth. The idea was to protect the poor and disadvantaged from the worst of the economic calamity caused by rising oil prices. Marginal income-tax rates rose to 70 percent, but raising taxes and redistributing wealth didn't work. By 1979 the nation faced double-digit inflation and was headed for a recession. Why did redistribution fail? The only logical answer is that there wasn't enough wealth to go around. There were too few rich and too many poor. Rising income-tax rates slowed the already inadequate growth of the nation's wealth.

In the 1980 presidential race, Ronald Reagan produced an appealing concept that was fathered by a California economist, Arthur Laffer. The Laffer curve, as it was called, made national headlines. The idea was that high tax rates were the primary culprit. Reduce tax rates, it was argued, and the nation's economy would respond by creating new jobs and new wealth. Voters embraced the concept, and President Reagan put the idea into practice. Tax rates were reduced significantly, and the economy did improve. Millions of new jobs were created. But when 1989 came to a close, the country was still faced with daunting economic problems. In the end, both redistribution (with its high tax rates) and the Laffer curve (with lower tax rates) failed to save the economy. Redistribution ended in double-digit inflation and recession. Falling tax rates ended with a nation deep in debt and a banking system in crisis.

The common denominator in the 1970s and the 1980s was the size of government. President Reagan increased defense spending and thereby kept government relatively large compared to the overall economy. In 1980 total federal government spending was 21.6 percent of the economy. In 1989 the figure was 21.8 percent. That was the similarity between the Carter and Reagan years.

In 1945, after World War II, total government spending (federal plus state and local) was 19 percent of the economy. In the 1980s total government ran between 36 and 38 percent of the economy. The clear message from the 1980s is that this level of total government spending is too large for the American economy to support. If we were richer, as we were in the 1960s, perhaps we could afford this much government. But we aren't richer. Our economy has suffered blows—from rising energy costs to intense foreign competition. We need to redirect resources away from government and into private enterprise—and we have a chance.

In 1989 defense spending totaled 5.8 percent of the economy. With peace breaking out in Eastern Europe, we should be able to cut defense spending. If we only cut 2 to 3 percent and redirect that money, energy and manpower to private enterprise, it will make a difference. That alone may not set the U.S. economy right, but it would be an important step in the right direction.

To get the full benefit from a reduction in defense spending, however, a change in our attitudes will have to occur. We will need to place a greater importance on business and slightly less importance on politics. If we use the defense savings to finance other political programs or stand by as rising health-care costs gobble up what we used to spend on defense, we won't change the balance between politics and business in the United States. To keep American living standards intact in the 1990s, we must make business a top priority. If we don't, our standard of living will suffer and the U.S. stock market will remain a difficult place for investors to hunt for profits.

For the 20 years from 1970 through 1989, the U.S. stock market limped ahead, disappointing investors. We think there was a great bull market in the 1980s, but when the two decades are combined, a different picture emerges. The Morgan Stanley Capital International Perspective U.S. stock index gained only 200 percent in those two decades, compared with more than 400 percent for the world stock index. The gains of the 1980s barely made up for the lackluster performance of the 1970s.

Now that those two frustrating decades are over, are there better days ahead for investors in U.S. stocks? There could be, as there is enormous potential in the United States. The problem is twofold: first, there is the national attitude; and second, there is the specific problem of the negative attitudes of American investors toward their own country, currency and markets. For U.S. stocks to do significantly better in the 1990s, both will have to change.

It's clear that American business can compete effectively when running free, without handicaps. In the two decades that ended in 1969, U.S. business dominated the world economy. But when handicapped, U.S. business struggles to keep from falling too far behind.

THE HANDICAPS OF AMERICAN BUSINESS

In the 1970s American business was handicapped by an overvalued currency, rising oil prices, increased government regulation, rising taxes and rising interest rates. Slowly but surely we either adjusted to the new circumstances or changed the rules. For example, the dollar came down, we adapted to higher costs and the tax laws were moderated. But as soon as we dealt with one set of challenges, another set emerged.

In the 1980s U.S. business faced a deep recession and wild fluctuations in the dollar and interest rates. In the second half of the decade, business again was burdened by rising taxes.

As we come to the 1990s and the sunset of a century, we face new challenges. Health-care costs are high and rising fast. The issue of who will bear the cost for health-care insurance has become a major national labor issue. The health-care issue is likely to have a direct bearing on the ability of American business to be profitable and competitive.

We spend more than our competition (Germany and Japan) on education but get less in return. A well-educated and motivated work force is essential for business to prosper. If too many Americans are poorly educated, business will have a handicap that is very difficult to overcome.

For years our rate of capital investment has been too low. Without a significant increase in capital investment, the competition will continue to get ahead.

As a nation, we have not yet found the right balance between government or politics and good business. For some puzzling reason, we remain antibusiness.

For investors, the U.S. stock market in the 1990s requires a clear understanding of both the risks and the potential rewards. In the 20 years from 1970 through the end of 1989, the popular Dow Jones Industrial Average climbed from 1,000 in 1969 to slightly more than 2,700 at the end of 1989, for a gain of 170 percent. To have kept pace with U.S. inflation, the Dow should have climbed to 3,880. By comparison with the cost of living in the United States, the Dow Jones Industrial Average was a poor performer.

That doesn't mean you couldn't make money in U.S. stocks in those 20 years. There were plenty of opportunities. American Airlines (or AMR Corp.), for example, traded at $9 in the early 1980s and soared to $100 on takeover rumors in 1989. Defense stocks, such as Loral, E Systems and Raytheon, were in the doldrums in the mid-1970s. Under the Reagan defense buildup in the 1980s, they prospered and their stock prices skyrocketed. Service Merchandise, a retailer, fell to less than $4.00 a share after the 1987 stock crash. From that low the stock rose to more than $20 in a little more than a year. Compaq Computer rose from $4 to $90, and Ralston Purina turned in outstanding gains for shareholders. Computer software companies likewise produced outstanding gains for investors. In fact, there were hundreds, if not thousands, of opportunities in U.S. stocks in the 1970s and 1980s.

Nonetheless the overall performance of the U.S. stock market was not up to par. The World Stock Index gained significantly more (460 percent in the 20 years that ended in 1989). There were opportunities in the United States, but you had to be selective and lucky. It was easier to make money in stocks in foreign countries than in the giant U.S. stock market.

Will the 1990s be a repeat of the past, or will the U.S. stock market keep pace with the rest of the world in the coming decade?

THE CONTINUING COMPETITION WITH JAPAN

In each of the last three years of the 1980s, Japan invested 20 percent of its economy into improving business. That was three times the rate in the United States. When you stop and reflect on these numbers, the magnitude of the American problem comes into focus. Even if we eliminated the entire defense budget and used every dime for capital investment, we wouldn't come close to the Japanese standard. On the other hand, every year that goes by with less than adequate U.S. capital investment means we fall further behind.

In the last three years of the Eighties, the United States did in fact fall further behind the Japanese competition. That doesn't mean that Americans understood the problem. In fact, there seemed to be little popular awareness of the growing gap between U.S. and Japanese business.

In 1988 and early 1990 the dollar was strong versus the Japanese yen. The greenback climbed more than 12 percent versus the yen in the 12 months that ended on March 31, 1990. Americans cheered. We were happy the dollar was strong. One television journalist remarked that if the trend continues, American tourists will again be able to afford a trip to Tokyo. However, the ominous aspect of the strong dollar wasn't appreciated.

A strong dollar by definition means a falling yen. A lower yen makes more than a trip to Tokyo more affordable for Americans. It makes all Japanese products cheaper. Not only did Japanese business have the advantage of three years of heavy spending to improve products, introduce new technologies and modernize factories, but they were enjoying a price advantage as well. The threat to American business intensified with each upward notch in the dollar. When we cheered the dollar, we set ourselves up for a terrible letdown.

Japan's rate of capital investment exceeded that of West Germany as well. The Japanese invested at twice the rate of the West Germans. By the beginning of 1990, Japan had established a foundation for growth.

The prospect of a new wave of exports from Japan was masked in 1990. Japan's trade surplus had been shrinking in 1989. A strong domestic economy and the past strength of the yen combined to increase imports and slow the growth of exports. Americans felt secure. Their currency was gaining strength, and Japan's published trade figures were encouraging.

What will happen in the years ahead? Japan's massive capital investment points in the direction of a new surge in Japanese exports. Once exports begin to surge, the yen is likely to reverse course and become strong again. The United States seems headed for a repeat of the mid-1980s.

In 1984 the Federal Reserve, in the name of fighting inflation, raised U.S. interest rates. The dollar soared. Americans cheered then, too! Japanese goods became cheap for American consumers, and the U.S. trade deficit soared. American business suffered. Interest rates finally came down, and in 1985 the dollar plunged from its peaks. The lower dollar helped American business but didn't mend all the wounds. Foreign businesses gained a significant market share during the days when the dollar was too strong. They held on and didn't give much back when the dollar came down.

In 1990 the dollar, while strong, stayed well below its 1984–85 level versus the Japanese yen. That might seem consoling, but it shouldn't because there's always more to the story of business than the exchange rate for the currency. The massive Japanese capital investments had increased Japan's competitive position just as if the dollar had soared. The Japanese had become tougher competitors and didn't need a superstrong dollar to give them the edge. A modest gain in the greenback probably would be enough to set the balance in favor of Japanese business once again.

Just as the Japanese grew stronger in the late 1980s, the United States remained weakened by deficits. The U.S. trade deficit stopped growing in the late 1980s but remained large as 1990 began. Under those circumstances even a modest increase in U.S. imports would be too much. A new trend toward a growing U.S. trade deficit would be apt to send the dollar down sharply.

In 1990 the United States needed every advantage to fend off Japanese competition. Instead of cheering when the dollar was strong, we should have been worried and should have fought hard to keep the greenback down, especially versus the Japanese yen. Because of our collective failure to understand the importance of keeping the dollar down, the United States may be headed for another rollercoaster ride in its currency and trade balance in the 1990s.

EMERGING COMPETITORS

The Japanese are tough international competitors; that is obvious. Less obvious is the competition—present and potential—from regions of the world where the standards of living are decidedly lower than in the United States. It's difficult to look at the pictures of poverty and desperation coming from Eastern Europe and believe those countries are potential tough competitors.

At the end of World War II, no one imagined that the devastated and defeated economies of Germany and Japan would rise to become victors in the economic battles of the 1970s and 1980s. We saw pictures of destruction, poverty and desperation in the newsreels. Nevertheless within two decades Japan and Germany were well on the way to economic success.

It probably won't take decades before the people of Eastern Europe emerge as tough competitors on international markets. Like Germany and Japan in the 1950s, they will benefit from an injection of capital. They will also adopt the newest methods and technologies and will work for less because they have no choice. It may take just a few short years before goods made in East Germany, Hungary or Czechoslovakia appear in large quantities on the shelves in American stores.

The Japanese were right to worry about their future and to invest heavily in new plants and technologies. By investing their capital, they stand a better chance of competing as goods made with low-cost labor begin to flow out of Eastern Europe.

Western Europe was right to worry about Japanese competition and move to eliminate red tape and politics by 1992. It's lucky for them that they started when they did. At that time there was no way of knowing the Berlin Wall would come down and Eastern Europe would open its borders. Now that this has happened, Western Europe is better prepared to meet the developing army of new competitors from the East.

Where is the United States on the spectrum of world competition? We haven't had the money to invest like the Japanese and haven't increased our competitive position through massive capital investment. We could have changed the balance between politics and business, but we didn't. We entered the 1990s with the same heavy government burden we had at the beginning of the 1980s. The harsh truth is that the United States entered the 1990s vulnerable to the old familiar competitors, Japan and West Germany, and to a new, emerging group of competitors from Eastern Europe.

The people of Eastern Europe have suffered under the burden of too much politics. They have a clear idea of what responsible government means and know that providing for the economy must be the highest priority or nothing else will matter. In the United States we still find the siren song of ideas (such as tax the rich and give the money to the poor) alluring. We haven't buckled down and decided that the best idea is to work hard and try to make the whole nation wealthier. We dream that somehow the politicians in our state capitals or in Washington will solve all our problems.

Americans must awaken quickly to the limits of big government, learn to set priorities and balance short-term desires against our long-term welfare. The stakes are high. We won't fall off the cliff into chaos and poverty, but there is a risk that we will fall further behind in the intense global competition of the 1990s.

FOREIGN INVESTORS AND U.S. MARKETS

Each month the Federal Reserve publishes a bulletin. Included is a page showing the net buying and selling of U.S. stocks and bonds by foreign investors. The statistics show that in almost every year since 1972 foreign investors were net buyers of both U.S. stocks and U.S. bonds.

In the case of bonds, the figures aren't so troubling. The U.S. government has been running deficits and borrowing and issuing new bonds every year. American business has likewise been borrowing heavily. There have been plenty of new bonds for foreign investors to buy. Net foreign buying of U.S. bonds doesn't mean that American investors have been selling. In fact, the opposite is the case. American investors have preferred bonds over stocks and have bought heavily. What the net foreign buying of U.S. bonds means is that there have been more than enough new bonds coming on the market to satisfy U.S. investor demand. Foreign investors have purchased the excess.

The statistics on stocks are more worrisome. New issues of common stocks were sparse in the United States in the 1970s and 1980s. Because of stock buy-back programs and mergers, the quantity of U.S. stocks available to the public declined in the second half of the 1980s. Under these circumstances net foreign buying of U.S. stocks means that American investors have been selling. That is discouraging.

You can argue that there have been good reasons for Americans to sell their own stocks, but that is a half-truth, a self-fulfilling excuse. A healthy stock market, one where individuals are willing to buy and hold, is important to the overall success of business. For example, suppose Americans had not been net sellers. U.S. stock prices might have been higher in the 1980s, or at least less volatile. Higher stock prices would have permitted business to sell stock to raise low-cost, long-term capital instead of borrowing. Less debt and more long-term capital would have been a major help to American competitiveness in the 1980s. With a stronger stock market, the United States might have withstood the battering of foreign competition much better. Perhaps we would have ended the 1980s in a less vulnerable position. American investors can explain why they sold stocks and bought bonds or certificates of deposit from local banks, but they cannot deny that their selling contributed to the loss of American economic might. Investors' attitudes toward common stocks are just as important as our attitudes toward politics and business.

In case there is any doubt about the benefits of a robust stock market, consider the story of the competition in the 1980s between U.S. and Japanese banks. In the 1970s Citicorp had a large traditional commercial banking business in Europe. By the end of the 1980s that business was all but gone, lost to Japanese banks. The Japanese took business away from U.S. banks by offering loans to major corporations at a lower rate of interest. The Japanese could do that and still make money because they had access to a source of low-cost capital—their own stock market. Japanese banks sold new shares of stock in Japan at very high prices and used the capital to drive the U.S. banks out of selected, lucrative markets. The U.S. banks were powerless to respond because their stocks sold at depressed prices in their home market. They were faced with meeting the Japanese competition and suffering huge losses or getting out of the traditional banking business when they met stiff Japanese competition, so they got out. The difference between the high-priced Japanese bank stocks and the low-priced U.S. bank stocks was the determining factor in giving away what once had been a huge and profitable market for U.S. banks.

It's puzzling, to say the least, that while American investors shied away from their own businesses, foreign investors saw a different picture. Between 1972 and 1989 foreign investors accumulated $86.2 billion worth of U.S. common stocks (see Table 9-1). But that doesn't mean the United States can always count on foreign buyers. There have been wide swings in foreign attitudes about U.S. stocks.

In 1986 net foreign buying of U.S. stock surged to more than $18 billion, as indicated in Table 9-1. The volume of foreign buying remained high until the crash in October, which was assisted by computer-program trading. The American fascination with a possible

Table 9-1. Net Foreign Buying (Selling) of U.S. Common
Stocks

Year	Dollar Amount (In Billions)
1972	2.188
1973	2.790
1974	.540
1975	4.678
1976	2.753
1977	2.675
1978	2.423
1979	1.679
1980	5.418
1981	5.830
1982	3.976
1983	5.410
1984	(2.980)
1985	4.941
1986	18.719
1987	16.272
1988	(2.062)
1989	10.948

Note: 1989 data are for 11 months.
Source: Monthly Bulletin of the U.S. Federal Reserve.

crash produced a panic that not only drove the U.S. stock market
down but scared foreign buyers away. In 1988 foreign investors became the net sellers of U.S. common stocks.

In the great stock market crash of 1929 the headlines reported at
one point that the market's plunge was due to massive selling by
foreign investors. Prior to the crash of 1987, foreign investors had
accumulated enough billions of dollars worth of U.S. common
stocks to effect a repeat performance. Fortunately, that isn't what
happened. Although they stopped buying because they were frightened by the panic in U.S. stocks, they didn't try to liquidate all their
holdings. By 1989 foreign investors were once again substantial net
buyers, providing renewed support for the U.S. stock market.

The swing from substantial net foreign buying in 1987 to modest
net selling in 1988 was the direct result of the crash of 1987. It wasn't
that foreign investors lost faith in the American economy or American business; they became terrified of U.S. investors. We proved to

the world in 1987 that we can deliver a stock market crash even in a time when business is good and on the verge of a significant increase in profits.

As long as Americans are prone to devastating fantasies about possible depressions and market crashes, we risk being left behind as the rest of the world gets on with the task of preventing such calamities. In 1987 American investors panicked when computer-program trading caused a stock market accident. Individual investors fled the stock market because they believed it to be too risky. Contrast that experience with the steep fall in the Japanese stock market in early 1990. Tokyo also suffered from computer-program trading, but there was no panic or massive fleeing from the Japanese stock market by individual investors.

In 1990 Hungary was busy constructing a stock market. Even the Soviet Union commissioned a study on how to open a stock market. Why would the Soviet Union and Eastern European countries want stock markets? They certainly didn't talk to the average American investor about stocks. An American would have explained how risky stocks can be and would have offered dozens of personal reasons why not to invest in stocks. The Soviets and other struggling economies didn't have to ask, for they already knew about economic risks. Bitter experience had taught them that an economy without a healthy stock market is worse off than one with a healthy stock market. The bottom line is that economic progress demands having more than a few citizens willing to assume the long-term risks of buying and owning common stocks. A nation of risk takers can provide low-cost capital for business. That in turn benefits the entire economy.

In 1929 the U.S. stock market crashed. The consequence was not just a depression in the United States; it was a worldwide economic calamity. In the late 1970s, *The Crash of 1979,* by Paul Erdman, was a best-seller. Soon after its publication, investment analysts and journalists became worried about long-wave cycles. They reasoned that after 50 years, we must be at least exposed to another crash and depression. After the 1987 world stock crash, fear of a coming depression intensified. In all the anxiety, the unspoken assumption was that the U.S. stock market and economy remained so important that a crash here would spread to the rest of the world. In 1987 that assumption still had enough believers that most other world stock markets followed the U.S. plunge.

The collapse of the Berlin Wall and the opening of Eastern Europe has, among other things, defeated that assumption. While the rich, developed nations of the West indulged in fantasies about a depression, the people of Eastern Europe were already suffering a full-blown, real depression. Once the television cameras focused on the plight of Eastern Europe, fantasies about a depression faded. Instead of worrying about such dismal possibilities, people in Europe began to put their energies, capital and efforts into the task of rebuilding the devastated economies.

Pessimism was the chief export from the United States in the 1980s. We tried—and in the end failed—to convince the rest of the world that risk taking in stocks was foolish, that another world crash and depression were coming and that the future would be just like the dismal past of the 1930s. The world decided it was better to try and prevent a depression than to sit by with cash in the bank waiting for a catastrophe. The dismal reality of life behind the Iron Curtain changed attitudes for the better. There is no point in worrying about a possible future depression when you have a current one to deal with.

Will attitudes from Europe spill over to the United States? Will American investors return to their own stock market? If they do, it will be easier for American business to raise low-cost, long-term capital, and the chances of restoring American competitiveness will improve.

Foreign buying in the 1970s and 1980s provided support for U.S. stock prices. Without foreign buying, the performance of the U.S. stock market might have been worse. In the 1990s it remains to be seen if foreign investors will still find the U.S. stock market attractive. No stock market can remain attractive indefinitely without the support of its own citizens. It is possible that this decade will bring less enthusiasm for U.S. stocks as foreign investors look to opportunities in Europe and other regions.

U.S. STOCK PRICES AND THE DOLLAR

There has been a changing relationship between the U.S. stock market and the fate of the dollar on foreign exchange markets. In the 1970s we still had a love affair with the strong dollar. Having a strong currency made Americans feel like royalty when they traveled abroad, and American business was able to buy foreign assets cheaply. But by the end of the 1970s attitudes changed. We still longed for a strong dollar, but for different reasons. A falling dollar became associated with rising inflation and high interest rates. We thought that if the dollar were strong again, we could languish in the pleasure of low inflation and low interest rates.

In the middle of the 1980s our wish for a strong dollar came true, but we learned another painful lesson. The strong dollar of 1984 pushed inflation down but in the process it nearly destroyed American business by allowing a flood of imports. By the end of the 1980s we were ambivalent. On the one hand, we still wished for a strong dollar; but on the other hand, we feared its consequences.

The sad truth is that U.S. after-tax corporate profits in 1989 were only slightly greater than in 1980 (see Table 9-2 for figures for 1980–1989). American business didn't make much progress in the 1980s, nor did profits keep up with inflation. Since after-tax corporate profits represent the capital available to pay dividends to shareholders and to invest in improving business, inadequate after-tax profits explain why U.S. capital investment in the 1980s was so much less than that of Japan or West Germany.

There were several reasons for the poor performance of U.S. corporate profits. Rising taxes and rising costs, for example, made it hard for American businesses to maintain profit margins. However, to its credit, American business adapted to higher taxes and rising costs. The blow that set U.S. profits back was the superstrong dollar

Table 9-2. U.S. After-Tax Corporate Profits

Year	Profits in Billions of Dollars
1980	152.3
1981	145.4
1982	106.5
1983	130.4
1984	146.1
1985	127.8
1986	115.3
1987	142.0
1988	168.9
1989	159.3

Source: Economic Indicators, a monthly publication of the President's Council of Economic Advisors.

of 1984. Since there is a direct connection between U.S. corporate profits and the dollar, one also exists between the dollar and U.S. stock prices.

Even though so many investors behave as if the U.S. stock market were a casino, the truth is that stocks represent ownership in business. Their value is tied to the fortunes of the economy, the industry and the individual businesses. The most popular measure of the worth of a business is its profits. When profits rise, stock prices tend to follow. Likewise, when the outlook is gloomy for profits, stock prices tend to fall.

How will U.S. stocks perform in the 1990s? This question can only be answered after assessing the outlook for U.S. corporate profits. The starting point for an analysis of possible future trends begins with a look at the past. The story of U.S. corporate profits in the 1980s is a tangled web of recession; economic growth; rising and falling interest rates; and most important, the U.S. dollar's fate on world currency markets.

U.S. corporate profits fell sharply in 1981 and early 1982. The obvious explanation for this decline was the existence of high U.S. interest rates and the worst recession since the Great Depression. From the depths of the recession, a recovery developed, but that ran out of steam in early 1984. For most of the rest of 1984, profits again declined. What caused U.S. corporate profits to fall in 1984 and 1985 when there was no recession? Interest rates did rise in the first half of 1984, when the Federal Reserve overreacted to slightly higher inflation, but they turned down again before year-end and fell sharply in 1985.

The culprit that stopped U.S. corporate profits in their tracks in 1984 was a rising dollar. The dollar soared in 1984 after the Fed's interest-rate hike. It kept on soaring until March 1985, when it finally reversed course and began to fall. The superstrong dollar made foreign goods (such as Japanese cameras, fax machines, television sets and automobiles) bargains for U.S. consumers. American business cut prices to match the low-cost competition. Falling prices cut into U.S. corporate profits and produced the decline in 1984 and 1985.

The dollar fell sharply in the summer and fall of 1985. By mid-1986 the U.S. currency had come back down enough to restore profit margins, and corporate profits began to rise again. The dollar kept falling in the new year, not reaching a low until the last day of 1987. The result of the dollar's fall from its 1985 peak was an upward explosion in U.S. corporate profits in 1988, when after-tax corporate profits rose to 14.3 percent. Even as profits were growing in 1988, the seeds of the next decline were sprouting. The dollar didn't stay down at its 1987 low. The U.S. currency gained strength in 1988, and the result was another corporate profit reversal. After-tax profits fell again in 1989.

Looking back to the early 1980s, the effect of the dollar on profits can be seen beneath the maze of recession statistics. There was more to the story of the steep fall in corporate profits in 1980, 1981 and 1982 than high interest rates and recession. The dollar gained strength in the early 1980s. For example, the U.S. currency rose 38 percent versus the Swiss franc between the last day of 1979 and the fall of 1982. The combination of high U.S. interest rates, a recession and strong dollar all but crushed the life out of U.S. corporate profits in the early 1980s.

As the 1980s wore on, the connection between the dollar and U.S. corporate profits became more and more obvious. The fundamental explanation for this connection is that when a nation (such as Japan) invests heavily in new equipment, new factories, product development and new technologies, it gains an advantage over a nation that invests less. All things being equal, Japan would wipe out their competition. The truth of this can be seen clearly if you take away the nationalities and discuss two competing companies located in different states. Suppose both companies make a common product—washing machines. One company takes a significant portion of its profits and invests to improve its methods of manufacturing and the quality of its products. The other company spends all its profits on advertising. In the short run, the advertising is likely to pay off; but in the long run, a company that doesn't keep up with the competition loses, and advertising won't help. (Not even the cleverest ads will sell hand-wringer washing machines in the 1990s.) Although this example is an exaggeration, it makes the point that Japan's massive capital investments in the last few years of the 1980s present a significant challenge to the United States.

Fortunately for the United States, countries have a tool that doesn't exist between two states, namely, currency. All states use the U.S. dollar. Once behind the competition, there is no help available from the currency for trade between two states; but in international trade the situation is different.

The United States fell behind Japan in capital investment in the 1980s. That is a fact, but it doesn't mean that the United States is doomed to a competitive nightmare in the 1990s. If the dollar comes down far enough, it will change the playing field and offset the advantage the Japanese gained through capital investment. A lower dollar would make Japanese goods more expensive and American goods cheaper. The currency markets, by altering relative pricing, can buy time for the underdog. With a lower dollar, Americans could sell their products more cheaply. Putting it another way, Japanese products wouldn't be that cheap for American consumers.

There is always much arguing whenever it's suggested that the United States should welcome a lower dollar to give business a chance of competing, restoring profits and accumulating capital for investment. Economists are quick to point out that a falling dollar, by making imports more expensive, tends to increase U.S. inflation. Investors worry that a falling dollar will push interest rates up and stock prices down. The key, however, is in the word "falling." No country should welcome a currency that keeps falling indefinitely. That shouldn't be necessary. If the dollar comes down to a level where U.S. business is competitive and stays there, the negative effects from higher inflation and rising interest rates will dissipate.

A lower currency can be compared to medicine. If a patient needs medicine all the time, there can be serious negative effects. However, if the medicine works and the patient's health improves, the medicine had a positive effect and need not be taken anymore.

The problem faced by American business in the 1980s was that first of all, the dollar didn't stay down. After each fall, it began to rise again. U.S. business never enjoyed the benefit of a lower dollar long enough to build profits and capital and to make new investments. The second problem was the continuing higher level of capital investments in Japan and West Germany. The competition kept growing stronger as we struggled to cope. Thus the competitive gap between the United States and its principal opponents, West Germany and Japan, grew wider by the end of the 1980s. This growing competitive gap amplified the currency effect. By the end of 1989 the United States was more vulnerable and sensitive to changes in the value of the dollar. In 1984 it took a skyrocketing dollar to damage U.S. corporate profits seriously, but in 1988 a slightly higher dollar caused a downturn in U.S. corporate profits.

In the 1990s U.S. business needs two things. First, the dollar has to fall to a level low enough to even the playing field and close the competitive gap. Second, business needs the dollar to stay down long enough to enjoy several consecutive years of higher profits.

The managers of U.S. businesses are just as tough as those of foreign businesses. Witness the tremendous past successes of U.S. business. At the end of 1989, after a long period of significant foreign buying of U.S. assets, U.S. holdings overseas stood at $785 billion, compared with $466 billion of foreign investment in the United States. In terms of who owns how much of whom, American business and American investors still held the edge at the end of 1989. The reason for this is that in decades past, American business was the leader and had the capital to invest abroad. If American business did so well in the past, it's fair to assume that given the right circumstances, it could happen again.

Likewise, the Japanese aren't the only tough competitors in the world. England, often pictured as a lightweight in international competition, dominated the U.S. foreign buying spree in the 1980s. British business and investors accounted for 31 percent of the total of U.S. assets held by foreigners in 1989. At the end of 1989, British investments totaled $122.8 billion, compared with $66.1 billion held by the Japanese. If the British can benefit from a lower value for their currency and significantly increase their U.S. investments, there is no doubt that with the help of a lower dollar, U.S. business can do very well even against the Japanese. But if the dollar stays too high, U.S. business will have a difficult time and the competitive gap could grow wider.

WHAT WILL HAPPEN TO THE DOLLAR IN THE 1990s?

In the fourth quarter of 1989 a record amount of capital flowed into West Germany. Investors and businesses, excited by the prospects of the opening of East Germany, rushed to buy stocks and invest in German businesses. The West German mark soared. In the four months from November 1, 1989, to the end of February 1990 the mark rose 7.5 percent versus the U.S. dollar. In the United States this was seen not as strength in the mark but as weakness in the dollar. Americans were concerned, but they should have been overjoyed.

The Bundesbank (West Germany's equivalent of our Federal Reserve) felt it was necessary to have a strong mark to make sure that growth from the opening of East Germany didn't ignite inflation in West Germany. The rise of the mark made U.S. goods cheaper in West Germany. The cost of an American-made computer, for example, went down as the mark went up.

Capital is apt to keep flowing into West Germany and other European countries for years. That inflow of money will probably keep the German mark and the other European currencies from coming back down to the levels of the late 1980s. With respect to Europe, American business received a gift at the end of 1989, one likely to have lasting value. Instead of the United States having to drive the dollar down, the German mark and other European currencies went up. These rising European currencies didn't favor just the United States. The Japanese yen, like the U.S. dollar, stayed down as the European currencies rose. Computers made in Japan also became cheaper in Europe by the end of February 1989. The competitive gap between U.S. and European companies narrowed, but the competitive gap grew between the United States and Japan.

In the opening months of 1990 the Japanese stock market and the yen came down. The U.S. dollar actually rose 7 percent versus the yen in the first three months of 1990. What the United States gained as a result of rising European currencies it lost to its prime competitor, Japan. However, all was not lost. The rise in the dollar or the fall in the yen, depending on your point of view, was due to special factors. Chances are that the yen won't keep falling in the 1990s. Japan's extremely strong competitive position will, in all likelihood, eventually produce the opposite—a strong yen—as money flows into Japan to buy Japanese goods.

Japanese insurance companies, pension funds and other investors had invested billions of dollars in U.S. assets, government bonds, real estate and stocks. In Japan in 1988, it was widely believed that the U.S. dollar would fall sharply versus the Japanese yen. Since the Japanese count their fortunes in yen—not dollars, a fall in the U.S. currency would mean losses in terms of yen. To guard against that possibility, they hedged against the dollar.

Hedging comes in various forms, but in its simplest form it means borrowing dollars and selling them, expecting to buy them back later at a lower price. Hedging is always expensive. At the least, you have to pay interest on the borrowed dollars and commissions on the currency sales. When a hedge doesn't work and the market goes the other way, it can be disastrous. That is what happened to the Japanese in late 1989 and early 1990. The dollar gained strength versus the yen. By early 1990 the Japanese were faced with huge and growing losses on their hedging activities, and they were forced to reverse the hedges. That meant buying dollars to repay the loans. The dollar climbed further and more investors panicked and closed out their hedges. The dollar's rise against the yen in early 1990 was an event made in Japan and was the direct result of exaggerated Japanese concern in 1988 about a weak dollar.

This story of the yen and the European currencies in late 1989 and 1990 shows how difficult it is to predict short-term currency movements. It also shows why investors shouldn't make long-term judgments about business profits based on short-term changes in the currency markets.

Capital flowing into Europe to take advantage of major changes, such as the collapse of the Berlin Wall and the opening of Eastern Europe, is real and long-term in nature. The rise in the dollar versus the Japanese yen in early 1990 was quite different. That was the result of a collective error in judgment by Japanese investors. The effect of such errors can linger beneath the surface for a year or more. When they surface and force activity (as in the reversing of all the Japanese dollar hedges), the impact can be sharp, sudden and confusing. In the long run, however, other fundamental factors, such as capital flows and trade balance, reassert their normal importance.

It is highly likely that the real, fundamental differences between the United States and Japan will surface and drive the yen higher. In 1985 the yen reversed and shot to higher ground. From March 1985 until the end of 1986 the Japanese yen rose 40 percent versus the U.S. dollar. The reason for this was Japan's long-standing trade surplus and huge competitive advantage over the United States. The currency markets adjusted in 1985, and they are apt to do the same again. The yen could rise by 30 to 50 percent in the 1990s. That would make a significant difference in international competition. After the yen's 1985 rise, U.S. corporate profits rose significantly. Even a 25-percent rise in the yen would have a meaningful and positive impact on U.S. profits.

Japan's massive capital investments alone indicate that another steep rise in the yen is likely in the 1990s. The question is not whether the yen will rise versus the dollar, but if it will rise soon enough to help U.S. business in the 1990s. The odds are that it will.

OPPORTUNITY #12: WATCH THE DOLLAR

In March 1985 the dollar peaked and began to fall. As it came down, anxiety increased in the United States. Investors began to fear that a falling dollar would mean higher interest rates and rising inflation. Instead, the falling dollar helped American business. The following year, 1986, was a good one for both corporate profits and investors in U.S. stocks.

Watch the dollar. When it falls, take advantage of uncertainty in the U.S. markets by buying stock in a well-managed U.S. company that is either faced with tough foreign competition or engaged in sales of its products abroad. The odds are that a lower dollar will lift the profits of such companies and produce handsome profits for savvy investors with an international perspective.

CHAPTER

10

Investing in U.S. Stocks

There was a bull market in U.S. stocks in the 1980s. It began in August 1982 and was triggered by massive buying of U.S. stocks by foreign investors. Once the market began to move higher, more and more American investors joined the buying parade. The Dow Jones Industrial Average climbed from 791.48 in the summer of 1982 to 2,722 in August 1987. It then crashed and finally moved higher—to 3,000—in July 1990.

On the face of it, the 1980s looked like a good decade for stocks. From low to high, the Dow Jones Industrial Average rose 255 percent. The problem, however, was that the upward thrust of U.S. stock prices in the 1980s was an overdue compensation for the dismal showing in the 1970s. When the two decades are combined, the U.S. stock market showed only a 210-percent gain. This was far below the gains shown on stocks in Denmark, Belgium, Norway, Japan, Hong Kong and others. The world stock index gained 459 percent, and that index includes the U.S. stock market.

The sensible conclusion is that the decade of the 1980s was a time of catching up after a poor showing in the 1970s, rather than a genuine upward movement in U.S. stock prices. Stocks were down in one decade and up in the next, and this leaves open the question of what comes next. Have U.S. stocks simply reached a new equilibrium level? Will we now have two similar decades, with the 1990s a time of poor performance and the first decade of the next century the next good time for U.S. stocks?

U.S. STOCK PRICES IN THE 1990s

When investors go sour on stocks, they tend to stay that way for a long time. The best way to see how investors feel about stocks is not by watching stock prices but by watching both earnings and stock prices.

All things being equal, stock prices will rise and fall as earnings or profits rise and fall. But things are almost never equal. Not only do earnings change, but confidence in the future changes as well. When investors have confidence, they will pay relatively high prices for low earnings. When confidence is low, however, not even strong earnings produce a rising stock market.

The way to measure investor sentiment is through the price-earnings ratio. This ratio is calculated by dividing the stock price by the earnings to see how many times today's earnings investors are willing to pay for any given stock. Suppose there are two companies, both earning $1.00 per share. One stock sells for $10, and the second sells for $5.00. If you look at the price-earnings ratio, you find that the second company sells at five times earnings, or half the ratio of the first company. This indicates that investors have confidence that the first company will continue to do well and earn $1.00 a share or more for years to come. However, that is not the case for the second company as investors worry that the $1.00 per share today won't last and so they pay a lower price for the same amount of earnings.

Price-earnings ratios are published for all the major markets of the world. By watching these ratios for whole markets we can get a good idea of the trend in investor confidence. In the 1970s the trend in investor confidence in the United States was steadily lower. In 1969 the stocks in the Dow Jones Industrial Average traded at 15.4 times earnings. In 1979 the price-earnings ratio on the Dow stocks was down to 6.8. High oil prices, a sinking dollar, rising interest rates and high inflation so disheartened investors that they were willing to buy stocks only at very low prices compared with earnings.

In 1979 the logical question was this: how low can price-earnings ratios go? So dismal was confidence at the end of 1979 that few even dared to ask the question. Most simply assumed that earnings would collapse as the world edged ever closer to the next depression. In that event, there was no point of even discussing price-earnings ratios. Stock prices, it was argued, were down and would go lower.

In the first two years of the 1980s the United States and much of the rest of the world fell into a deep recession. Earnings didn't collapse, but they did go down. The decline of earnings and the recession acted as a cleansing agent. Some of the ugly fantasies of a dismal economic future were swept away. Investors were impressed that we survived the battering of 20-percent interest rates and a dramatic slowing in economic growth.

While recession was evolving and American investors were still glum, a strange thing happened on stock markets around the world. International markets began to display signs of growing confidence. Japan, as you might guess, was one of the brightest spots. From 16.1 times earnings at the end of 1980, Japanese stocks sold at 22.2 times earnings by the last day of 1982. That was a 38-percent rise in price-earnings ratios in two years marked first by high inflation and high interest rates and then by a deep recession. The Japanese weren't the only group of emerging optimists. Price-earnings ratios on British stocks also expanded—from 6.2 to 9.8 between 1980 and 1982.

The United States, on the other hand, refused to follow the new world trend. Price-earnings ratios on U.S. stocks rose only modestly in the first two years of the Eighties—from 9.1 to 10.1. As late as the summer of 1982, optimistic predictions for U.S. stock prices were greeted with ridicule. Few watched foreign stock markets. Fewer still believed that what was happening around the world had any bearing on the fate of the U.S. stock market. In the fall of 1982, however, the emerging optimism, so evident on world markets, suddenly began to pierce the veil of gloom in the United States. The Dow Jones Industrial Average shot to a new record high, launching what was to become a long and magnificent bull market with sharply higher stock prices. But U.S. pessimism didn't go away. It slid into the background, where it lurked in seething anger until October 1987. It then emerged with a vengeance to remind everyone that the forecasts of a stock crash and depression were not ridiculous after all.

In 1988 corporate profits soared and stocks recovered. The pessimists were wrong about the fundamentals, but they enjoyed one victory anyway. By the end of the decade of the Eighties investors still lived in fear, not so much of a crash and depression, but of another steep fall in stock prices brought on by latent pessimism and computer-program trading. Many decided that the stock market was just too much for their nerves, so they sold their stocks and stayed out of it.

In spite of the pessimism, the crash of 1987 and the loss of so many individual investors, the surprise was that when the sun went down on the last day of 1989, price-earnings ratios on U.S. stocks were significantly higher than at the beginning of the decade. At the end of 1989, U.S. price-earnings ratios were 14.1—55 percent higher than at the end of 1980. Somehow the U.S. stock market managed to confound the pessimists and turn in a respectable performance, one that was much better than the 1970s.

The best explanation for the relatively good performance of U.S. stocks in the 1980s is that the United States became more a part of an international phenomenon than generally appreciated. Foreign buying of U.S. stocks and a more positive attitude toward stocks in other major markets had a positive impact on U.S. stock prices.

The argument over what stocks should be worth didn't end on December 31, 1989. Confidence in the future improved in the 1980s. Price-earnings ratios on European stocks, for example, rose from 6.9 in 1980 to 13.0 in 1989. Nevertheless one market, Japan, had become so optimistic that skeptics worried about a Japanese plunge that would reverse all the progress of the 1980s by leading all world stock markets back to their previous lows. At their peak in 1987, Japanese stocks sold at 64 times earnings. Thanks to rising earnings, that ratio declined to 52 by the end of 1989 but was still too high by current international or historical standards.

In the opening months of 1990 the Japanese stock market convulsed, falling 30 percent in a few months. The rest of the world, while showing signs of anxiety, didn't follow Japan's plunge. Instead of panic selling, investors from Australia to West Germany waited anxiously for the fall in Japanese stocks to run its course. These investors recognized that stock prices in Japan were too high, but did that mean that all stocks were too high?

What lies ahead for the 1990s? There is no doubt that the superoptimists in Japan led the parade to greater confidence and higher stock prices in the 1980s. They went too far and got so far out in front of the rest of the world that they had to pull back. Did the retreat on the Japanese stock market in early 1990 signal the end of rising investor confidence? Will world stock markets fall back to the extremely low price-earnings ratios of the early 1980s without the Japanese to lead the way?

These questions are critical for the U.S. stock market. If pessimists regain the upper hand, the 1990s could undo all the gains of the 1980s. It would take a huge gain in corporate profits just to hold stock prices steady if price-earnings ratios fell from 14.1 back to 9.1. Business could do well, but if investors lose confidence, stocks will suffer anyway. That, after all, is what happened in the closing years of the 1970s.

In 1990, as the Japanese stock market fell, the German stock market rose. Price-earnings ratios on German stocks increased to 19 from 10.7 at the end of 1987. The Japanese leadership was replaced by new optimists in Europe. The collapse of the Berlin Wall and the promise of a long period of sustained economic growth in Europe provided the basis for buying German stocks at high prices.

Confidence isn't apt to run away in Europe as it did in Japan. German stocks are unlikely to ever sell at 50 to 60 times earnings. But it's also unlikely that pessimists will regain control of the world stock trend. The promise of long-term economic growth as Eastern Europe is rebuilt, plus a world moving toward peace and prosperity, should keep the pessimists at bay. The gains in confidence won in the 1980s are apt to be permanent, sustaining world stock markets in the 1990s.

If the U.S. stock market has trouble keeping up with other major stock markets in the Nineties, the problem won't be lagging world investor confidence but poor performance by U.S. businesses. If U.S. companies have the help they need from a lower dollar and a shift away from too much politics, U.S. stocks should at least keep up with the world trend and might do even better. On the other hand, if U.S. after-tax corporate profits lag again in the Nineties as they did in the Eighties, U.S. stocks will have a hard time keeping pace with the world stock trend.

WHAT LIES AHEAD FOR U.S. CORPORATE PROFITS?

For the nation as a whole, there are two major considerations: (1) the dollar and (2) the deployment of our resources. The dollar is particularly important because it is key in determining the price of American goods on world markets. If our prices are too high, we will lose out to countries that produce quality products at lower prices. If our prices are low and our quality competitive, we stand a good chance of increasing our share of markets at home and abroad—that is, we have a chance if we don't throw away the opportunity by refusing to solve our fundamental problems. If we gain a price advantage by keeping the dollar low enough only to dissipate the advantage by excessive inflation at home, we will have gained nothing.

The key to future success is a shift away from spending to savings and investment. This is often said and usually taken to mean spending less on frivolous things such as the latest stereos or stylish fashions. Consumer spending accounts for two thirds of the U.S. economy. There clearly is room for some change in consumer habits, but it's wrong to look at U.S. consumers as wild spendthrifts. The Japanese, for example, have profited by selling things to U.S. consumers at a profit. If we had been able to keep those profits at home, no one would today be arguing in favor of less consumer spending because we'd be happy that consumers spend and business prospers. The reason we lament the low U.S. savings rate is that too much of our consumer profits are ending up in foreign countries. What we really need is to make sure that U.S. business regains its competitive edge so that future consumer spending will produce after-tax corporate profits at home. It would do the United States little good if consumers spent less and saved more if, at the same time, foreign business took more of the U.S. markets away from U.S. business. What we would gain on additional savings would be lost to more profits ending up in foreign pockets.

In the 1980s the United States deployed valuable resources to make military weapons. In the 1990s that will change, but two other critical issues will rise to take its place—health care and education. The United States spends more per pupil on education than either Germany or Japan. In spite of the higher spending, our educational system doesn't produce graduates as capable in the basics, such as math and literacy, as our competitors. People are the most critical of all national resources. It isn't possible to improve standards of living, make quality products and improve the economy without well-trained, capable and motivated people. Spending more on education but getting less cuts to the heart of the issue for the 1990s.

To regain our competitive edge, we need both capital for investment and capable people to produce better products. When we spend more and get less, we lose twice. Our capital is reduced and we still don't have the trained, motivated people we need. Meanwhile Germany and Japan win twice. They spend less, so they have more to invest and they get better results, namely, highly trained and motivated people.

When we say the United States needs to spend less and invest more, we don't mean for consumers to tighten their belts. What we mean is that the United States must find a way to improve the results we get from the dollars we spend.

It is said that 70 percent of all U.S. high-school graduates cannot go to college. The reason is that there aren't enough colleges to take more than 30 percent of the graduates. This isn't peculiar to the United States; it's true the world over. The Europeans and Japanese have addressed the issue of training beyond high school for those that won't go to college. In Europe there are government-sponsored vocational schools. High-school graduates in Switzerland, for example, cannot just go and apply for bank positions. First they must attend vocational school and then they serve as apprentices. In Japan the need for vocational training is taken care of by business, but in the United States little has been done to address this fundamental issue. Instead of looking at the basics of proper training, we look at the dollars and cents of the educational question.

As the 1990s began, the popular cry unfortunately was for more spending on education. If politicians answer that cry, we could end up spending more and still not get the results we desperately need. Spending more on education but still getting less would make the U.S. international competitive position worse, not better.

The same is true when it comes to spending on health care. If we continue to spend 12 percent of the economy on health care while our competition spends 6 percent, we will have a growing competitive problem. A 6-percent difference is too much for a nation that started out the 1990s in less than a solid competitive position. If we spend twice as much on health care, much less money will be available to spend on improving factories, products and technology.

In the 1970s and 1980s the United States fell behind in capital investment because we spent too much on defense. While we made missiles, bombs and guns, our competitors made cars, television sets and other products. By 1989 this disadvantage was well understood. Moves to reduce defense spending were well entrenched by the start of 1990. Less well known was the impact of excessive spending on health care, and it should have had the attention of the nation. By 1990 health-care spending was running at a rate twice that of defense spending. In fact, the excess over our competitors, at 6 percent, was just about equal to defense spending before the cuts. In other words, excessive health-care spending threatens to be just as much of a competitive drain on our national resources in the 1990s as defense was in the 1980s.

Will the United States awaken and deal effectively with health-care costs and improve the quality of education? The answer will hopefully be yes, but you never know in advance. These two issues, more than any others, are likely to determine the general course of U.S. corporate profits in the 1990s.

There were positive signs as the 1980s came to a close. The U.S. personal savings pool more than doubled from 1987 to 1989. In 1987 the total annual savings pool increased by $101.8 billion, or 3.2 percent of personal income. In 1989 the savings pool grew by $204.4 billion, or 5.4 percent of personal income. These figures suggest that American spending and savings habits were changing. If the savings rate rises a bit more and returns to its old early-1980s average of 7 percent, there will be enough savings to change the financial landscape. With personal income rising, a 7-percent savings rate would mean a savings pool of more than $300 billion a year within a year or two. That would make it easier for the United States to finance its deficit as well as the savings and loan bail-out. A growing U.S. savings pool would also increase confidence in the United States.

Another area of improvement was the trade deficit. From $152.1 billion in 1987, the U.S. trade deficit shrank to $109.0 billion in 1989. The dollar's long slide from its 1985 peak made U.S. goods competitive, and U.S. business took advantage of the situation. The upward march of the European currencies in late 1989 and early 1990 added to U.S. competitiveness. If there is a rise in the Japanese yen, U.S. business will be in a good position to start the new decade.

HOW WILL U.S. INVESTORS REACT
IF THE DOLLAR FALLS?

The U.S. stock market hasn't always greeted a lower dollar with enthusiasm. In fact, the opposite was usually the case in the 1970s and 1980s. Americans looked at the dollar as the score in an international game. When the dollar went down, they assumed the United States was losing.

In the 1960s the dollar was king. One U.S. dollar bought four German marks, four Swiss francs and three hundred Japanese yen. Everything in Europe was cheap for Americans. We liked it that way! The strong dollar was our reward for having helped Europe and Japan rebuild. It was a symbol of all our success.

When President Nixon cut the link between the dollar and gold in 1971, the dollar began to fall. It fell each year for ten consecutive years, finally hitting bottom at the end of 1979.

At first the U.S. stock market didn't notice. Corporate profits sagged in 1970, and the Dow fell to 753. Attention was focused on the familiar—profits and stock prices. Profits recovered in 1971 and continued to climb to a 1974 peak; the Dow also recovered, reaching 1,052 in 1973. Severing the link between the dollar and gold plus a falling dollar didn't seem to bother the stock market too much.

Then, from 1,052 in 1973, the Dow began to sink. In 1974 the U.S. stock market plunged, having been battered by rising oil prices, beaten by the fear of a never-ending oil shortage and stunned by a steep fall in the dollar. In late 1974 the Dow finally found a floor at 577.6, which was 45 percent below the 1973 peak.

American investors would never be the same again. The world of investing, as it had been for over two decades since World War II, came to an end. The extreme confidence in the ability of American business to compete that marked the U.S. stock market of the 1960s was replaced by its opposite—pessimism. Stocks that once sold for 50 times earnings plunged to extreme lows.

From the depressed low in 1974, the Dow fought to recover, managing to edge above the 1,000 mark again in 1976. But U.S. investors were so discouraged that the Dow was not able to hold at 1,000 that it soon began to sink again. The popular Dow Jones Industrial Average closed the 1970s below 900.

During the 1970s profits reported by the companies in the Dow Jones Industrial Average rose from $51.02 per share in 1970 to $124.46 per share in 1979. That was a dramatic improvement in earnings. U.S. business benefited from the ten-year slide in the dollar, but investors didn't see it that way. In 1979 the Dow Industrial Average sold at 6.8 times earnings compared with 15 to 16 times earnings in the early Seventies. There were all sorts of explanations offered at the time for the extremely low prices paid for U.S. stocks.

Such explanations included "the earnings are puffed up by inflation" and "the good earnings can't last because the world is running out of oil, and business will crumble when oil reaches $100 a barrel."

With the benefit of hindsight, we can see that President Nixon would have been smarter to raise the price of gold first to say $100 an ounce and thereby officially sanction a major devaluation of the dollar before setting gold and the dollar free to float on world markets. A lot of the inflation of the 1970s was caused by the fact that the dollar kept falling year after year. Had the dollar plunged and then leveled out for a few years, there would have been a burst of inflation followed by a return to more normal conditions. Investors would have been shocked but probably less confused.

As it was, politicians, economists, investors and American business leaders watched in disbelief as the dollar kept sinking. Each year they would say "Don't worry. The dollar will come back." After several consecutive years of disappointment, they became disheartened and lost confidence not only in the currency markets but in stock markets, bond markets and in the ability of Americans to cope.

The kindest analysis is to say that Americans were caught by surprise. They didn't fully appreciate the extent of the dollar's overvaluation in 1970. For that reason, they didn't anticipate the need for a significant devaluation of the currency. But the truth is that Americans simply didn't want the currency to go down. They didn't want to accept their loss of energy independence and acknowledge that Germany and Japan had become major competitors.

Finally, at the end of the 1970s American investors threw in the towel and concluded that the United States and the rest of the world must be headed for a repeat of 1929 and the Great Depression that followed. In effect, by our collective investment attitude, we said that if America had lost so much, the rest of the world must be in deep trouble. If we could not continue to be the dominant economy, we would prove that our power had not diminished by leading the world into economic chaos and catastrophe.

Our general attitude and overreaction to the dollar's devaluation in the Seventies didn't change with the start of the Eighties. Fascination with a possible stock market crash and depression was still alive and well and expressed itself in the October 1987 stock market plunge. However, our awareness of the dollar's importance did improve. By the mid-1980s American investors realized that there was a connection between U.S. interest rates, inflation and the dollar's value on world currency markets. When the dollar was strong, markets anticipated lower interest rates. When the dollar fell, markets convulsed in fear of higher interest rates. This overly simplistic view of the connection between interest rates and the dollar left investors with the feeling that the old impressions about the dollar were correct. A falling dollar was considered a negative in the 1970s because it symbolized the loss of American economic might, and in the 1980s it was considered a negative because it meant rising interest rates and trouble for U.S. stock and bond markets.

As late as 1989 the markets were only dimly aware of the notion that the dollar's exchange rate was critical in fending off foreign competition and making U.S. business competitive. That is likely to change in the 1990s. American awareness of the currency markets and how they impact costs, competitiveness and corporate profits should continue to evolve in the Nineties.

If the German mark remains strong due to capital flows into Europe and the yen gains strength due to Japan's strong competitive position, the dollar will, by definition, be pushed down. Before the 1990s are over, Americans will probably realize that the currency market is a two-way street. There can be benefits from both strong and weak currencies. We may continue to wish for the day when the U.S. economy supports a strong dollar but may also learn to appreciate the benefits of a low currency. A low dollar may make travel to faraway vacation spots more expensive, but it also makes U.S. goods more competitive, helps fend off foreign competition at home, lifts corporate profits and aids us in the struggle to restore our economic strength.

Before too many years of the Nineties slip by, the U.S. stock market is likely to change and react to the dollar's impact on corporate profits as well as on interest rates and inflation. Don't be shocked to see U.S. stock prices rise in the Nineties if the dollar is low enough to help U.S. business and fall if the dollar becomes too strong.

Investors in Europe are able to assess the impact of currency market movements on not only interest rates and inflation but on the profits of individual companies as well. This is something Americans have had trouble doing because of lack of experience with foreign currencies. In the 1970s and the 1980s American investors learned a lot. In the 1990s they will undoubtedly show the same savvy ability to assess the complex effects of changes in the dollar as do their counterparts in other countries.

Individual investors who haven't taken the time to understand the currency markets will have trouble. They can expect to be confused and befuddled. Understanding the interaction of currency markets, business profits and stock prices will be a prerequisite for good performance in the years ahead.

DEALING WITH UNCERTAINTY ABOUT THE FUTURE FOR AMERICAN BUSINESS

American business began the 1990s with both significant opportunity and daunting challenges. The dollar was down far enough versus the European currencies to give U.S. business a meaningful price advantage. The threat of Japanese competition remained, especially because the yen was too low (but that is subject to change). The yen rose sharply in 1985 and can do it again. A rising yen would be the final touch on the opportunity side of the issue.

The challenges of rising health-care costs, a tough tax law and a less than satisfactory educational system were also there at the start of the 1990s. The future was hardly clear. In fact, the presence of so much opportunity and so many handicaps made it impossible to determine the course for U.S. business in the 1990s. American business could prosper, as it did in the 1950s and 1960s, or the opposite could be the case. After a brief period of rising profits (thanks to a lower dollar), American business might again fall prey to all its handicaps and end the decade with inadequate corporate profits.

A U.S. STOCK MARKET STRATEGY FOR THE 1990s

You definitely want to own U.S. stocks in the 1990s. They could be a source of enormous profits. However, a stock market strategy for the 1990s has to take into account the possibility that we won't arrest the rise in health-care costs, improve our educational system or save and invest more in time to close the growing competitive gap. U.S. business profits, overall, may not keep up with the world corporate profits trend in the 1990s.

The solution to the dilemma of a world headed towards peace, prosperity and economic growth and an America still clouded by uncertainty is to focus on individual U.S. companies rather than on the market as a whole. Don't worry as much about the trend for the popular averages, such as the Dow Jones Industrial Average, as about the fundamentals of a handful of chosen U.S. companies.

The nation may not move fast enough, but many individual companies will find ways of coping under adverse circumstances, developing new products and successfully competing on world markets. The United States is so large that even when things aren't good for the nation as a whole, there are still many individual companies that prosper. If you succeed in picking just two or three prosperous companies in the 1990s, your portfolio will grow no matter how we address the challenges and opportunities that face the nation.

CHOOSING U.S. STOCKS FOR THE 1990s

Merger, takeover or deal stocks were the rage in the last years of the 1980s. In 1990 the bankruptcy of the junk-bond king, Drexel Burnham Lambert, reduced the amount of financing available for takeovers. There still were deals made, but they tended to involve foreign companies buying American companies. Without daily news releases of another takeover, the U.S. stock market fell on hard times in the early days of 1990; and without instant profits, many investors decided to sit on the sidelines holding cash. Takeovers, mergers and deals may continue in the 1990s, but is this a reliable way to invest?

Low-priced stocks attract attention. Cheap stocks in good companies are tempting targets for corporate raiders and other companies looking for a less expensive route to expansion. When a whole market (e.g., the United States in the 1980s) languishes behind the rest of the world, takeovers and mergers tend to increase.

There were hundreds of companies (especially in the second half of the 1980s) whose stocks suddenly shot to higher prices when a buy-out deal, merger or takeover was announced. In a few cases individual investors who had been holding their shares for decades became instant millionaires. Predicting which companies will be next in line for quick profits through merger or takeover isn't easy. The buyers want to pay as little as possible and therefore keep their intentions secret as long as possible. Once a proposal is made public, everyone knows that a deal is coming and the stock rises quickly.

Analysts tried to formulate the characteristics that make one company more attractive as a takeover target than another, but this didn't really help. Being attractive is not enough; you need to have a buyer. No formula was ever found that would identify a match between a buyer of a company and the target.

If you had advance information about a deal, you could obviously buy the stock of the target company and make a fortune. The laws of the United States make such "inside" trading illegal, but that didn't stop people from trying. Ivan Boesky went to jail for violating the insider-trading rules and for making a fortune with advance information about mergers. He also had to give most of the profits back in the form of fines.

Making money is the primary objective of investing. However, there is a second and equally important goal—staying out of jail in the process. Investors want to profit legally and to be able to keep their profits and enjoy them in freedom. Unfortunately, there is no safe, legal way of knowing in advance which companies will be taken over next. As a practical matter, this means you have to find some other way of profiting from American stocks in the 1990s. The U.S. stock market may continue to languish in the Nineties, and mergers and takeovers may also continue. But unless you are lucky or willing to tempt the law and risk a jail sentence, you are best off not relying on deal stocks to produce portfolio profits.

There are other ways of making money in carefully selected U.S. stocks. For example, there are always pockets of excellence in American industry. Compaq Computer produced spectacular profits for shareholders in the 1980s by beating not only other U.S. computer makers but the Germans and Japanese as well. How did Compaq succeed where others failed? They succeeded by excellence in product design, controlling manufacturing costs, being responsive to the needs of customers and having a capable management and motivated work force. Why can't all other U.S. companies follow the Compaq example? The answer is that there aren't enough capable people or risk takers to go around. We may not be able to field an entire national team of excellent companies, but we do have enough resources to produce some.

Compaq is an example of what is called a growth stock. Sales and earnings grew rapidly, and the stock price rose accordingly. Growth in sales and earnings isn't the only route to profits in American stocks, however. The prospects of established companies seldom proceed in a smooth line. Even well-managed companies experience ups and downs in their fortunes. Sometimes the downs come after a well-intentioned management decision goes the wrong way. At other times, the profits fall due to economic trends beyond management's control. In either case, when profits fall, investors frequently overreact. Once in a while a fall in profits coincides with a weak stock market to create an outstanding opportunity.

Service Merchandise, a nationally recognized U.S. retail chain, went on an expansion binge through acquisition. Unfortunately, the purchased companies ended up with more problems than the management of Service Merchandise anticipated. As is usually the case, management took steps to correct the mistakes. Just as the corrective action was about to pay off (but while the earnings and stock price were still down), the crash of 1987 came along. Service Merchandise's stock price plunged. Within a year, the recovery in the stock market (plus a recovery in Service Merchandise's profits) pushed the stock significantly higher. Investors who bought after the 1987 crash multiplied their investment by five in a relatively short time.

Compaq Computer and Service Merchandise are examples of two legal strategies for selecting U.S. stocks that can produce extraordinary profits. One is to look for growth and the other is to invest in recovery.

HOW DO YOU FIND GROWTH STOCKS?

You don't have to find many growth stocks to do very well. If you had only found Compaq and invested $10,000 at $10 a share, you would have multiplied your money by nine in a few years.

To grow, a company needs to have a product in demand that it can make at a cost low enough to earn a meaningful profit. What products are in demand? Some are purchased by business, and they can be more difficult for the ordinary investor to spot. Others are sold to consumers. As a consumer, you stand as good a chance of spotting them as any professional.

The search for growth stocks begins by looking for products that are in demand. The next step is to look carefully at a company to make sure it can make the products at a profit. The final step is to look at the competition and the stock price. Remember that even with a growth stock, you want to buy low and not after the whole world has already discovered the company.

The quest for growth stocks is a never-ending process of watching the world around you and then investigating the financial aspects of what you see. You may be lucky and find several in a decade. Then again, you may look and look, research, study and never find one at the right price. Frustrating though the search may be, it's worthwhile because if you find one, the profits on a single growth stock will pay for all the endless hours of work.

RECOVERY STOCKS ARE EASIER

Making money in stocks that fall too far and later recover is easier. The process begins by developing a manageable list of companies that you will follow.

The secret to making money when a stock falls too far is to have studied the company over a long period of time in advance. When a stock plunges, you either won't have much time to act or else the newspapers will be chock-full of negative articles about the company. Either way, you must be confident and decisive.

How many companies can you follow? Reading quarterly and annual reports is time-consuming. Don't take on more than you can handle with the time available. Then read the reports and become familiar with the management, the business and the problems faced by the company. Make no mistake: all businesses face problems. From time to time even the best companies run into periods of slow sales and slumping profits. That's what you are waiting for. When sales growth slows or profits decline, investors become discouraged and often overreact. The selling can drive the stock price down so low that you can buy and make a significant profit when business improves and the stock recovers.

If you know a company and have followed its stock for months or years, you will be in a position to take advantage of the market when the price falls too low. General Public Utilities (NYSE: GPU), the company that owns and operates the nuclear power plant at Three Mile Island, is a classic case of a recovery situation that was easy to find and produced handsome profits. The nuclear accident at Three Mile Island made national headlines. The company's stock plunged, falling from $20 to a low of $3¼. Investors panicked on the early reports, fearing there would be claims for personal injury as a result of the accident that could run into the hundreds of millions of dollars.

The stock didn't stay down for long. It immediately bounced back to $7.00 a share. After the bounce, the stock reversed course again and slowly sank back to $4.00 over a period of several months. Between 1980, when the accident made headlines, and 1984, when the stock began a new upward move, there was plenty of time for investment research. In 1983 General Public Utilities' earnings began to recover, and by year-end it was clear that the company had survived the blow from the Three Mile Island accident. On a fundamental basis, the stock looked attractive. From $8.00 a share in 1984, it climbed steadily, reaching $46 at the end of 1989. In addition to handsome capital gains, investors were rewarded when the company's directors reinstated the dividend.

The story of General Public Utilities makes two things clear: (1) it's easy to find recovery stocks; just watch the headlines for companies in trouble, and (2) there's no need to rush into a stock. If you had been following General Public Utilities in advance of the accident (unlikely), you could have bought stock after the initial plunge and doubled your money quickly. But the real profits came not from a smart trade but from patiently following the company and its stock until the fundamentals improved. If you didn't buy the stock on the initial bad news and patiently followed developments until 1984, you would have paid $8.00 for the stock—more than twice the low. But from then on, you had an investment that proved to be among the best in the second half of the 1980s.

BUY BOTH GROWTH AND RECOVERY STOCKS

Make a list of companies to follow and continually keep your mind open for potential growth stocks. Use both of these strategies in your quest for profits in U.S. stocks in the 1990s.

Don't rush out and buy stocks. Develop your list or universe of companies you will follow. Then take your time, be patient and get to know the companies and the way their stocks act on the market. Invest only after you are convinced that you have a stock at a price low enough to load the odds in your favor.

Following this approach should keep you out of jail and in the black on your U.S. stock portfolio in the years ahead. If the United States manages to keep the dollar down and solve its fundamental problems, your portfolio will do even better. Either way you are likely to enjoy significant profits in your personal portfolio.

OPPORTUNITY #13: PICKING YOUR FIRST RECOVERY STOCK

Set aside a portion of your savings, $2,500 should be enough, to invest in a recovery stock. What you are looking for is a stock in a sound company that has fallen out of favor. The stock price and the company's business are different. The stock price is supposed to move up and down in sync with the business, but in the real world of real markets that is seldom what happens. More often than not stocks move up and down based on investor sentiment rather than changes in the company's fortunes. It is not uncommon for a stock to plunge even though the company is financially sound. That is what you are looking for, a stock that has plunged in a company that is financially sound.

Scan the financial papers for stocks at new lows to find a candidate. When you see a stock that looks right, call the company and ask for the recent quarterly report and any news releases. Don't be shy! Ask the company's spokesperson if there are any fundamental problems. In this day and age of legal disclosure requirements and shareholder lawsuits, companies are usually quick to point out their problems.

Armed with a newspaper, a telephone, your wits and patience you should have no trouble finding a low-priced stock in a sound company that will provide you with above-average profits over the following year or so.

There is nothing quite like success to inspire confidence. Once you have made a profit on a recovery stock of this type, you will be ready to go the next step and look for companies that have fallen on hard times and are struggling to recover. Such situations are more difficult to analyze, but these are the stocks that can produce extraordinary profits for savvy investors.

CHAPTER

11

The Future

Professor Joseph Campbell said it best: "Life is no longer an adventure to be sought, just a series of risks to be avoided." This is how Professor Campbell, psychologist, philosopher and close observer of man's inner character, described life in the 1980s. His words have the ring of absolute truth. We don't enjoy the adventure of living. We continually look for risks and have no trouble finding them in drugs, street violence, nuclear power-plant meltdowns, cancer-causing chemicals, food, high cholesterol, the greenhouse effect, pollution, inflation, stock market crashes and, of course, the ever-present risk of a coming depression. What a shame. What an awful way to look at the world around us. Don't we realize that the world has always been a risky place?

If we didn't have man's destructive inclinations to worry about, we could worry about earthquakes, volcanic eruptions and meteors. They have threatened the earth, spoiled the environment and caused mass extinctions in the past. Now that we have conquered polio, smallpox and put men in space, perhaps we don't feel so threatened by nature. Maybe that's why we have turned toward our collective selves to find our list of unacceptable, unavoidable risks.

As individuals, we cannot expect to change the world overnight. Society and the financial markets are apt to remain stuck with their dismal approach to life for the foreseeable future. But that doesn't mean we have to fall in with the pessimists. We can keep the adventure in our personal lives and open ourselves to another possibility: that we might be entering a time of increased prosperity.

Fifty years ago the world was headed into World War II. Once the destruction ended, a 20-year period of prosperity began as the United States profited from the reconstruction of Europe and Japan. World War III didn't materialize. Instead, whole regions of the world were destroyed by the oppressive policies imposed by Communist regimes. The process was different. There were fewer guns and bombs used, but the destruction is nevertheless real. The economies of Eastern Europe, the Soviet Union and China, for example, are in ruins. They represent another opportunity for prosperity through reconstruction.

The gloom-and-doom crowd admits there is need for reconstruction but say it will never happen. They could be right. The world has missed plenty of opportunities in the past. Then again, the gloom crowd could be dead wrong. In fact, the odds are that there will be reconstruction, and it has already started. West Germany has taken East Germany under its economic wing. If that succeeds and both East and West Germans enjoy greater prosperity, there will probably be a rush from other countries to participate in the growth.

There is more. Europe has moved in the direction of reducing red tape and barriers to trade by 1992. Economists believe that this will unleash economic growth. When Europe 1992 is linked with the economic unification of the two Germanys, the future begins to look a good deal brighter.

It could be that we will have another depression some day in the future. But the evidence is growing that the next depression is a long way off. In the meantime the world may be headed into a new long-term up cycle, one that could produce extraordinary profits for investors.

NIKOLAI KONDRATIEFF WAS RIGHT AFTER ALL

In the 1920s Kondratieff observed a tendency for economic cycles to repeat themselves roughly every 50 years (see Figure 11-1). He predicted both a financial panic and a steep economic decline well ahead of the stock market crash of 1929 and the Great Depression of the 1930s. For a short time his work attracted attention. Then the arrival of World War II snuffed out interest in economic patterns.

In the 1970s Kondratieff's ideas resurfaced. His 50-year cycle theory became the basis for popular predictions of a repeat of the

Figure 11–1. Kondratieff's 50-Year Economic Cycle

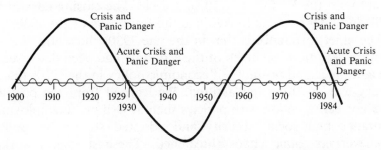

Source: Harry D. Schultz, *Panics and Crashes* (New York: Pinnacle Books, 1975).

crash of 1929. When the Dow Jones Industrial Average refused to plunge in 1979, prognosticators of economic gloom weren't discouraged. They explained that no theory, not even Kondratieff's, is perfect and claimed that the timetable must be slightly off. Finally, when the Dow fell from 2,700 to 1,700 in October 1987, they cheered. This was the long-awaited crash.

Well into 1988 the crash cult argued that we were headed into a depression. But they were disappointed again. The year after the crash of 1987 turned out to be one of the best in the decade for both the economy and corporate profits.

It may come as a shock to all those who waited expectantly for an exact repeat of the 1929 stock market crash and depression, but the Kondratieff cycle was repeated. There was a stock market crash in the 1970s and a 1980s equivalent of a depression right on schedule.

If we have already been through a stock market crash and depression, why are so many economists, market analysts and investors afraid these terrifying events lie ahead? The answer is twofold. First, the repeat of the 1929 crash and depression wasn't so obvious that everyone recognized it. Second, just as it was in the 1930s, climbing out of a depression isn't easy. In 1939 unemployment in the United States was higher than it was in the depths of the depression in 1932. Without the arrival of war in Europe, the U.S. economy might have stayed in an economic trough in the 1940s. Aircraft orders from France and England lifted the U.S. economy in the early 1940s. The road back from dismal economic failure is long, hard and fraught with risk. The frightening economic challenges that lingered in 1989—such as the banking crisis, high interest rates, the credit crunch, the trade deficit and the federal deficit—are consistent with the Kondratieff 50-year cycle. The closing days of the 1980s in many respects looked like the final days of the 1930s.

The chief difference is that in the late 1930s the world was still fighting deflation. So much of the economy had been destroyed by the ignorance and brutality of economic policy in the 1920s that recovery was anything but assured. We learned from the past and took corrective action with policies such as welfare, unemployment insurance and social security and adopted stimulative policies whenever economic chaos threatened. These strategies worked. They prevented the 1982 recession from destroying so much of the economy that a depression developed. But the cure produced a different problem—inflation. At the end of the 1980s we faced the challenge of the lasting effects of the great recession and the real threat of reversal if inflation got out of control.

If the 1930s and the 1980s are compared, but with the deflation/inflation difference in mind, it's easier to see that the Kondratieff cycles are still evident. The present is always different from the past until you take a closer look. Then you see the similarities.

We could slip back, just as we did in the late 1930s. Deflation tightened its grip on the economy in 1938. Prices fell 1.9 percent that year and 1.4 percent in 1939. In 1988 the rate of inflation rose not only in the United States but in other major countries as well. It was inflation that was our downfall in this cycle, and inflation could wreck recovery as well. That's really what terrifies so many people.

There is no World War II on the horizon to generate orders, sales and profits. The world is instead headed down the road to peace. That is new, different and therefore a source of uncertainty. When faced with uncertainty, economists, politicians and investors have two choices. They can look to the future with confidence or assume the worst and live with anxiety. Confidence in the United States was unfortunately at a low ebb as the 1980s came to a close. The result was continuing anxiety and fear of a major economic catastrophe in the 1990s.

The popular focus for anxiety in 1990 still was the last great stock market crash and depression. Few understood that we had already been through the equivalents of crash and depression. While the anxiety was misplaced, there was good reason to be fearful. Peace might not bring the instant economic rewards that war did in the 1940s.

Peace, however, is still consistent with Kondratieff's theory. What is often overlooked in thinking about economic cycles is the principle of opposites. Fifty years ago the world was headed toward war. Today peace is the global initiative. In cycle theory, an opposite development fulfills the expectation. Peace in the 1990s, the opposite of war in the 1940s, fulfills Kondratieff's cycle requirements.

THE STOCK MARKET CRASHED
RIGHT ON SCHEDULE

The Dow Jones Industrial Average of U.S. stocks started the 1970s at about 800 and finished the decade at the same level. On the surface that doesn't look like the 1929 crash at all. In the 1920s the Dow Jones Industrial Average started at 100, climbed to 381 in 1929 and then plunged. It finished the decade at 200 but didn't stop falling until 1932, when the Dow hit 42. There was a plunge of 89 percent from the peak at 381 to the 1932 low at 42. That's what a crash is supposed to look like.

The problem with history is that the second time around there is always a difference, a new twist. To see the parallel, you must take the difference into account. The chief difference between the 1920s and the 1970s was that by the 1970s we were no longer on a gold standard. The dollar was free to rise and fall on world currency markets. The financial tensions had two ways to be released: in stock prices and in the currency markets. The dollar fell precipitously in the 1970s. For example, it fell from 4.10 to 1 versus the Swiss franc to 1.59 to 1 by the last day of the 1970s. The dollar lost 61 percent of its value on foreign exchange markets.

If the currency market and the stock market are taken together, a picture quite similar to the great crash of 1929 emerges. In the late 1960s the Dow peaked at 1,000. In terms of Swiss francs, that was 4,100. At 800 on the Dow in 1979 (when the dollar was at 1.59), the Dow in terms of Swiss francs had fallen to 1,272. Combining the two (the Dow plus the dollar), there was a fall of 69 percent. While not exactly the same as the fall in the 1929 crash, that decline in the 1970s was enough to qualify as a crash by any definition.

From the low in 1932 the U.S. stock market reversed course and began a long climb that culminated in 1937. Likewise, the Dow began to climb in 1982 and ended its rise in 1987, right on the same schedule. In 1937 the stock market plunged again, falling from 194 to 100, for a loss of 48 percent. Fifty years later in 1987, the Dow fell from 2,700 to 1,700, for a loss of 37 percent.

What was missed by so many market observers was the fact that the stock market crash of 1987 had a precedent in 1937. In the closing years of the 1930s, just as in the final years of the 1980s, the U.S. stock market recovered but ran out of momentum as the new decade began.

This look at the U.S. stock market reveals that the parallels between 50 years ago and recent history are in fact remarkable.

THE SIMILARITIES DON'T END
WITH THE STOCK MARKET

The economy slumped in the early 1930s and hit bottom in 1932, a time now described as the Great Depression. The U.S. and world economy also slumped in the early 1980s, hitting bottom in the recession of 1982. That recession has been correctly described as the worst since the depression. In other words, the recession of 1982 was the present-day equivalent of the Great Depression.

Just as with the stock market, there were economic differences in the 1980s. We learn from history, make adjustments and do things differently the second time around. After the depression of the 1930s, social security and unemployment insurance were introduced. Those programs were in place in 1980, and they cushioned millions of Americans from the economic downturn. Without social security and unemployment insurance, the recession of 1982 might have been a full-blown depression.

There were other differences. In the 1930s J.P. Morgan was asked by the British for a loan to pay unemployed workers. He refused, saying that to make such payments would eradicate the natural curative process of economic cycles, and he was supported by U.S. government policy. It is unthinkable today, but in the 1930s it was believed that human suffering and extreme poverty were natural and to be welcomed. If Morgan and other economic leaders in the 1930s had the wisdom of the 1980s, the Great Depression might have been just a severe recession, as was 1982.

The fact that we learned important lessons from the Great Depression doesn't mean that we didn't make mistakes in the 1980s. When you make an economic adjustment to head off one problem, you often move too far and head toward an opposite but equally threatening problem. In the 1930s the world plunged into deflation.

In the 1980s the opposite, inflation, was the challenge. By preserving consumers' buying power through expansive monetary policies, federal government deficits, social security, welfare and unemployment, we also preserved inflation.

Inflation came down from double-digit rates in 1982 to the single digits in the mid-1980s but remained stubbornly high. In 1986 the Federal Reserve decided the way to curb inflation was to slow down the rate of U.S. money growth. The Fed was quite successful in its efforts. By 1987 the rate of growth of a popular measure of the money supply, M-2, was down to 3.5 percent. That was a dramatic change. M-2 had grown at 10 percent in 1981, 11.8 percent in 1983 and 9.5 percent as late as 1986.

The plunge in money growth led to a chorus of dire predictions. A book entitled *The Depression of 1990* made the best-seller list. Its basis was slow money growth. The author argued that slow money growth would lead us into a period of deflation and depression. This theory, plus the stock market crash in 1987, kept alive the fear that we might be headed for a repeat of the Great Depression.

In 1988, the year after money growth slowed, the economy did what was supposed to be impossible. Economic growth and corporate profits increased. Slow money growth didn't have the predicted impact. The explanation for this was to be found in yet another difference between the 1930s and the 1980s. Fifty years earlier the United States was the dominant world economy. We were the world's largest creditor, and what happened here affected other economies. By the second half of the 1980s the United States had lost its dominant position, and Japan had become the world's largest creditor. What happened outside the United States had an impact on us. The world had turned upside down in the 1980s. Those who looked to the past, concentrated on what was happening in the United States and ignored the rest of the world came up wrong in their predictions.

In 1988 world trade grew at a remarkable 8.5-percent rate; the ten-year average was 4.5 percent. That overrode the slow U.S. money growth and pulled the economy along to greater growth. In the 1930s our hard-hearted policies dragged the world down into a depression. However, in the 1980s the U.S. economy was rescued by a buoyant international economy.

After the stock market crash of 1987, economists at the Deutsche Bank in Germany asked whether in 1987 we were headed into a depression. While they didn't come to the conclusion that we had already been through the 1980s equivalent of a depression, they did highlight the major differences between the 1920s and the 1980s. They explained that in the 1920s we did just about everything wrong. We loosened monetary policy in the late 1920s when we should have tightened it. Then as depression gripped the world, central banks tightened when they should have loosened. From that dismal experience, we learned important lessons. Those lessons allowed us to fend off a stock market crash and depression in the 1980s.

The idea that we are living through a familiar economic cycle provides a useful perspective. From the experience of the late 1930s, we can see how difficult it was to recover from the depression. There is no way of knowing how the world economy might have fared without the economic benefits of World War II. If the world had been at peace in 1940, economic progress might have been slower, although we will never know for sure. The important point is to recognize that depressions—and therefore deep recessions— create long-lasting problems. True recovery requires drastic action. In the 1940s it was war, followed by the remarkable Marshall Plan, which finally lifted the U.S. and world economy out of the depths and back on a track of economic growth and prosperity.

In the 1990s we will first have to struggle through the last of the effects of the long economic down cycle that began in 1970. Once that has been accomplished, the stage will be set for another long-term up cycle.

THE STRUGGLE FOR RECOVERY

The popular press has heralded the longest economic recovery in postwar history. While technically correct, this description lacks perspective and is confusing. Inflation fools us all. When we see more cash in the bank, we feel richer even though we know that in real (or after-inflation) terms, the cash doesn't buy as much as we think. Because inflation "saved" us from a depression in the early 1980s, it's difficult for us to see the 1980s for what they really were. The Dow Jones Industrial Average didn't keep up with inflation in the 1970s and 1980s combined. Neither did most American pocketbooks. In real, or after-inflation, terms the United States in 1989 was still well behind compared with the early 1970s or late 1960s.

What we thought was a "recovery" in truth was no more than the effects of inflation.

The real recovery is still in the future. To get there, we first have to bring inflation under control and keep it that way for a long period of time so that we can finally begin to enjoy the benefits of real economic growth. The risk is that in our struggle with inflation, we will produce not a lasting recovery but another setback, a repeat of the recession of 1982.

ONE WAY TO SEE THE PROBLEM: THE GREAT AMERICAN CREDIT CRUNCH

In the dictionary of terrifying financial terms the words *credit crunch* rank not far behind *depression, market crash* or *hyperinflation* in impact and power. The fuel for the engine of economic growth is credit, the ability to borrow money on reasonable terms. If we shut off credit, the economy will eventually grind down to a recession or worse.

For years the United States worried not about too little credit but about the opposite: rapid growth of debt. Total U.S. debt—government, consumer and business—soared in the 1980s, reaching record-high levels. In early 1990 two major events marked the end of the long period of easy credit. The United States went quickly from easy credit to something frighteningly close to a credit crunch.

The first major event was the bankruptcy of Drexel Burnham Lambert, the giant of the junk-bond market. Junk, or high-yielding bonds, had been used to provide money for a wide range of business purposes, including the takeover of whole companies. Proliferation of junk bonds contributed in a major way to the growth of debt in the United States, especially in the second half of the 1980s. That came to an abrupt halt when Drexel, the junk-bond leader, filed for bankruptcy in early 1990.

The second major event was a policy change in the way federal bank examiners look at U.S. commercial banks. In 1990 the U.S. commercial banking system was rocked by a series of huge losses reported by commercial banks. For example, Bank of New England, the second largest bank in New England, lost billions. Federal bank regulators had to move into the bank to make sure that losses to taxpayers through federally guaranteed deposits were minimized. Extensive problems with loans on commercial real estate and condominium construction loans were the source of the trouble. In response, the federal regulators methodically went from bank to bank making a detailed examination of the loan portfolios. They used new and tough credit standards. Loans that were up-to-date on both principal and interest were classified as doubtful if there was any reason to think the borrower might default in the future. As the president of one large New England bank said, "We have a new class of loans—performing and nonperforming loans."

U.S. commercial banks were suddenly faced with a new set of credit rules. They had to be sure that new loans would meet the tough federal standards and were short of capital because so many loans had now been classified. Almost overnight it became more difficult to borrow money. Business could on longer find easy credit through the sale of junk bonds, and borrowing at the banks was equally difficult. In Massachusetts, where business was suffering due to a slowdown in the local economy dating back to early 1989, the governor got involved and pleaded with the banks not to shut off credit to business. The questions facing investors, economists, politicians and all Americans were (1) how did we get in this credit crunch mess and (2) what does it mean for the future of the economy.

The story of the credit crunch of 1990 began in the late 1970s when the Federal Reserve and Congress decided it was necessary to deregulate the U.S. banking system. In the good old days, the U.S. banking system was highly regulated. Banks were told what they could pay on deposits, and then in turn kept the cost of borrowing for home mortgages and other purposes low. However, double-digit inflation in the 1970s changed the thinking in Washington. It was concluded that the only way to bring inflation down was to raise interest rates. But raising interest rates while the banks were only allowed to pay 5$\frac{1}{4}$ percent on deposits would cause a run on the banks and the collapse of the system. Thus the banks were deregulated and allowed to pay open-market rates for deposits. (Notice how we might have marched right back into the old familiar 1930s problem of a run on the banks if the Federal Reserve hadn't remembered those dismal days of 50 years earlier. This is another example of the parallels between the 1980s and the 1930s.)

The new policy worked for a while. The great recession of 1982 was created and inflation came down, but the price was high. Savings banks were saddled with whole portfolios of low-interest-rate, long-term mortgages as their primary source of income but had to pay high interest on deposits. Whole categories of savings institutions suffered huge losses. Mercifully, interest rates came down in the mid-1980s after inflation fell to single-digit rates. That stemmed the losses but didn't solve the problem.

The U.S. savings institutions found themselves short of capital because of the losses in the early 1980s, and they were faced with stiff competition. They had to compete with money market accounts and a wide range of new financial instruments. No longer did the banks have a monopoly on deposits.

All sorts of strategies were tried in an attempt to resolve the shortage of capital among U.S. banks. Savings banks went public and sold stock to raise capital, and other banks combined their resources through mergers. In the end, the highly competitive nature of U.S. financial markets forced bankers to seek ever-riskier loans in an effort to make money. They desperately needed to make loans at interest rates higher than what they were forced to pay on deposits. Aggressive lending practices led to the savings and loan crisis of the late 1980s. In 1990 estimates of the cost of bailing out the distressed savings and loans rose to $325 billion. Until 1990 commercial banks didn't make the headlines, but they too had been feeling the heat of competition.

Our money center banks felt the pressure from Japanese banks. Japanese bankers enjoyed the benefit of a lofty stock market. They were able to raise low-cost capital through the sale of stock and used that capital to make low-interest loans to the best of international businesses. U.S. money center banks didn't have the benefit of a high stock market. In fact, U.S. bank stocks were depressed in the 1980s, and that left them at a disadvantage. Whole markets in Europe and Asia were lost to Japanese competition. When the plunge in the Japanese stock market came in 1990, it was too late to help the U.S. money center banks. The markets were lost and couldn't be easily recovered.

At home the commercial banks faced competition from the junk-bond market. Customers could raise more money through the sale of junk bonds than they could borrow from banks. The collapse of the junk-bond market, like the plunge in Japanese stocks, came too late to save the commercial banks from huge losses.

Faced with stiff competition, commercial banks adopted the same policies as their counterparts in the savings institutions: they began to lend more aggressively. The combination of excessive competition and inadequate access to low-cost capital was at the root of the problems facing both U.S. savings institutions and commercial banks in 1990.

The United States has a unique banking system, created in the 1930s to ensure banks of low-cost capital. The federal government guarantees depositors the safety of the principal of their bank deposits up to $100,000. That guarantee means that when the banks suffer, the bill ultimately is sent to the taxpayers. With hindsight, we can see the error that was made in Washington in the late 1970s. Deregulating the banks meant an end to low-cost deposits. At that point the federal deposit guarantee should have been amended. Guaranteeing deposits made sense only so long as the entire credit market was regulated. But federal deposit insurance wasn't amended. At the time no one imagined the problems that would follow by the end of the 1980s.

A bill of $325 billion for failed savings and loans was terrifying. The last thing the government wanted was another huge bill as a result of failed commercial banks. Thus federal bank examiners set out to make sure the commercial banks used high credit standards. They brought an end to aggressive lending practices. Their response is understandable. In fact, they may have had no choice under the circumstances. The United States truly couldn't afford another bill in the hundreds of billions of dollars should commercial banks go the way of the savings and loans.

For the economy, the abrupt change in lending practices was a shock. Business needs access to credit. With new tougher credit rules, many businesses were faced with the threat of bankruptcy.

In 1990 the United States faced a real credit crunch, and it wasn't the first time this had happened. In 1951, fearing that the Korean War would result in high inflation (as had been the case after World War II), the United States created a voluntary credit allocation system. Bankers joined forces and established rules for what was and was not a proper loan. Credit was tight, and the result was a steep fall in inflation. Prices rose 7.9 percent in 1951 but rose only 0.8 percent in 1953.

Starting in early 1987, the Federal Reserve aggressively fought inflation by clamping down on money growth. Not that long ago it was blithely assumed that money growth and inflation went hand in hand. By 1990, however, that assumption was called into question.

In spite of slow money growth, inflation remained stubbornly high. The probable answer to the money growth-inflation dilemma was debt. As long as debt levels rise too fast, inflation remains strong even though money growth is low. Bringing inflation down requires the same medicine it did in 1951. We need to be certain that credit is controlled and debt doesn't run wild.

Coming against a background of years of moderate-to-slow money growth, the credit crunch of 1990 may turn out to be just what was needed to bring inflation under control. Lower inflation will set the stage for sustained economic growth and a lasting recovery from the devastation of the 1982 recession. In 1990 interest rates in the United States and elsewhere were still high. They acted as an insurance policy against the forces of another deep recession, which could be countered by lower interest rates.

Have we learned from our experience? Will the new tougher credit rules stick? Or will we slip back into the old inflationary ways once this crisis is past and the economy begins to grow again? Only time will tell.

THE WONDER OF IT ALL

The American banking crisis of 1990 is one way to look at the continuing struggle to fend off the effects of the long economic down cycle that began in 1970. Persistent world trade imbalances, wild currency markets, high interest rates in Europe and Japan, and the sinking corporate profits of 1989 and 1990 provide other ways of looking at the continuing struggle. The important thing, however, is not to see all the problems, risks and ways the world could slip back into dismal recession, but to wonder at the marvel of Kondratieff's observations.

Kondratieff was not a soothsayer, nor was he a prognosticator of economic gloom. His published observations on the long-term economic patterns have been used and abused by economists and investment advisors. Too often in recent history his work has been abused by those who, for reasons of their own, feel they can profit by selling predictions of coming economic chaos. The truth is that Kondratieff, by careful and meticulous observation, saw a pattern. He had no way of knowing in the 1920s that the world would be lifted into the next long-term up cycle by war and its resolution. He simply concluded that after each down cycle a fresh up cycle was born, each time in a new form but with certain similar characteristics.

He could be right again. We have won major battles in the war against depression and in the fight to keep inflation under control. The reconstruction of Eastern Europe alone holds enough potential to produce a long period of economic growth.

The 1990s could become a time when the long down cycle finally grinds to an end and a new up cycle begins. The United States and the world economy could be headed for a new time of rising prosperity, especially for investors willing to take risks.

OPPORTUNITY #14: TAKE A CHANCE ON STOCKS

In the 1980s inflation was the investor's friend. It moderated the risks. Maybe the Dow Jones Industrial Average didn't fully recover from the combined inflation of the 1970s and 1980s, but it did get most of the way back. Investors who owned stocks in the 1980s enjoyed reasonable profits. Inflation is likely to remain the principal enemy in the 1990s. If we don't beat inflation and produce a period of lasting growth, it is likely that the 1990s, like the 1980s, will at least produce reasonable profits for investors, especially those holding internationally diversified portfolios. If the high interest rates and slow money growth of the last years of the 1980s prove to be successful in the fight to keep inflation under control, Kondratieff will be right again, and we will have another long-term up cycle with outstanding profits for investors with stocks in good companies.

In the 1950s and 1960s the United States was the prime beneficiary of the long-term up cycle that Kondratieff expected. In the 1990s things are likely to be different. There are no guarantees that the United States will be a major beneficiary at all. This time it may be Europe's turn. On the other hand, the benefits of growth may continue to fall into the laps of the nations of the Pacific Rim. You just don't know in advance.

The best strategy is to adopt an international perspective and invest in companies in different countries. That way you will both reduce your risk and enhance the potential for increasing your personal wealth.

Appendix

Information for International Investors

1. *Dessauer's Journal of Financial Markets,* a bimonthly investment advisory letter written and published by the author, John P. Dessauer. The annual cost of $195 includes 24 regular issues; four special quarterly reports; a biweekly telephone hotline; and plenty of advice, specific recommendations and readable research reports. Write *Dessauer's Journal,* P.O. Box 1718, Orleans, MA 02653, or call 1-800-272-7550.

2. Charts of U.S. stocks: Securities Research Company, 101 Prescott Street, Wellesley Hills, MA 02181-3319.

3. *Asian Wall Street Journal,* a weekly newspaper on Asian markets with charts and information on both companies and economic developments in specific countries. Write the *Asian Wall Street Journal,* 200 Liberty Street, New York, NY 10281. Telephone: (212) 416-2000. Cost: $225 per year.

4. The *Financial Times,* a daily newspaper from London containing a wealth of information on world markets, stocks, currencies and economic developments. Write the *Financial Times,* now printed and delivered in the United States, at 14 East 60th Street, New York, NY 10022. Telephone: (212) 752-4500. Cost: about $350 per year.

5. For an expensive monthly statistical service, write Morgan Stanley Capital International Perspective, 3 Place des Bergues, CH-1201 Geneva, Switzerland. Cost: approximately $3,500 per year. This service is purely statistical with ratios, charts and basic company data on companies in markets around the world. It's not for every investor but is the bible of the professional international investor.

6. Information on American Depository Receipts (ADRs) for foreign stocks traded in the United States:
    a. A list of all available ADRs was included in the April 16, 1990, issue of *Barron's*.
    b. There are four U.S. money center banks that act as custodians for ADRs: (1) the Bank of New York, 90 Washington Street, New York, NY 10286; (2) Citibank, 111 Wall Street, 5th Floor, New York, NY 10043; (3) Morgan Guaranty Trust Company, 23 Wall Street, New York, NY 10015; and (4) Chemical Bank, 55 Water Street, Room 620, New York, NY 10041. Each of the banks publishes a list of ADRs where they act as custodian. By writing to the individual banks, you can obtain copies of their latest listings.

7. *Swiss Review of World Affairs,* a monthly publication, in English, of the *Neue Zuricher Zeitung,* P.O. Box 660, CH-8021 Zurich, Switzerland. Cost: $48 per year. This monthly bulletin doesn't provide investment information. It provides general information on world political and economic trends. It is an interesting and valuable source of background information.

8. *Value Line Investment Survey,* 711 Third Avenue, New York, NY 10017. Cost: $495 per year. *Value Line* provides specific investment information and advice on dozens of foreign stocks and closed-end country funds.

9. *Investext,* Thomson Financial Networks, 11 Farnsworth Street, Boston, MA 02210. Telephone: 1-800-662-7878. *Investext* offers a comprehensive service based on institutional reports prepared by professional analysts. The reports are available both in hard copy through the mail and via a com-

puter with a modem. Charges vary depending on the service level and number of reports requested.

10. Information on closed-end, single-country funds:
    a. There are tables listing closed-end funds published in the Monday edition of the *Wall Street Journal,* Saturday's *New York Times* and Saturday's *Barron's.*
    b. Details on closed-end, single-country funds can be found in *Value Line* and the Standard & Poor's investment service. Both should be available at your local library.

Index